Conor Donlon

Wolfgang Tillmans

Conor Donlon

Wolfgang Tillmans

Verlag der Buchhandlung
Walther König, Köln

We See Conor

Alex Needham

This book is not only a long-term portrait of one person, but also a portrait of London and its nightlife. It chronicles a friendship and is a journey through different photographic formats and qualities. It embodies both the joy of happy memories and the bitter-sweetness of time passing. Everything has changed, yet nothing has, in the poignant but reassuring way you feel when meeting up with an old friend after a long time apart.

Though I can't remember for sure, I think the first time I met Conor (and Wolfgang for that matter) must have been in a club – almost certainly Ghetto, the scarlet-walled Soho sweatbox in an alley round the side of the Astoria. It was 2002, the heyday of electro-clash, when Ghetto hosted two unmissable nights – Nag Nag Nag on Wednesday and The Cock on a Friday – where pulsating, queer, electronic records by the likes of Miss Kittin, Crossover, Atomizer and Fischer-spooner would be played, while a magnificent mix of Central Saint Martins students, record nerds and the occasional famous person would dance, drink and cruise. Intimate and anarchic, Ghetto was one of the best clubs I've ever been to. Along with half a dozen other clubs and gig venues, it was demolished forever to make way for London's egregious Crossrail project. But here, reflected in a mirrored pillar, we see Conor, enjoying a cigarette break while dancers throw shapes and a DJ with extravagant eye makeup – maybe it's Tasty Tim – picks the next record, perhaps the Ewen Pearson mix of Goldfrapp's Train, one of the anthems of that era. In another picture, there's Conor dancing near the tiny podium on which stars like Pete Burns occasionally performed PAs, and in a third Conor and his boyfriend Alex giggling, Alex's bright red hoody matching Ghetto's walls. Could this have been the night Wolfgang also DJ'd, bringing the house down when he dropped Fleetwood Mac's Go Your Own Way in the midst of all the electro?

Wolfgang employed Conor in 2001 as his assistant upon the recommendation of the late Louise Wilson, professor at Central Saint Martins. It was clear when he showed an exhibition of power tools rather than a collection of clothes for his final year show that Conor was never going to be a fashion designer – he much preferred research to making clothes. At Wolfgang's studio he became a crucial ally in making exhibitions and books and discussing photographs. He was a sounding board but also an inspiration, becoming the subject of photographs himself. Their shared interest in popular culture, music, books and nightlife nurtured a friendship that continues to this day. In some pictures he's busy inside the studio, in others he's working (and sleeping) in museums in Hamburg, Chicago, Paris and Tokyo. He's photographed with packages in hand en route to the post office, a place where, thanks to his books business, he spends an inordinate amount of time.
Conor is now a book publisher and the proprietor of a shop, Donlon Books, an essential destination for anyone searching for rare, esoteric and fascinating books on art, fashion or folklore. In other words, Conor is a pillar of East London's creative community.

Many other nights out are chronicled in this book. There were the spectacular parties in Wolfgang's studio which lasted all Saturday night and a good part of Sunday, the closing stages captured here in the pictures of partygoers dancing in the morning light and then collapsed in a heap, surrounded by the rubble of a good time, Federico the last man dancing. Then there's Conor dressed in a morphsuit, taking part in a vogueing competition at the Vauxhall club Crash – Conor didn't win, but unlike many of the other participants, at least he didn't vogue right off the end of the stage.

Conor has a great awareness, admiration and reverence for London nightlife legends, and some of them crop up in this book – people like Jeffrey Hinton and Cyprian de Coteau; still out, participating in the ever-changing ecology of London's clubland. Like Wolfgang, Conor shares their spirit, understanding that clubbing is a release and a laugh, but also much more than that, a place to express yourself and to bond through music with your friends and comrades in a pocket of resistance to the normal world.

The nighttime pictures are full of this love and camaraderie, made more overt when much of the action moves outside as a result of the smoking ban, which came into force in the UK in July 2007. We see Conor standing on street corners, chatting, listening intently, being confided in, allowing his chest to be used as shelter to light a cigarette. The subjects of the conversations are long-forgotten, but not so soon will the boozers we're standing outside: for instance the George and Dragon, another much-loved queer venue now fallen victim to the relentless forces of gentrification. The same has happened to the Joiners' Arms, the place most featured in this book, and the Nelson's Head, both a short walk round the corner. In some ways this book memorialises an East London that has irrevocably changed, though obviously new scenes rise up as others are scattered.

Of course, this book doesn't entirely take place after dark – or even mainly. We see Conor and some colleagues on the November 2003 demonstration against George W. Bush's state visit, holding a placard with a slogan: "The axis of evil goes right thru George W.'s juicy manhole". There's a picnic in the park after an opening at Between Bridges, the non-profit art space Wolfgang and his assistants ran in the entrance of the studio. There are afternoons spent by the sea in Finland and France or by a lake in Berlin. Time spent talking, in the studio and around town, turning for a moment into an impromptu portrait sitting. Private life amidst the cosiness and bright yellow walls of Conor and Alex's home.

Conor started his bookshop in Herald Street gallery, under Wolfgang's studio, in 2005, then stayed working as a travelling assistant until 2008. As the shop became Conor's main focus, we can trace an evolution through Wolfgang's photos – Conor moving from a young man to the confident proprietor of his own store (and host of his own excellent launch parties). In this way, the book also has a wistful tang, as Conor the assistant learns to stand on his own two feet and inevitably grows away from Wolfgang.

The book is also a glorious chronicle of Conor's ever-evolving personal style, inspiration for anyone who needs it on how to be impeccably turned out while never spending more than £30 on an item of clothing – Conor's upper limit for years. Sportswear and stripes, knitwear and camo, hoodies and double denim; Conor has an instinctive eye for what looks amazing, not to mention an enviable physical thermostat – who else could remain cool while wearing woolly jumpers on a steaming dancefloor? Conor comes from the grand tradition of street style. Stratospherically priced luxury labels hold no interest for him – he'd rather spend the money on books. That said, some of the early images in this book were used as a subversive fashion story for Purple magazine, including the picture of Conor wearing a weird furry top, his face covered by a copy of The Economist with George W. Bush's face on the front, Conor's hand holding the issue of NME which protested against Marilyn Manson being blamed for the 1999 Columbine massacre.

Fundamentally, this book is a testament to the friendship between Conor and Wolfgang. Last September, Conor came to New York to attend the NY Art Book Fair and the opening of Wolfgang's most recent exhibition. As usual, the show included an image of him – also in this book – in which Conor lies on the sand by the sea with his eyes closed, his hair and beard flecked with grey, still the object of Wolfgang's deep love and admiration. Conor inspires those feelings because he transmits them himself. He always has and surely always will.

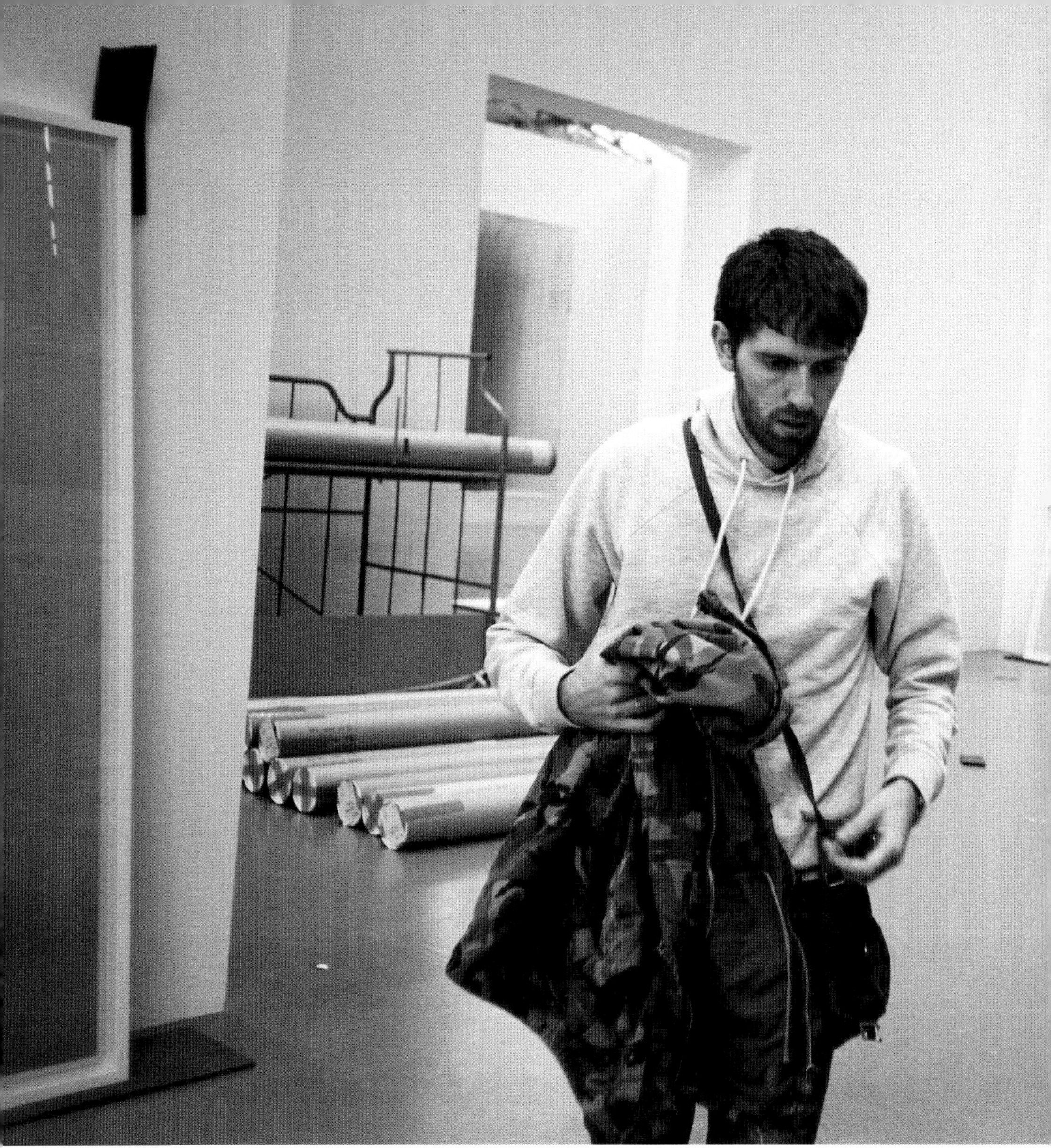

2001

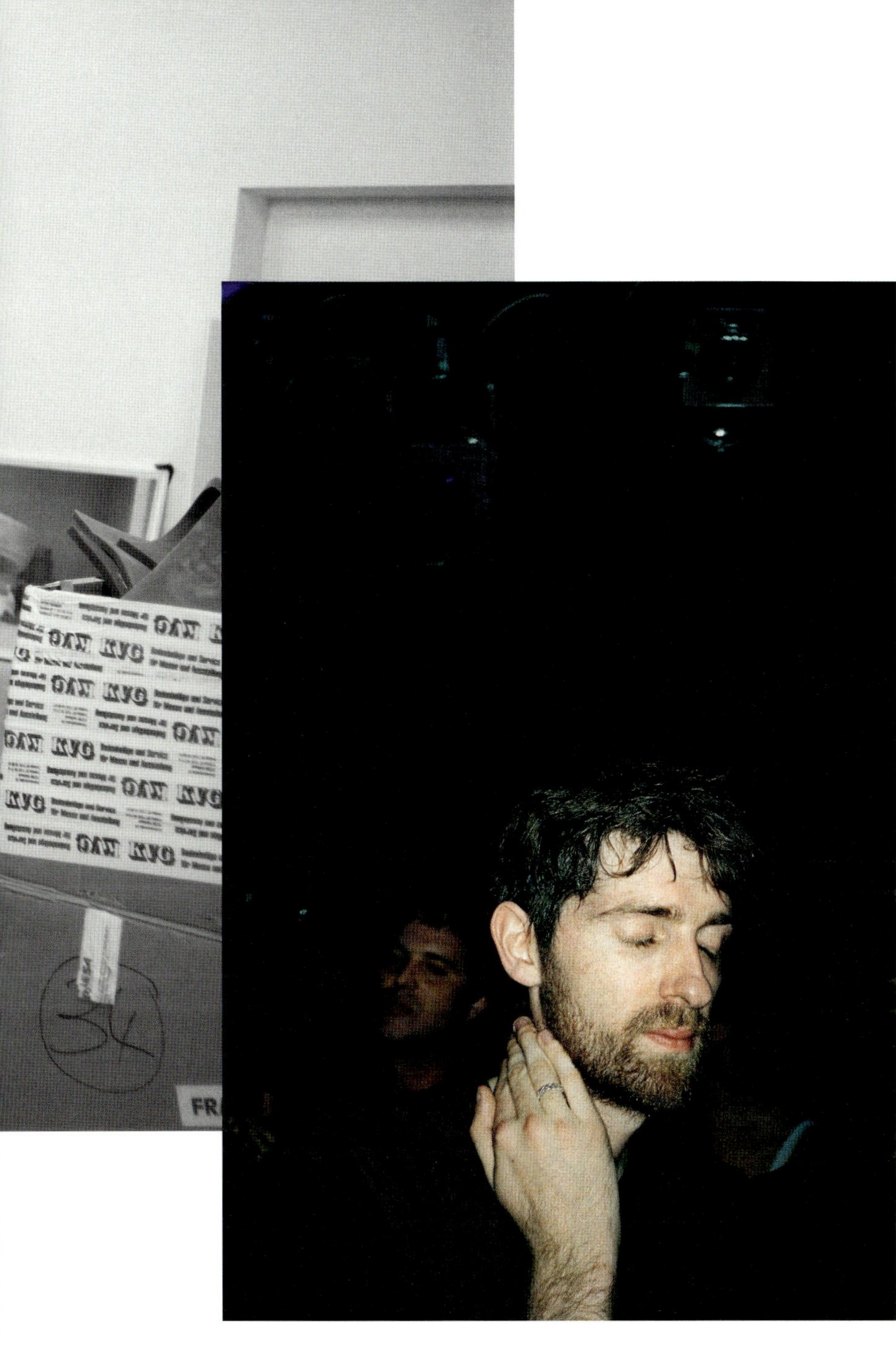

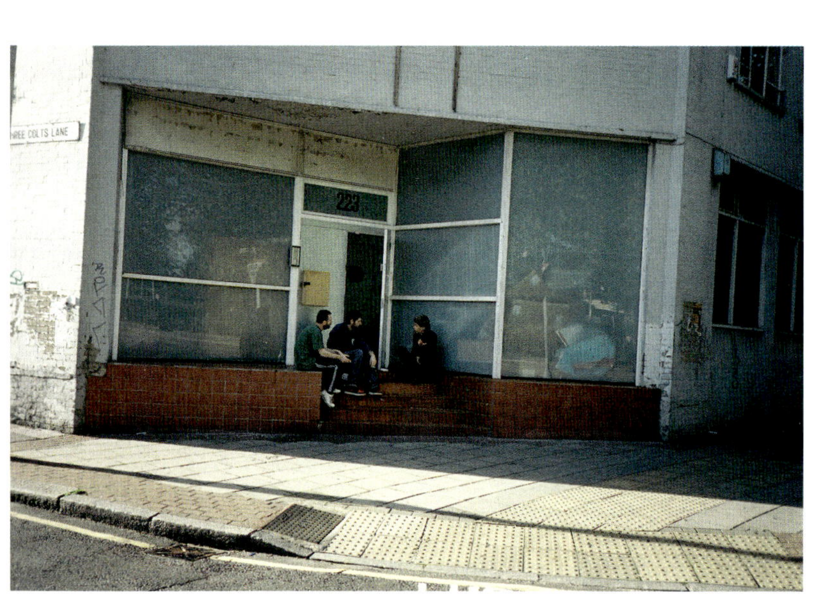
COLTS LANE
223

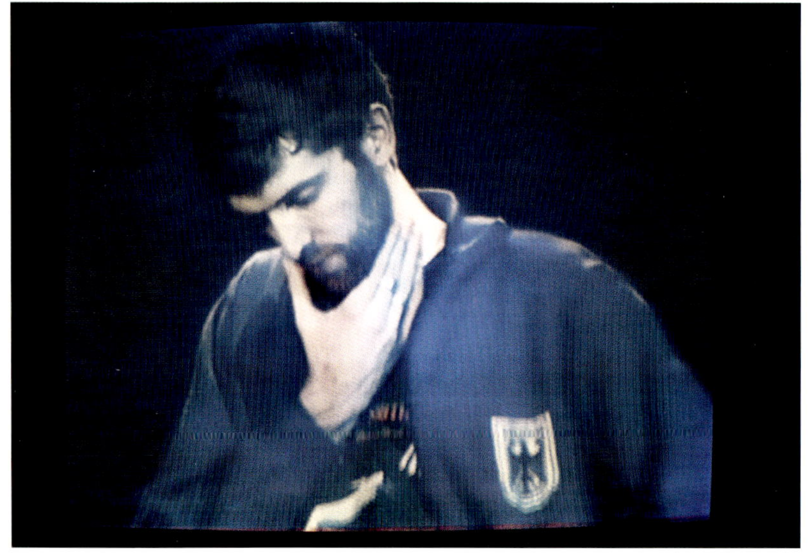

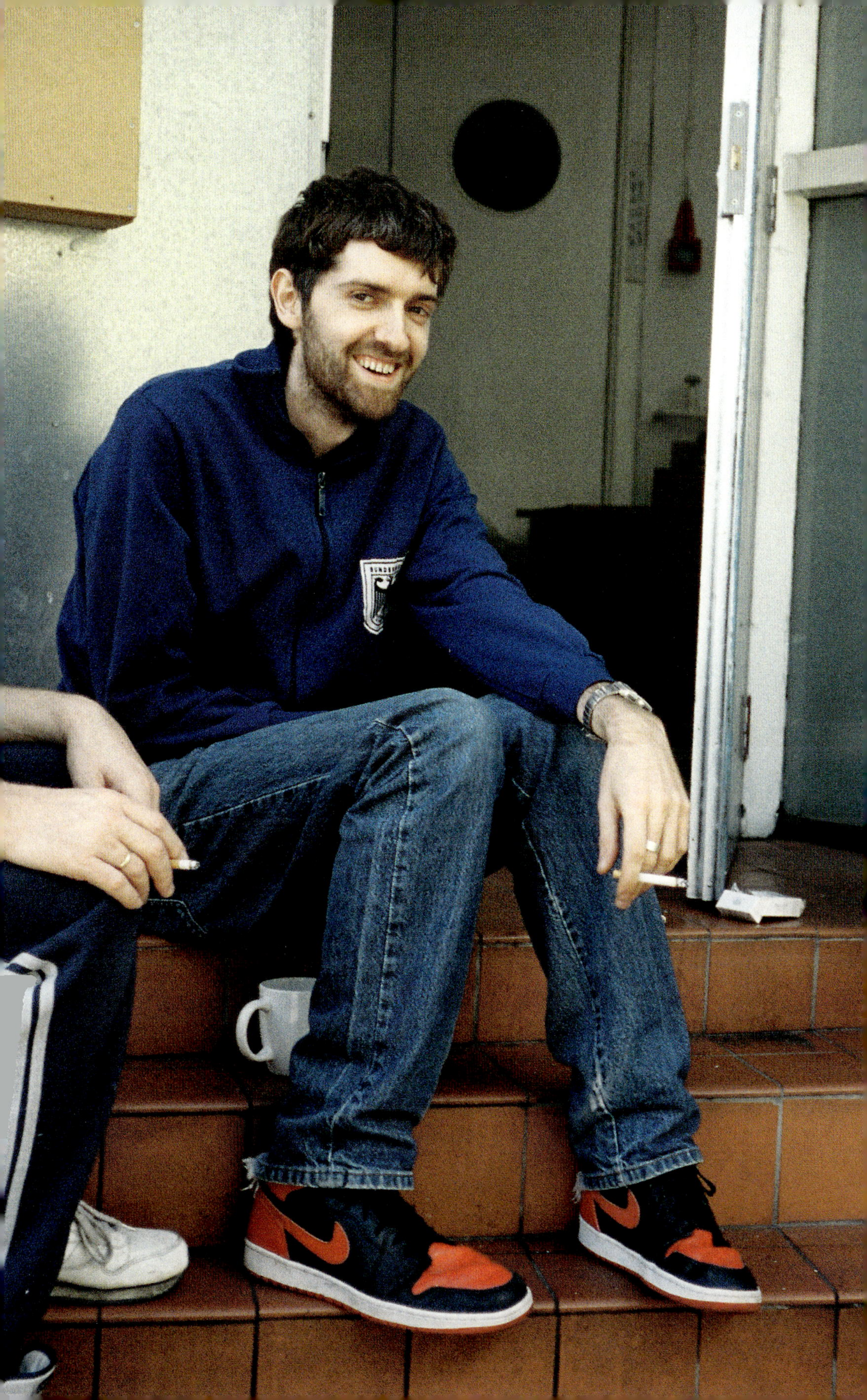

2002

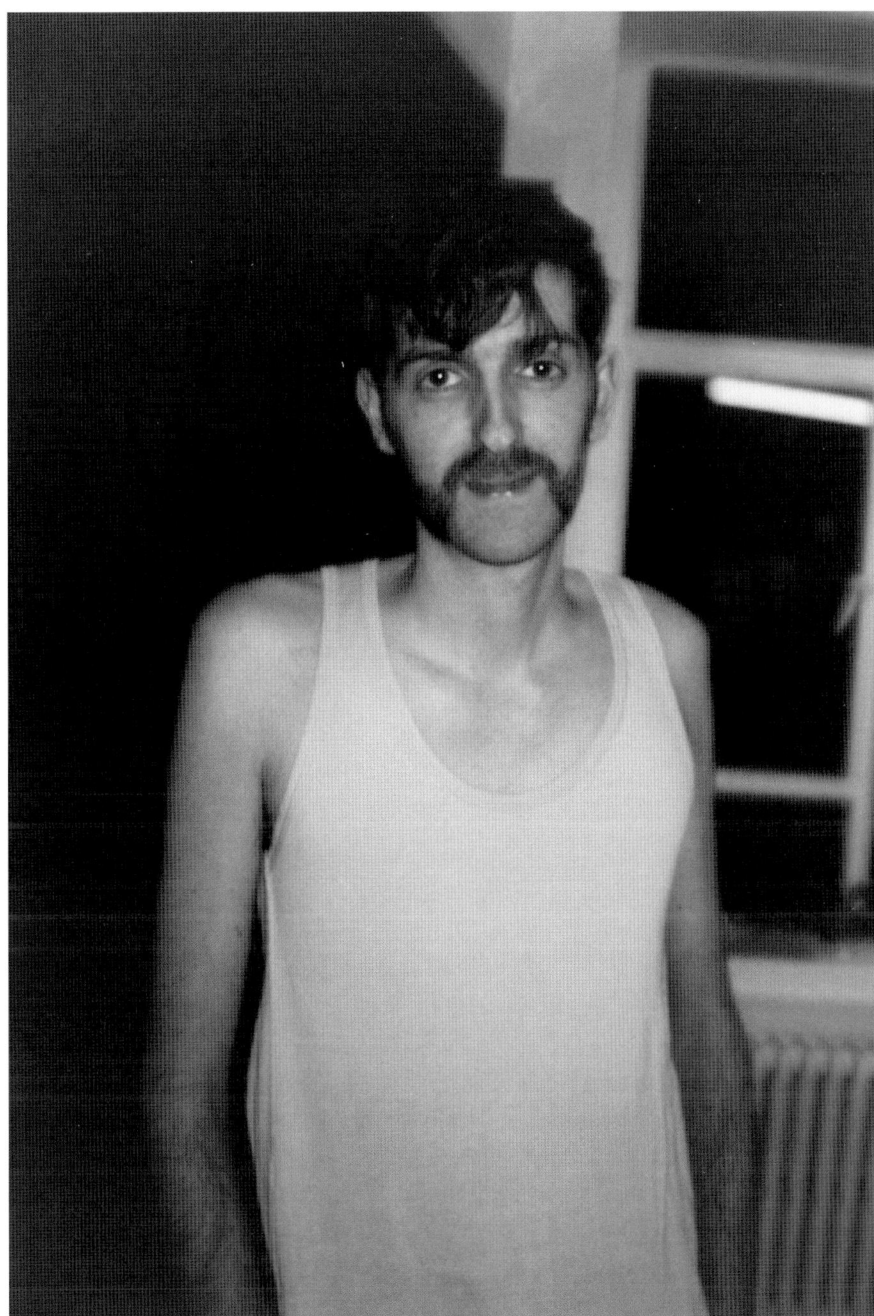

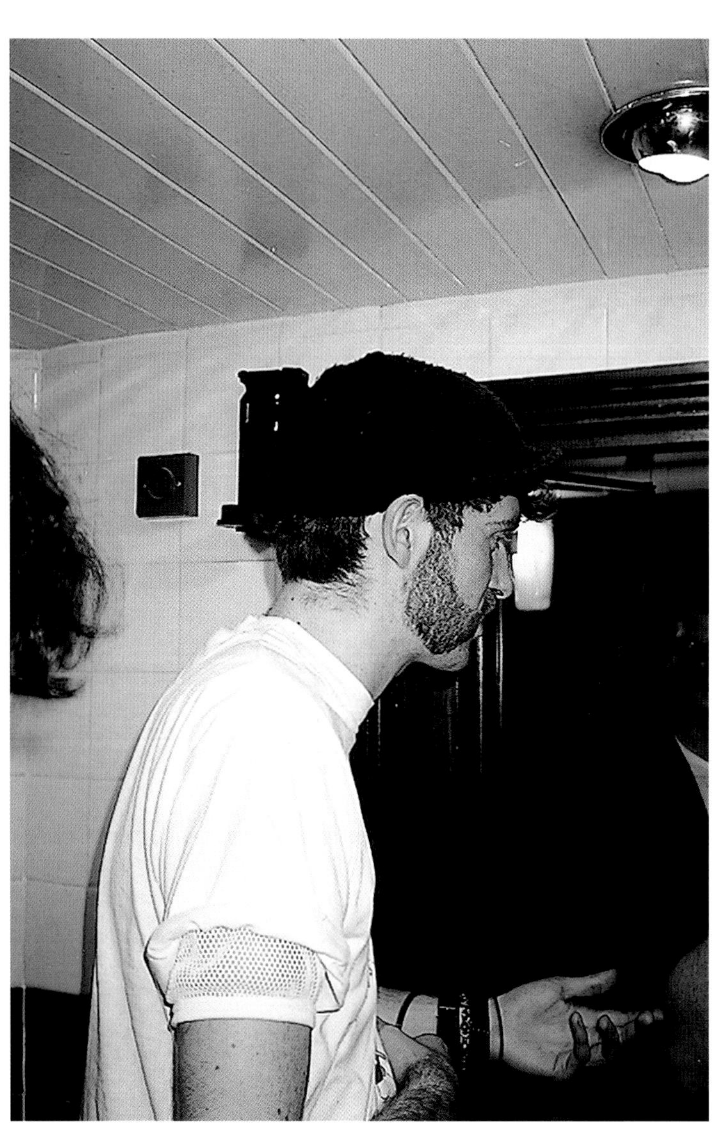

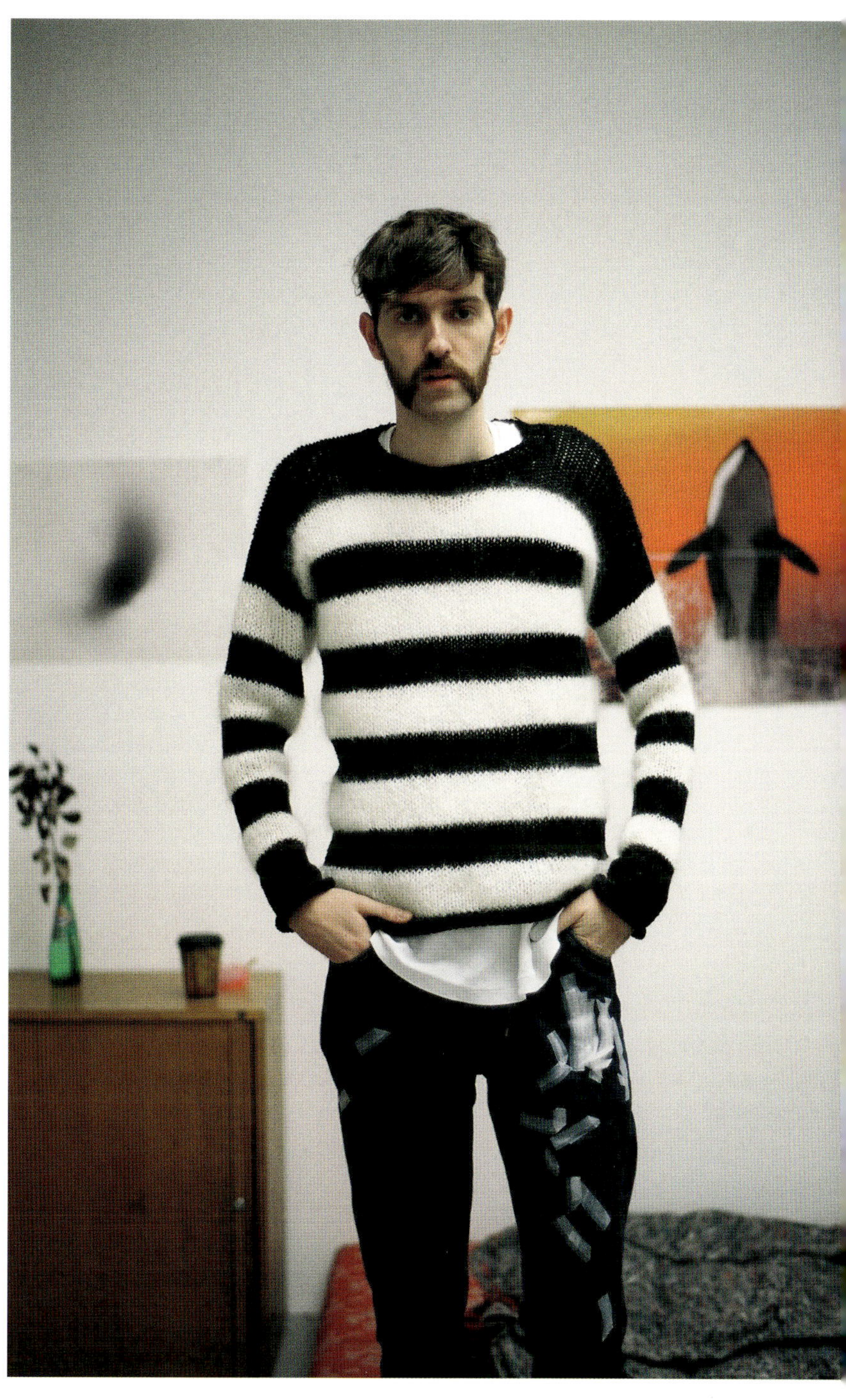

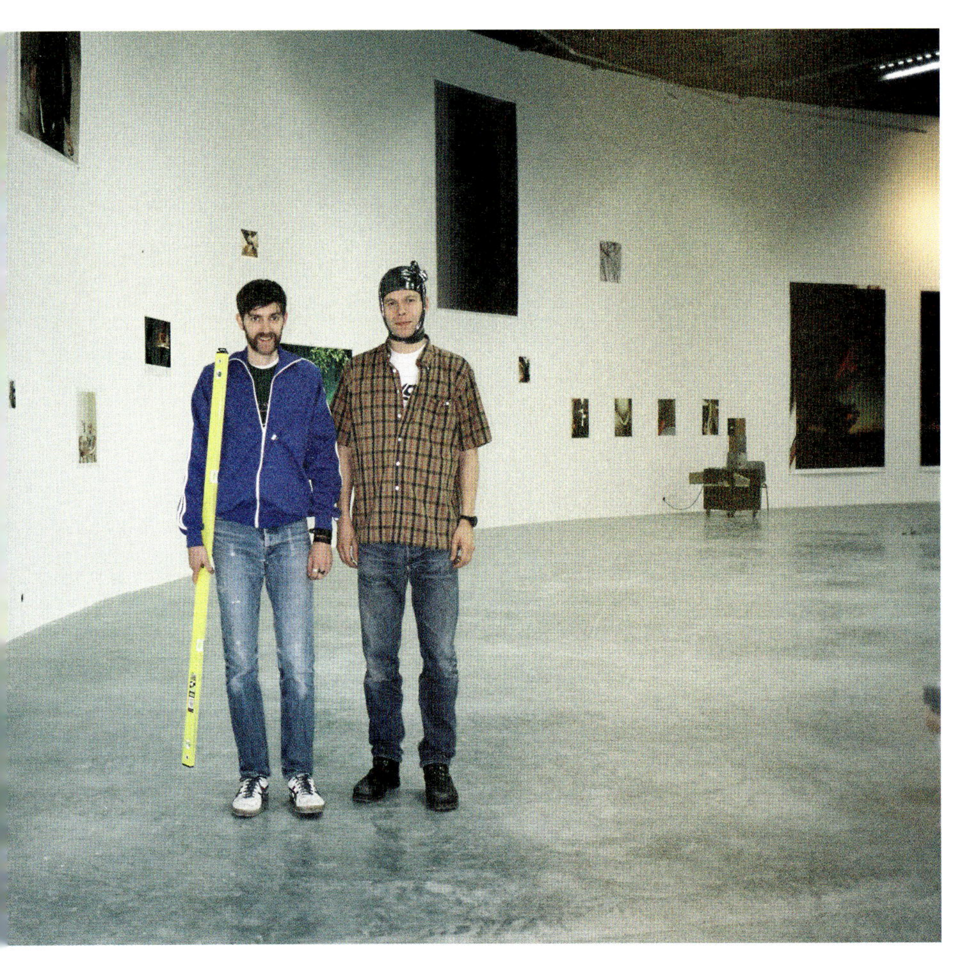

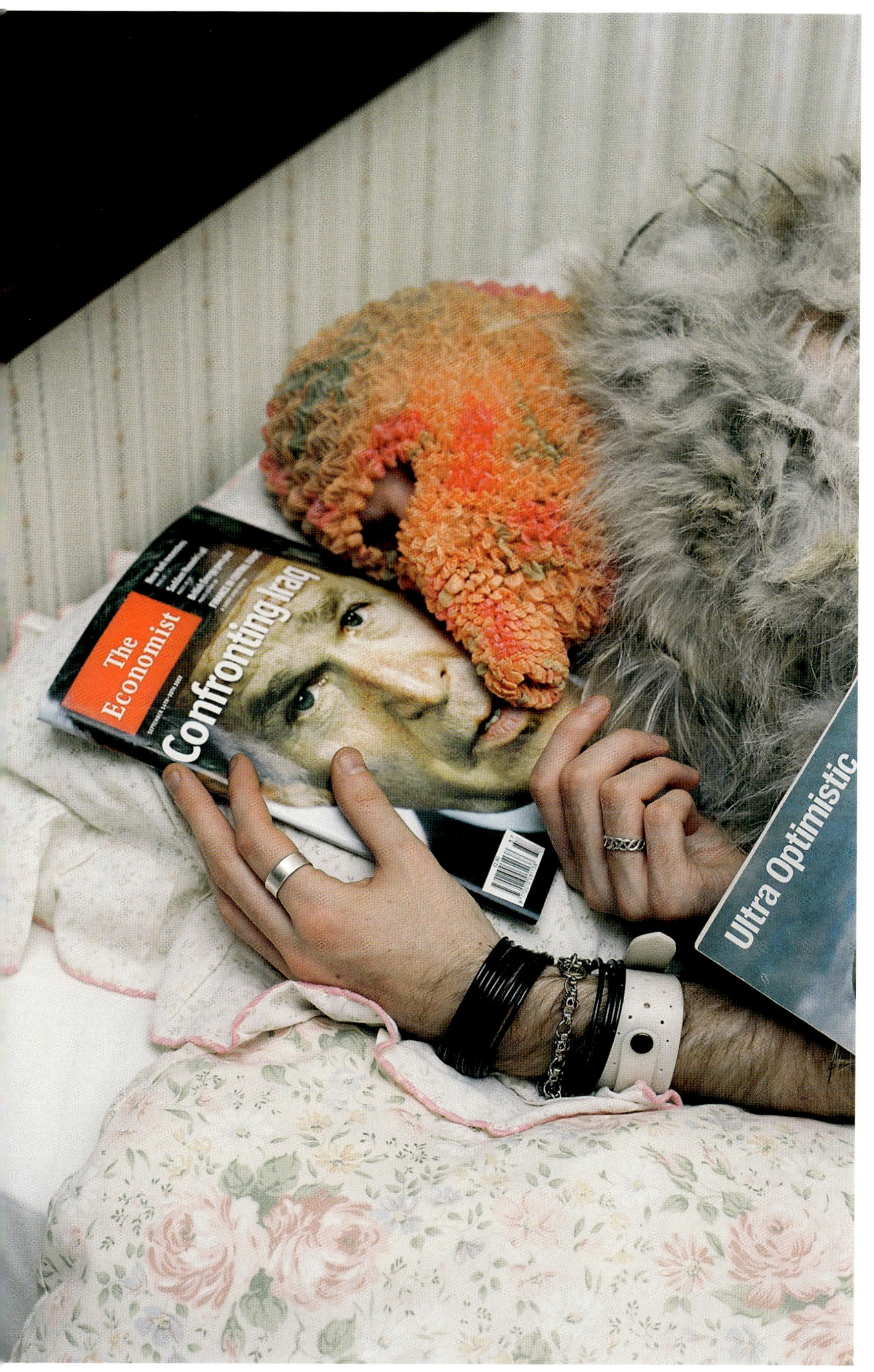
The Economist
Confronting Iraq
Ultra Optimistic

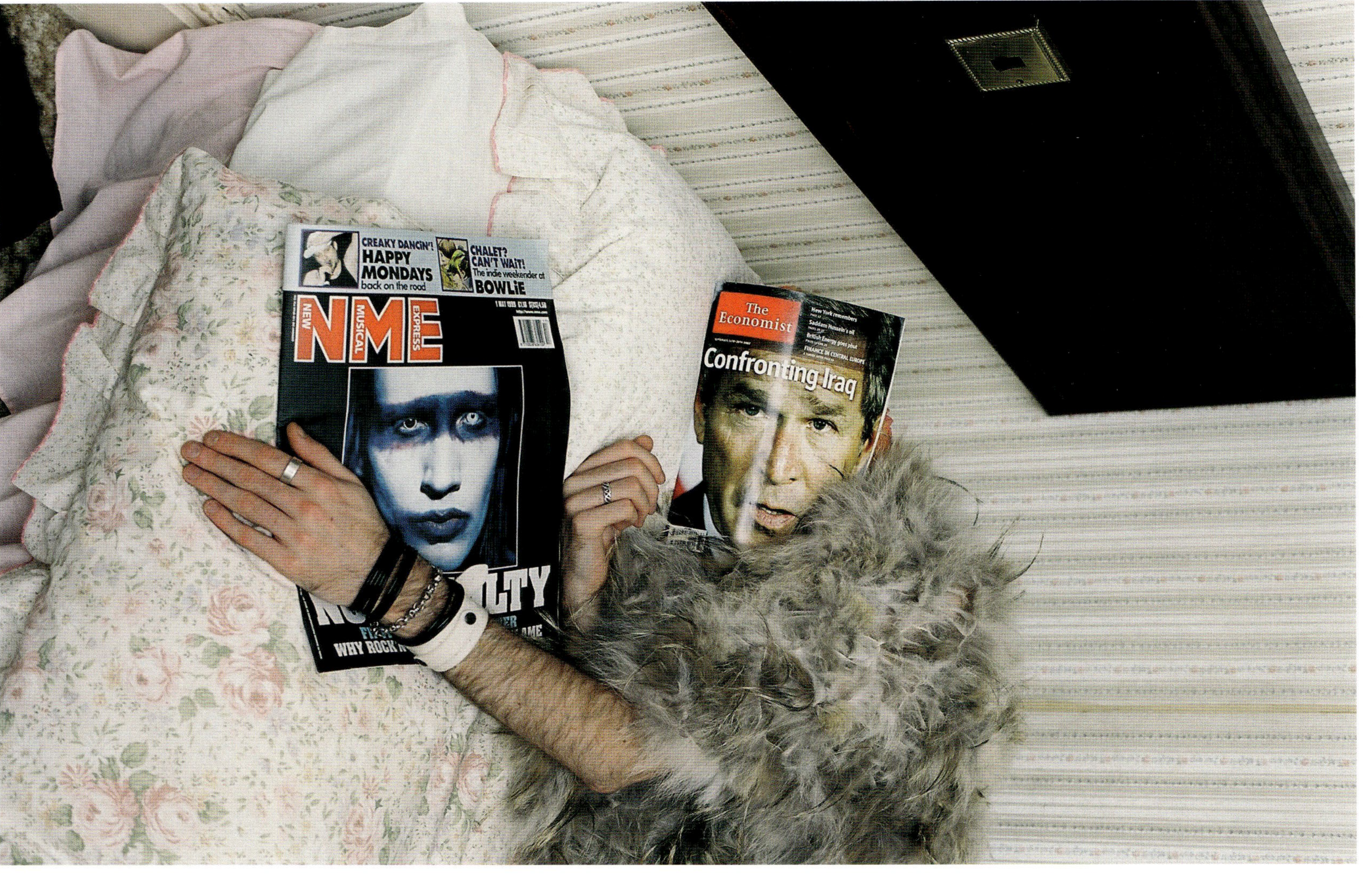

The Economist
Confronting Iraq
NEW
MUSICAL
EXPRESS
NME
CREAKY DANCIN'!
HAPPY
MONDAYS
back on the road
CHALET?
CAN'T WAIT!!
The indie weekender at
BOWLIE

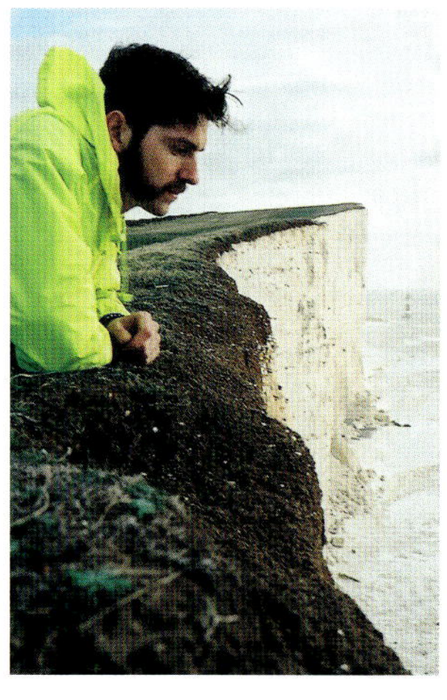

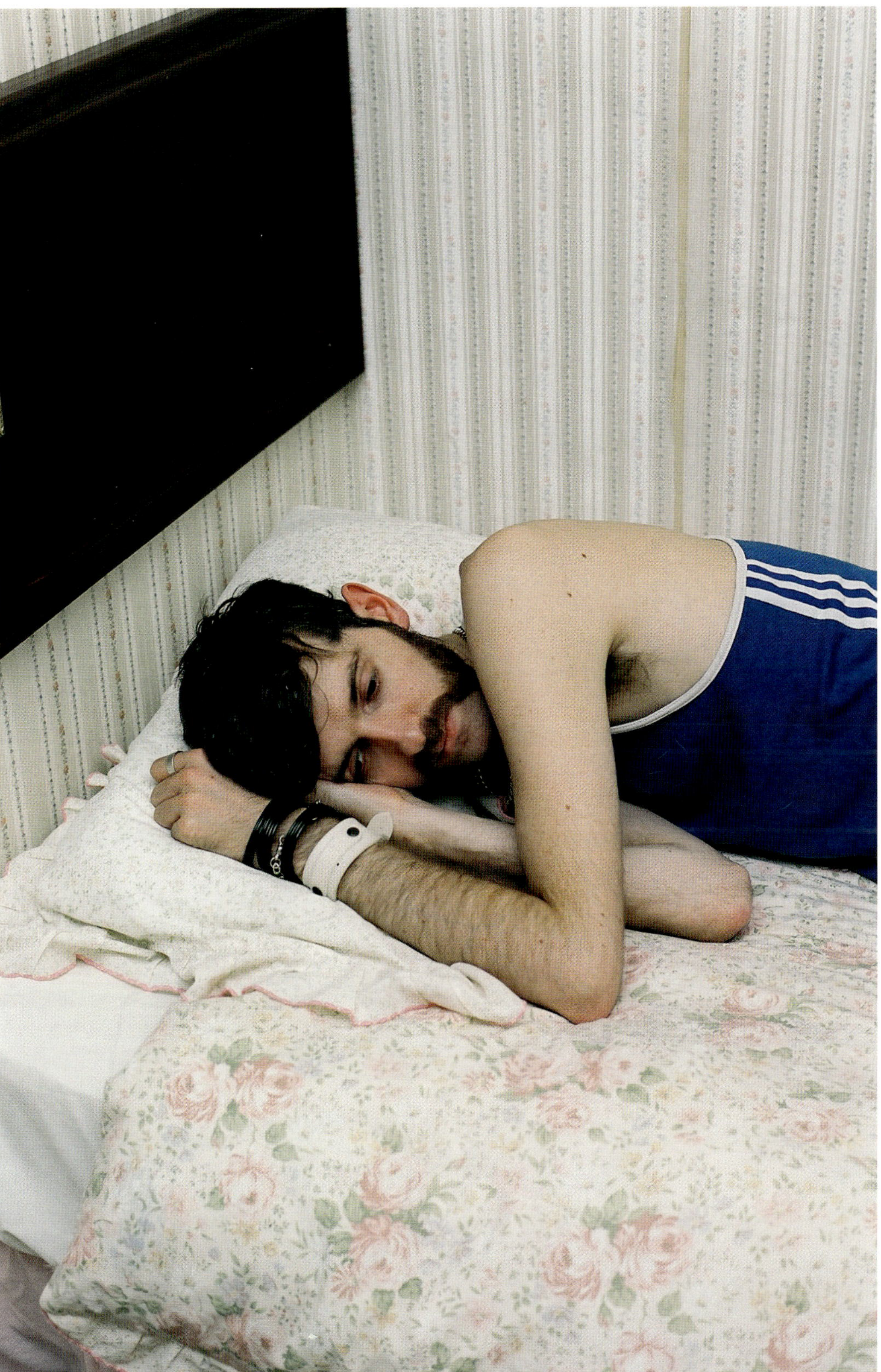

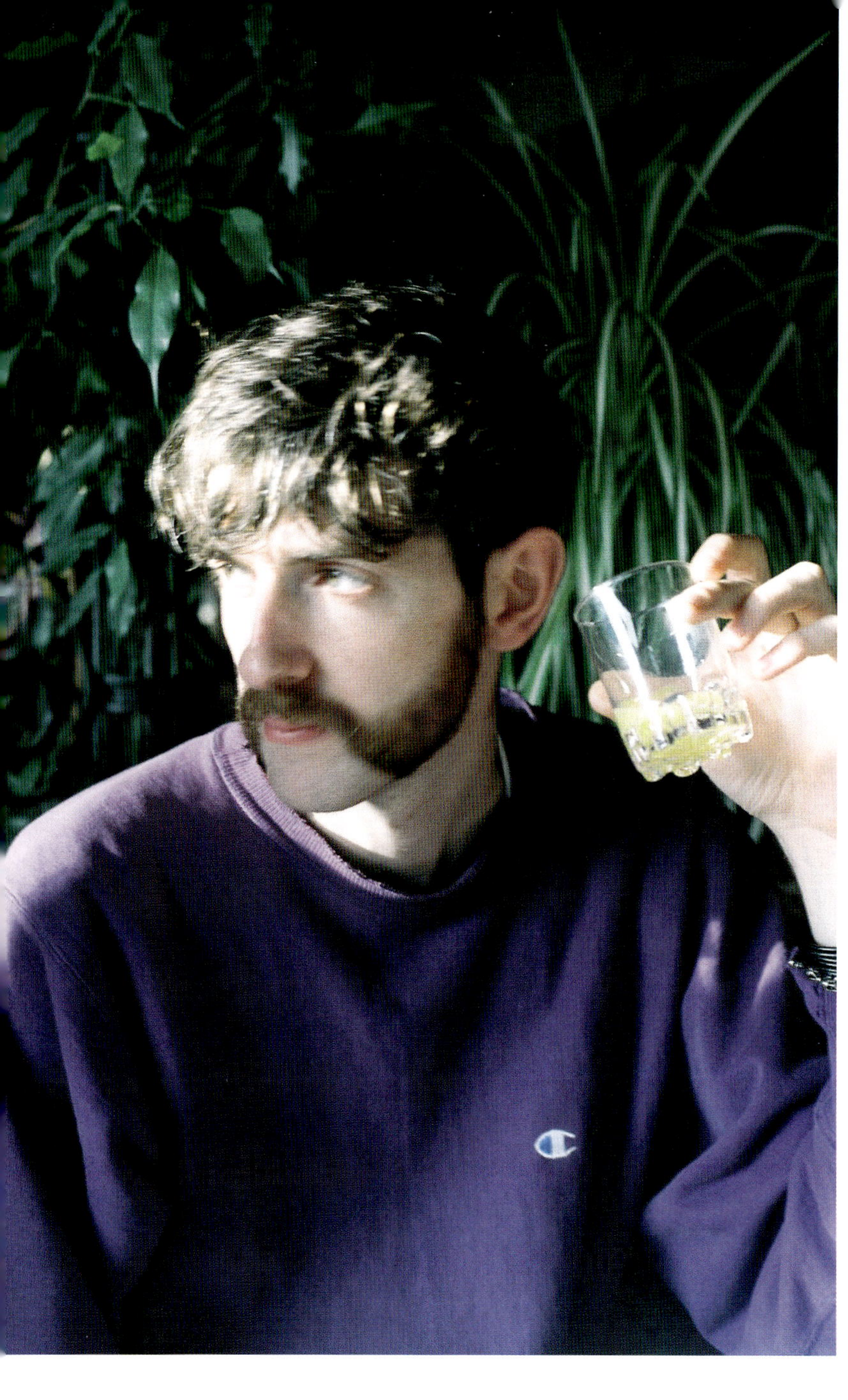

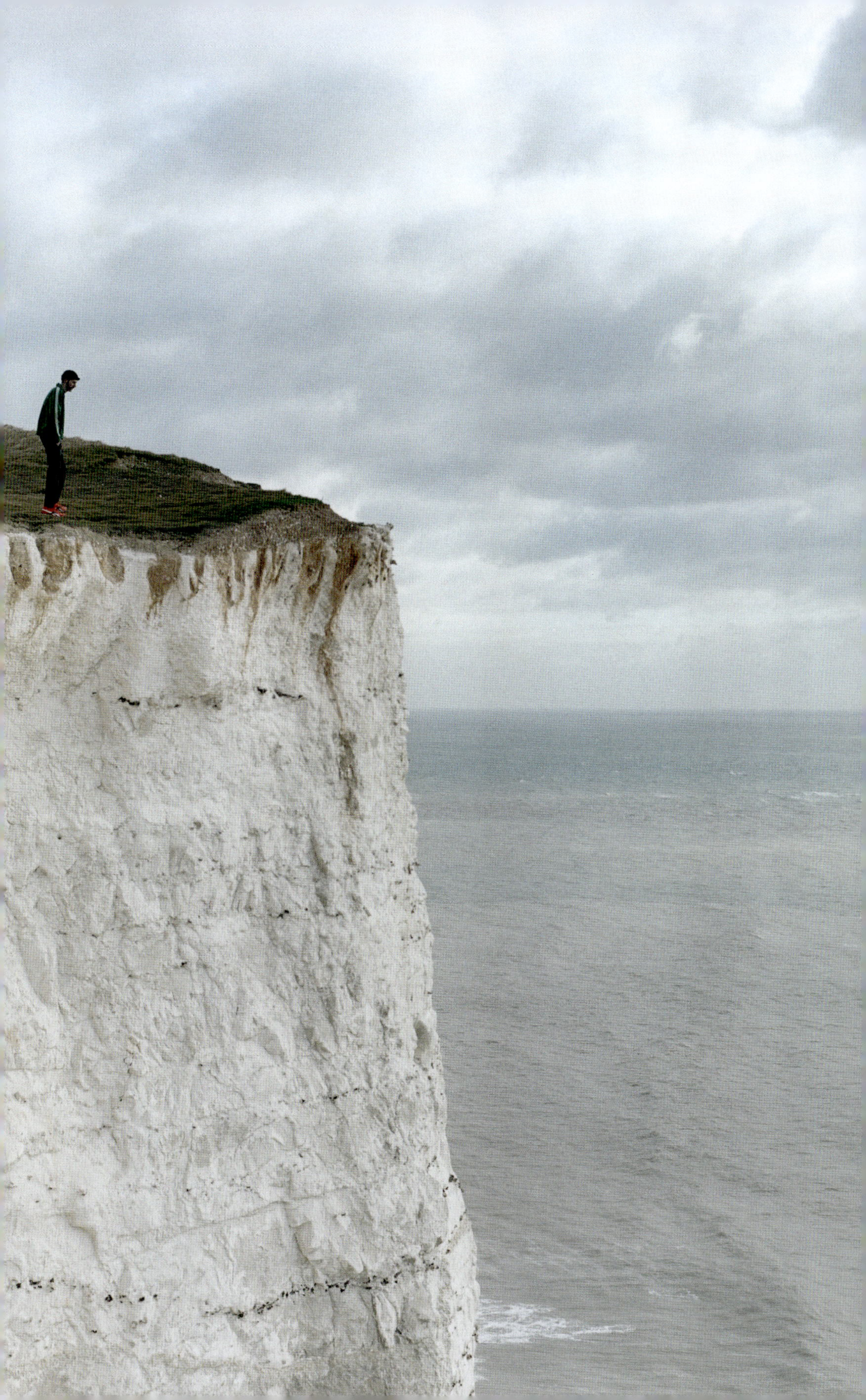

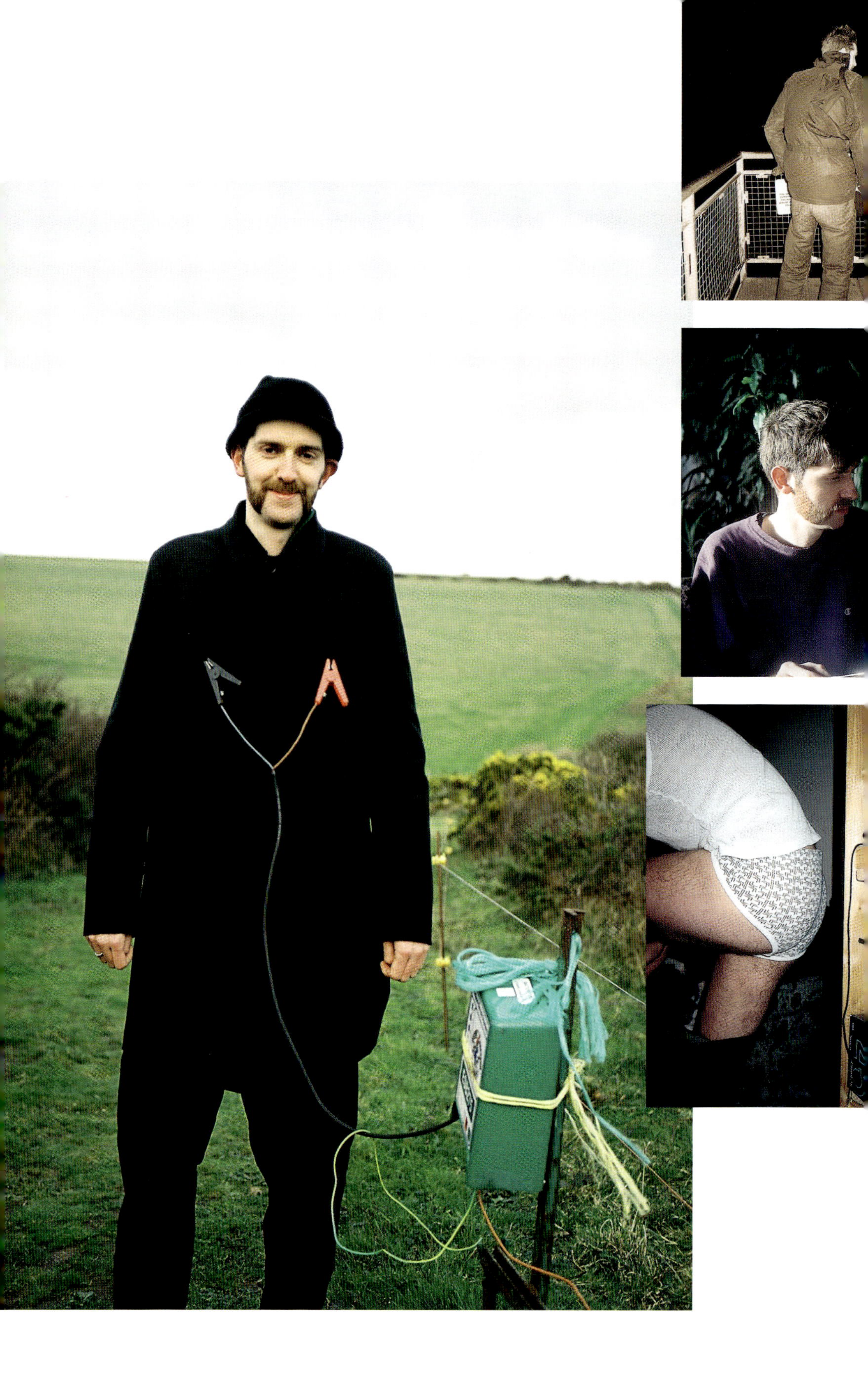

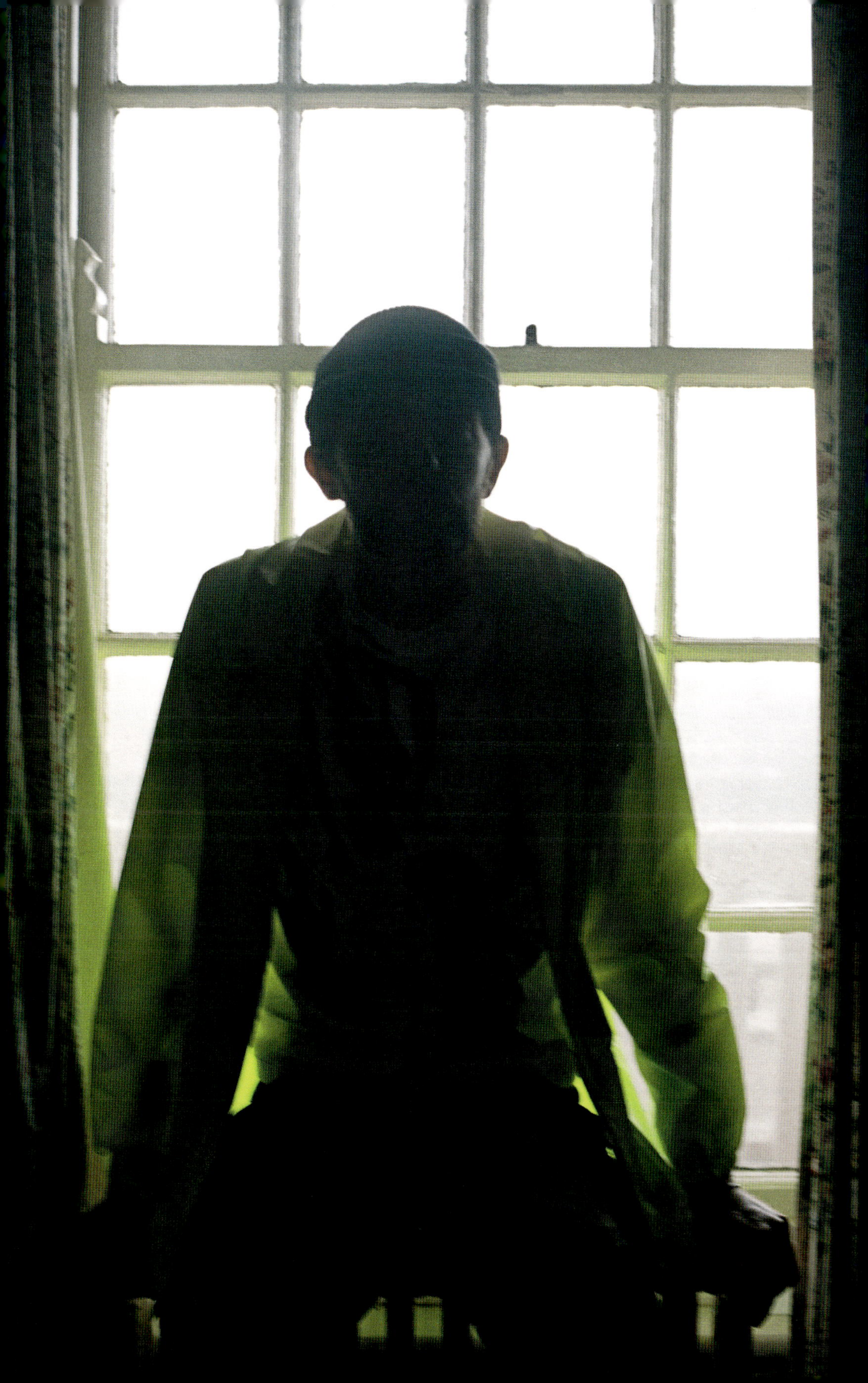

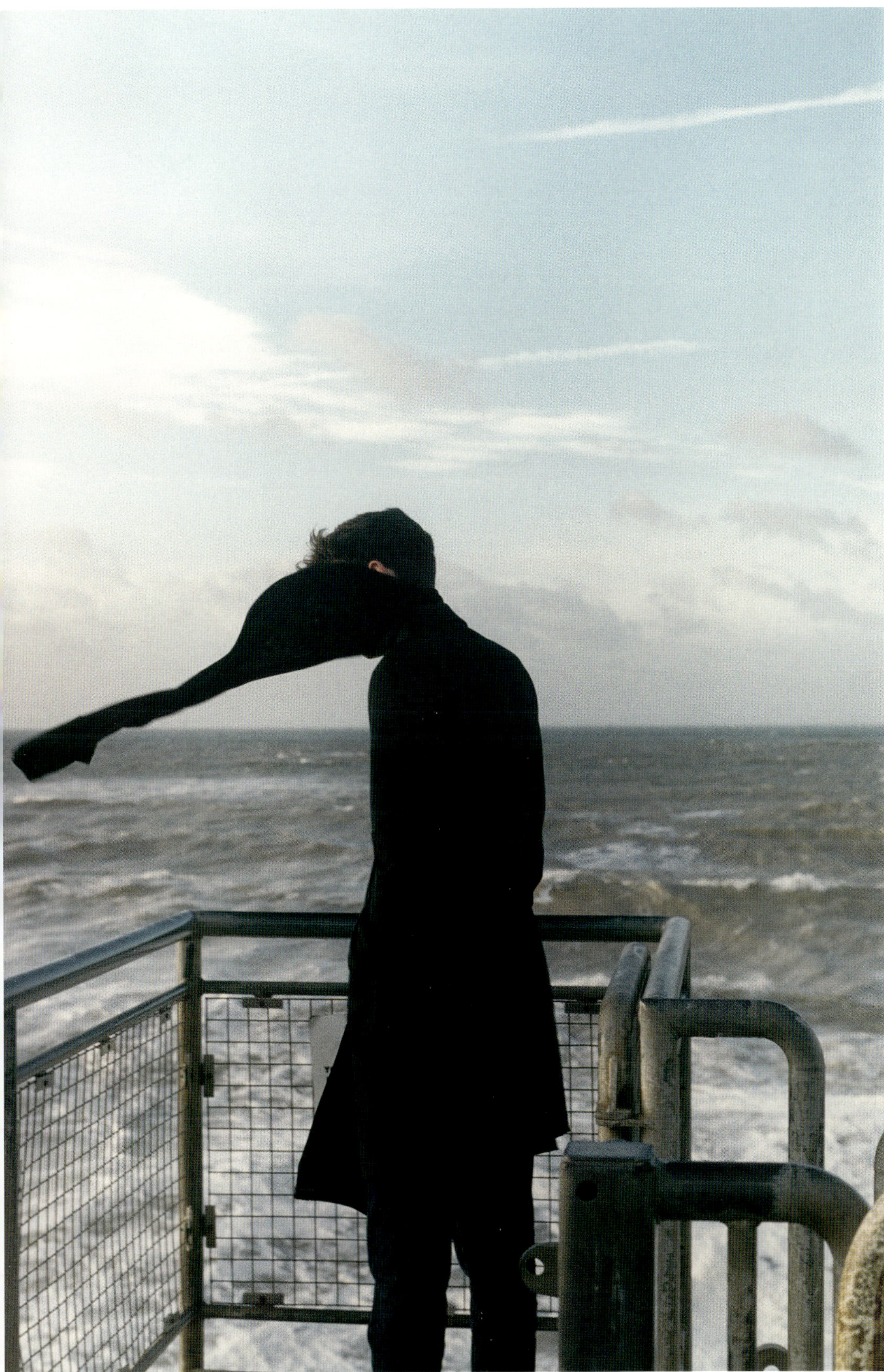

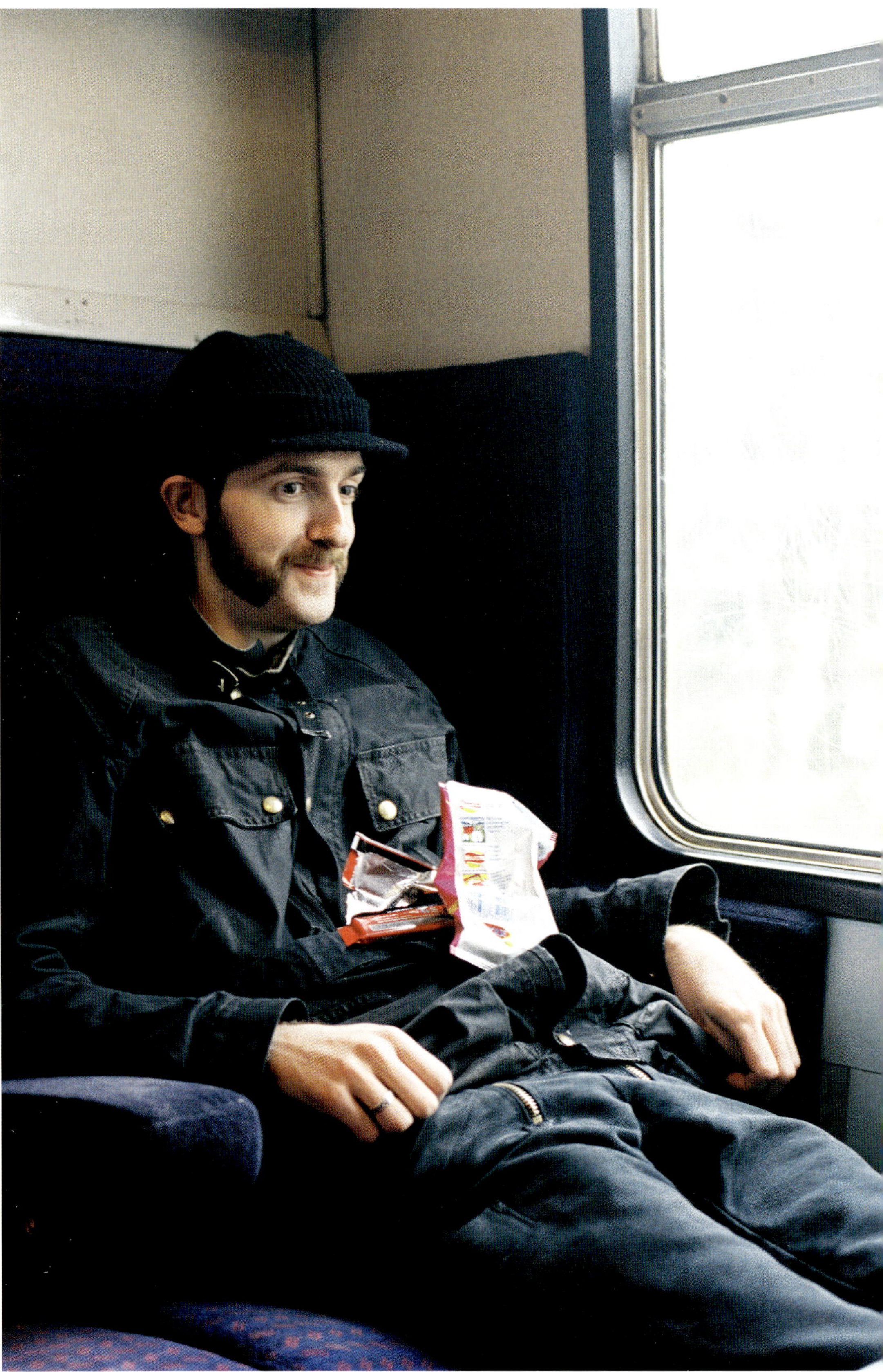

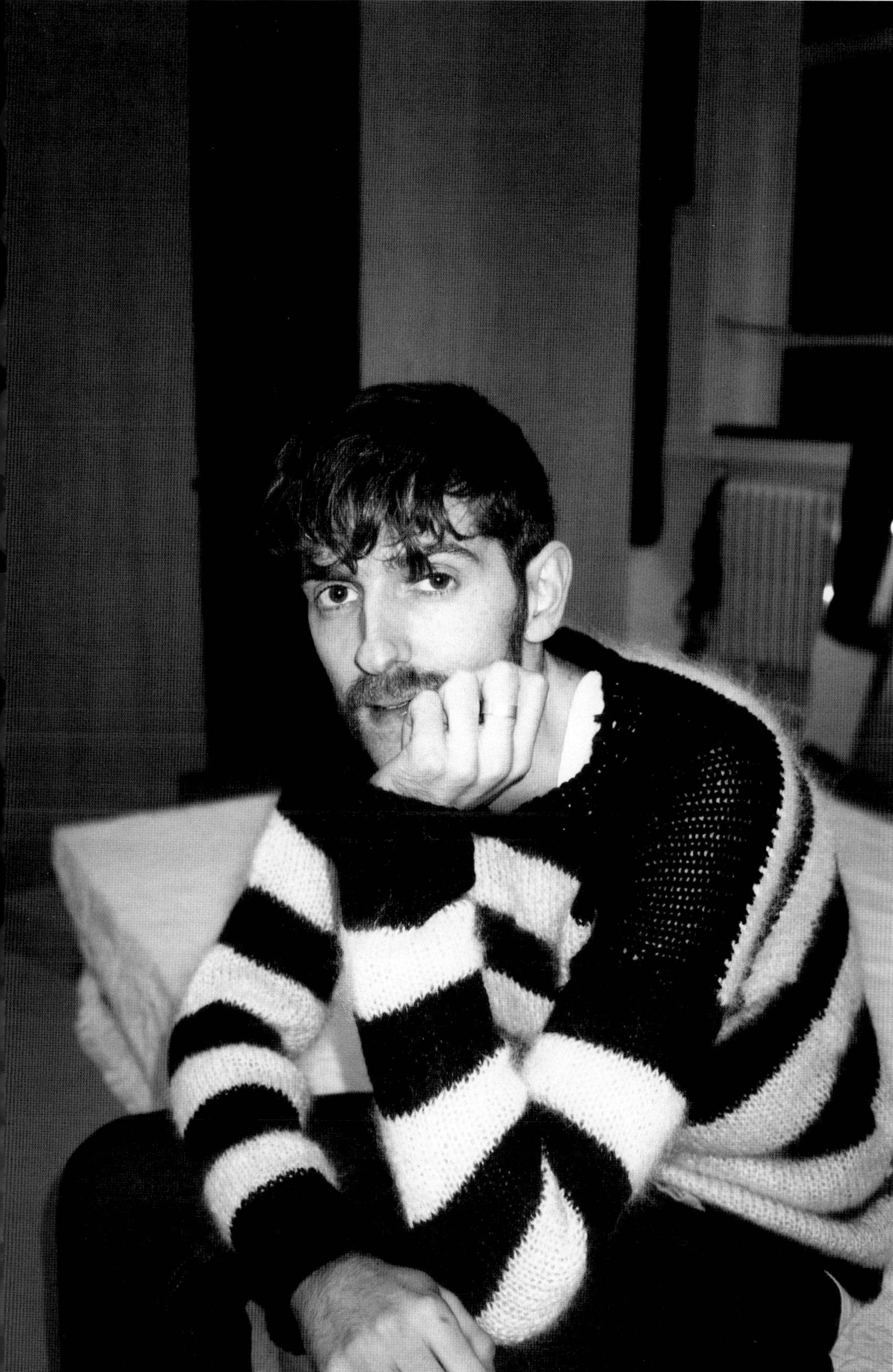

2003

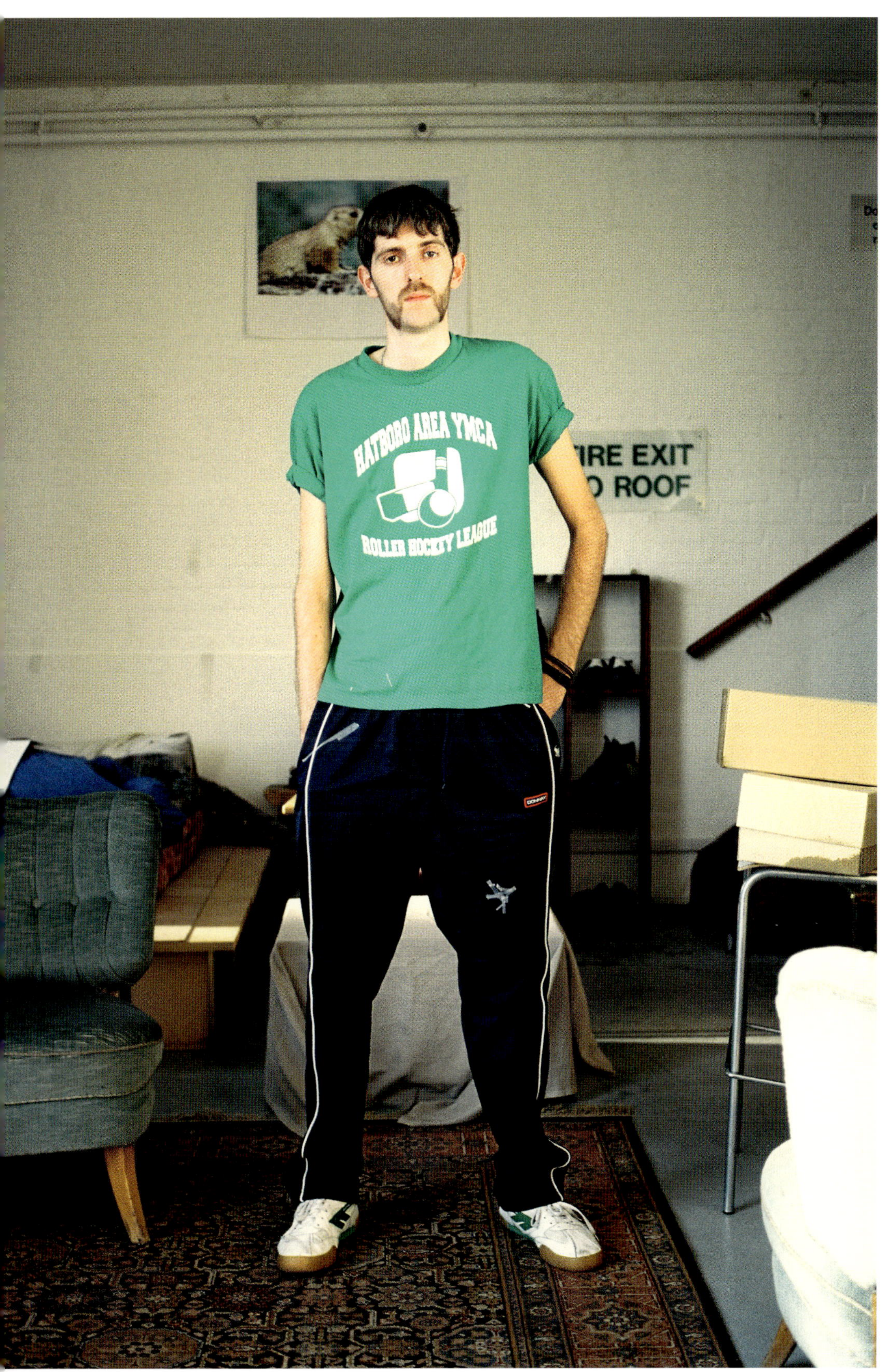
HATBORO AREA YMCA
ROLLER HOCKEY LEAGUE
IRE EXIT
O ROOF

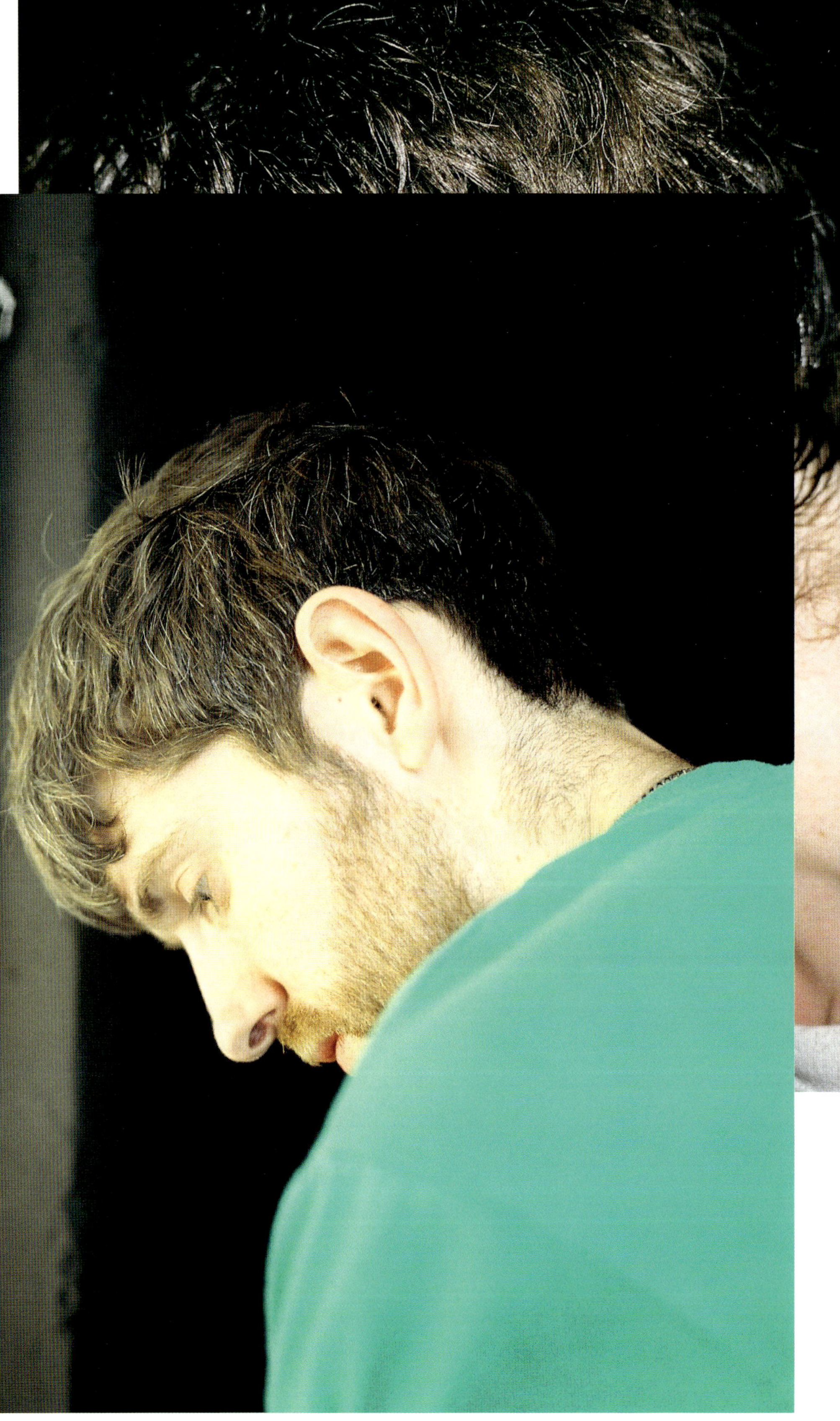

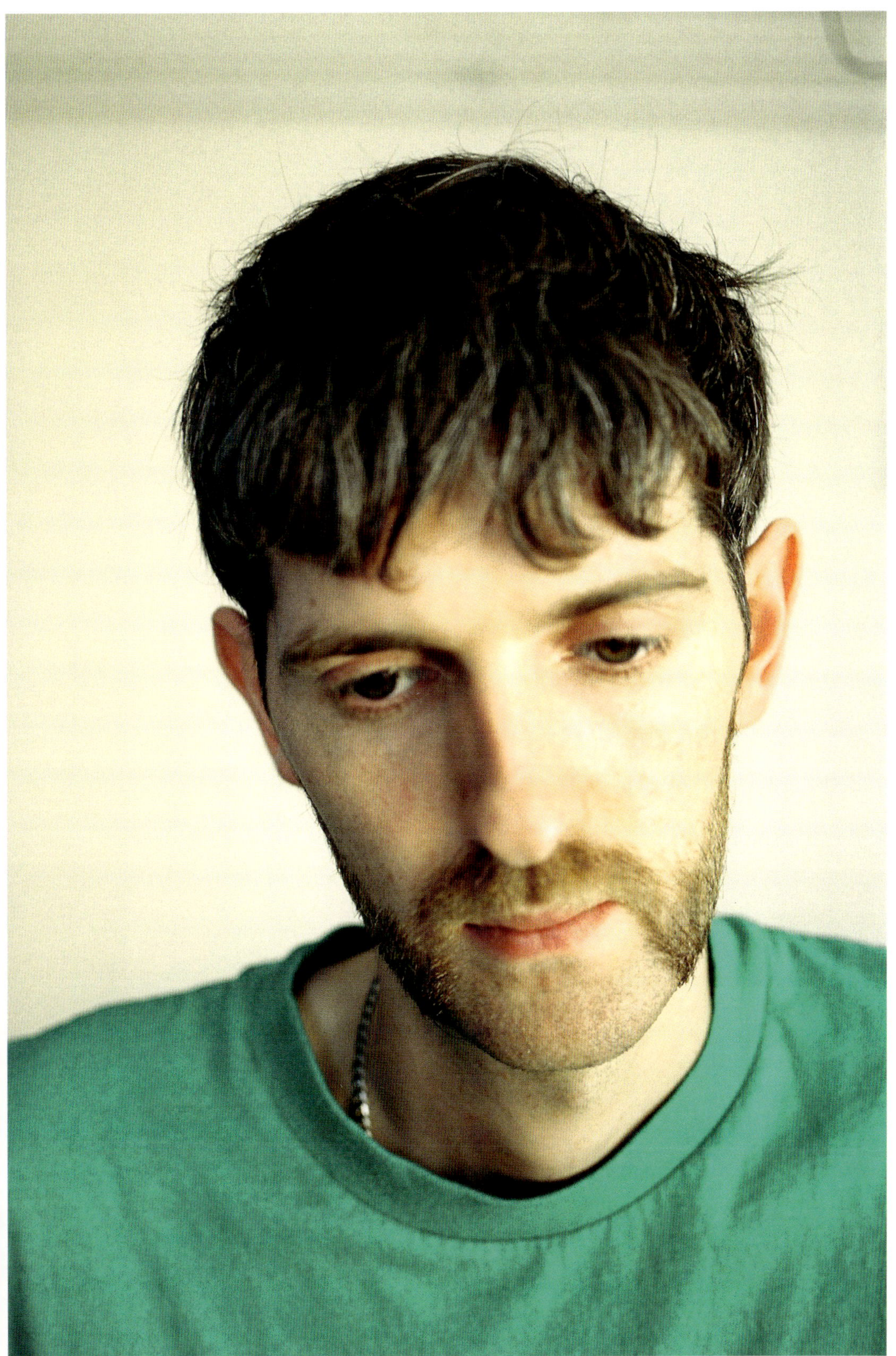

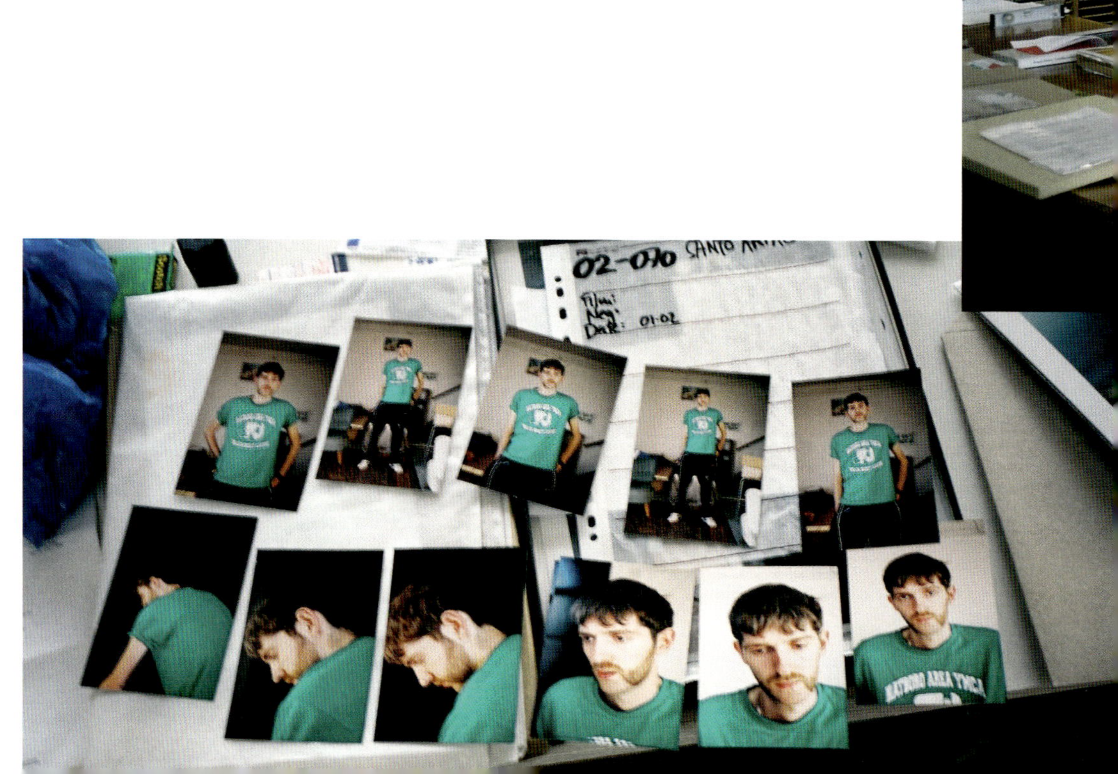
02-070

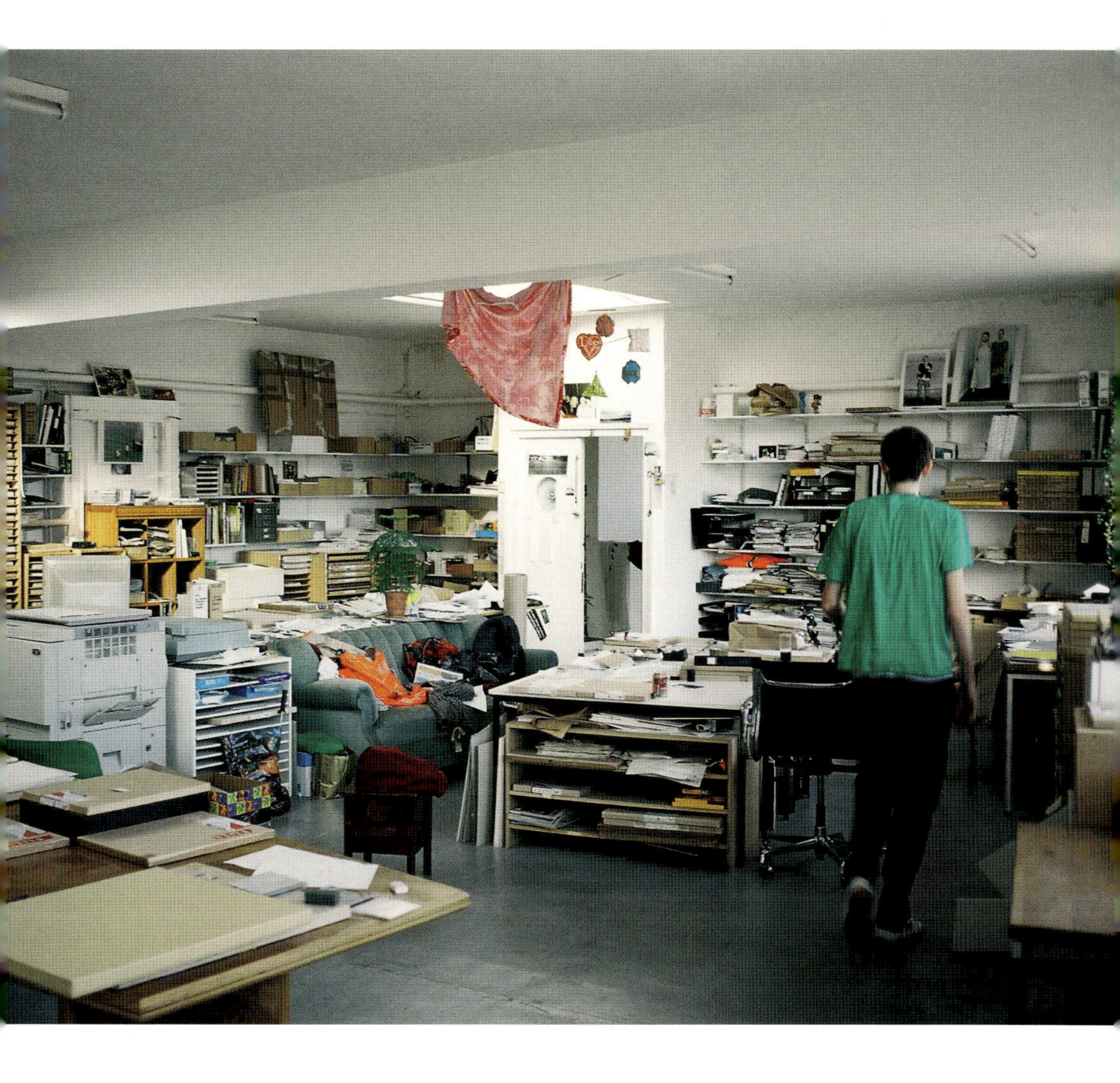

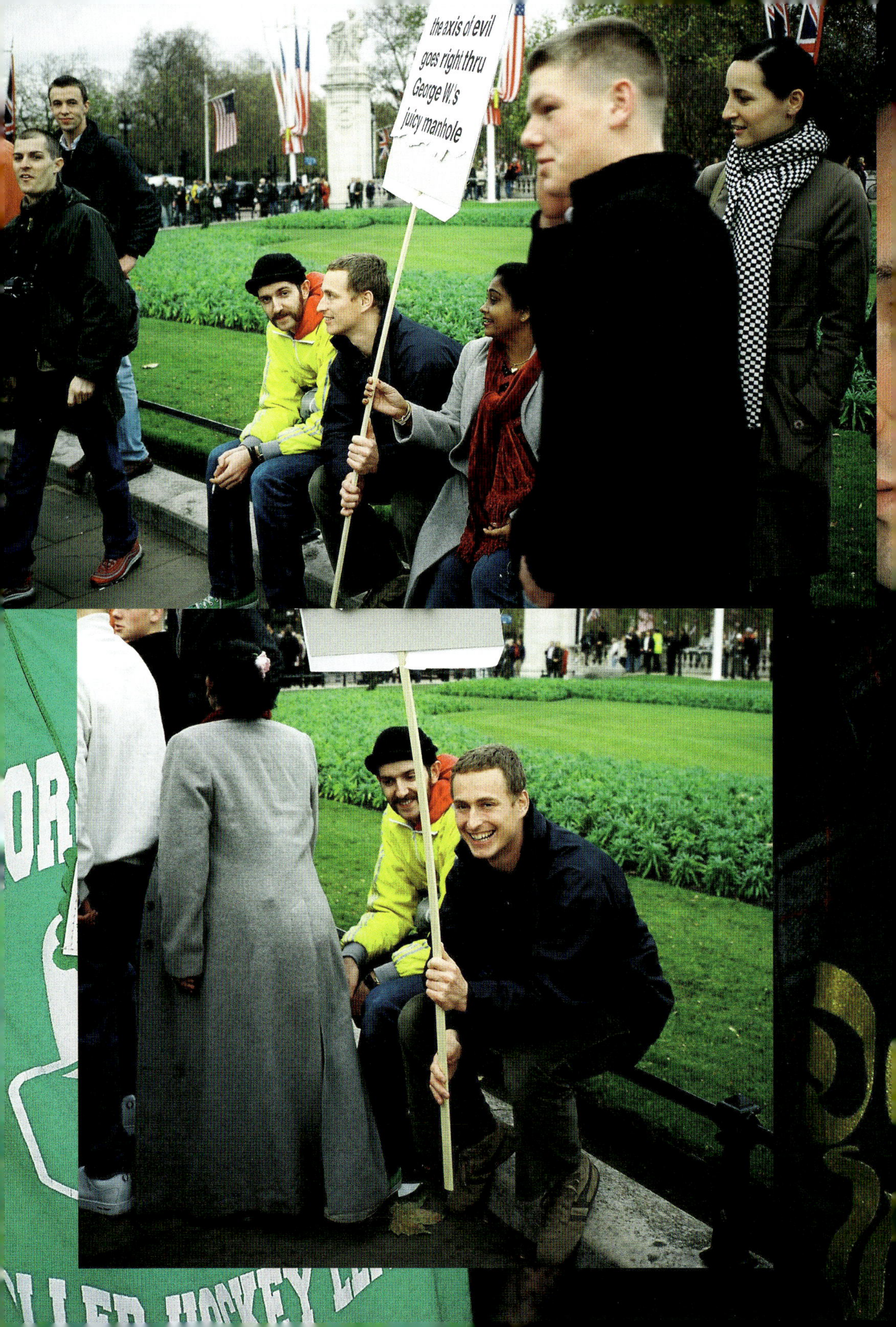
the axis of evil
goes right thru
George W.'s
juicy manhole

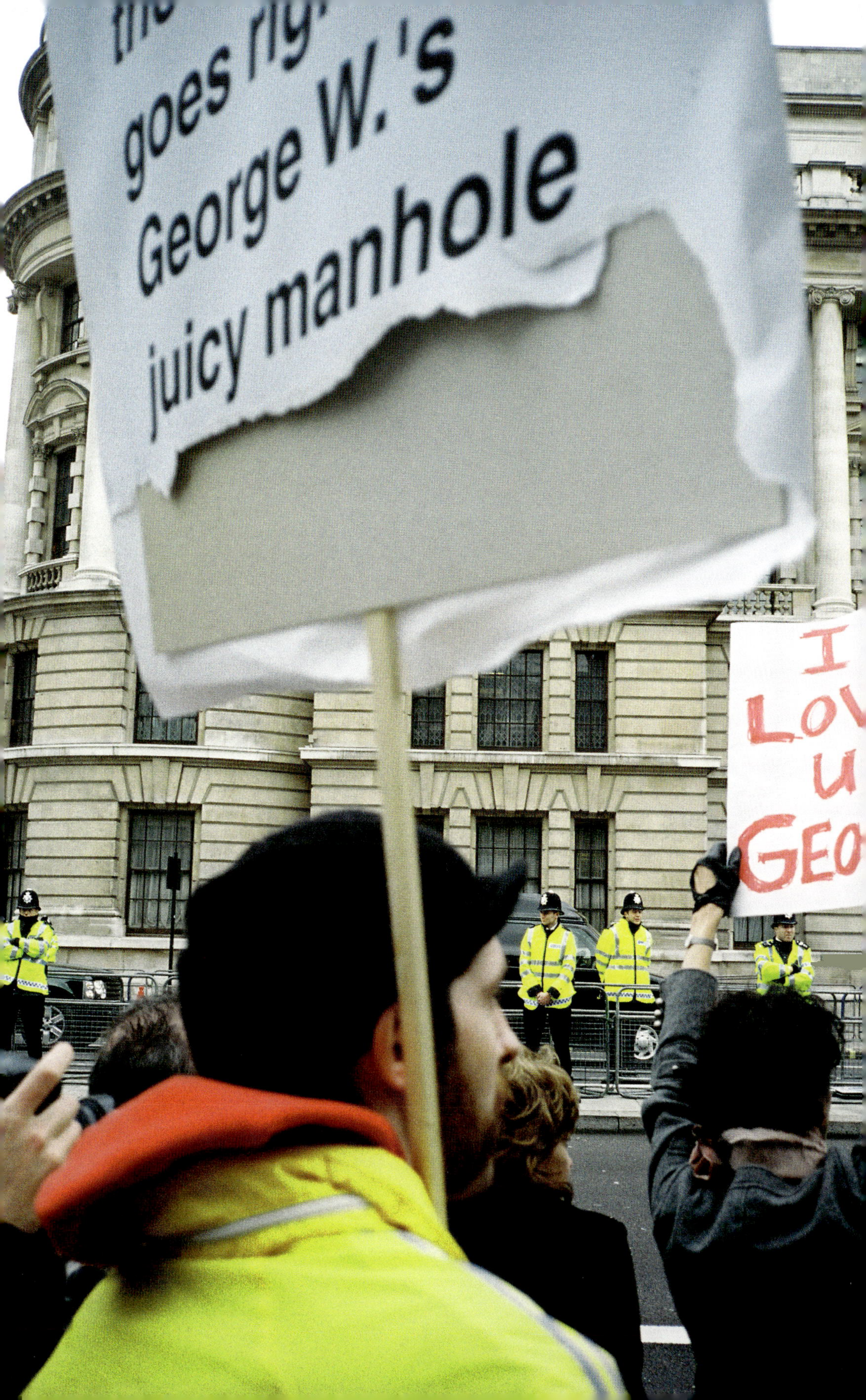
goes rig
George W.'s
juicy manhole
I
LOV
U
GEO

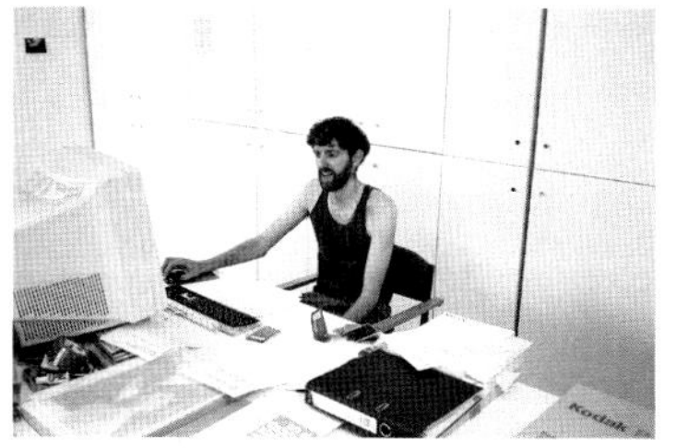

2004

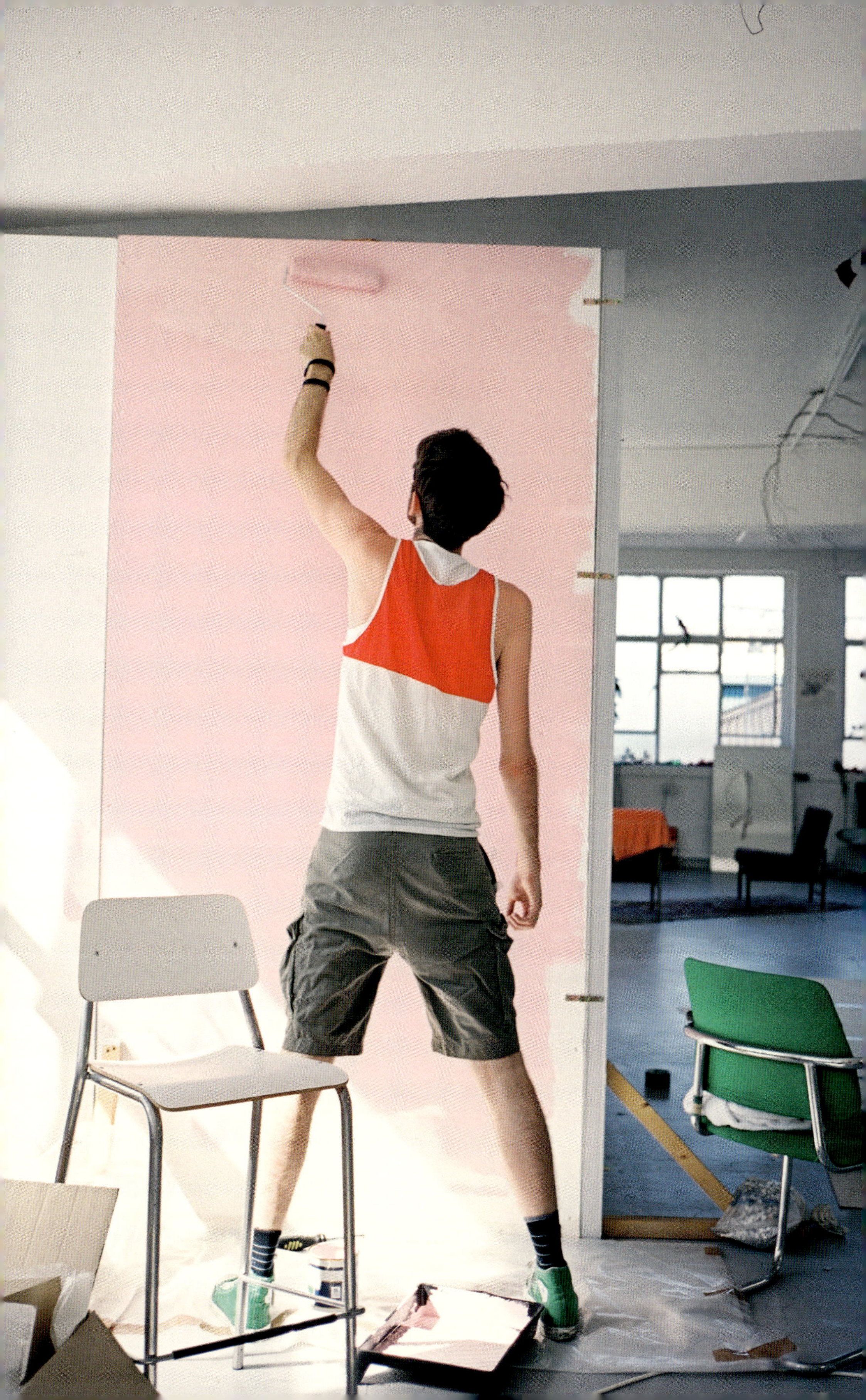

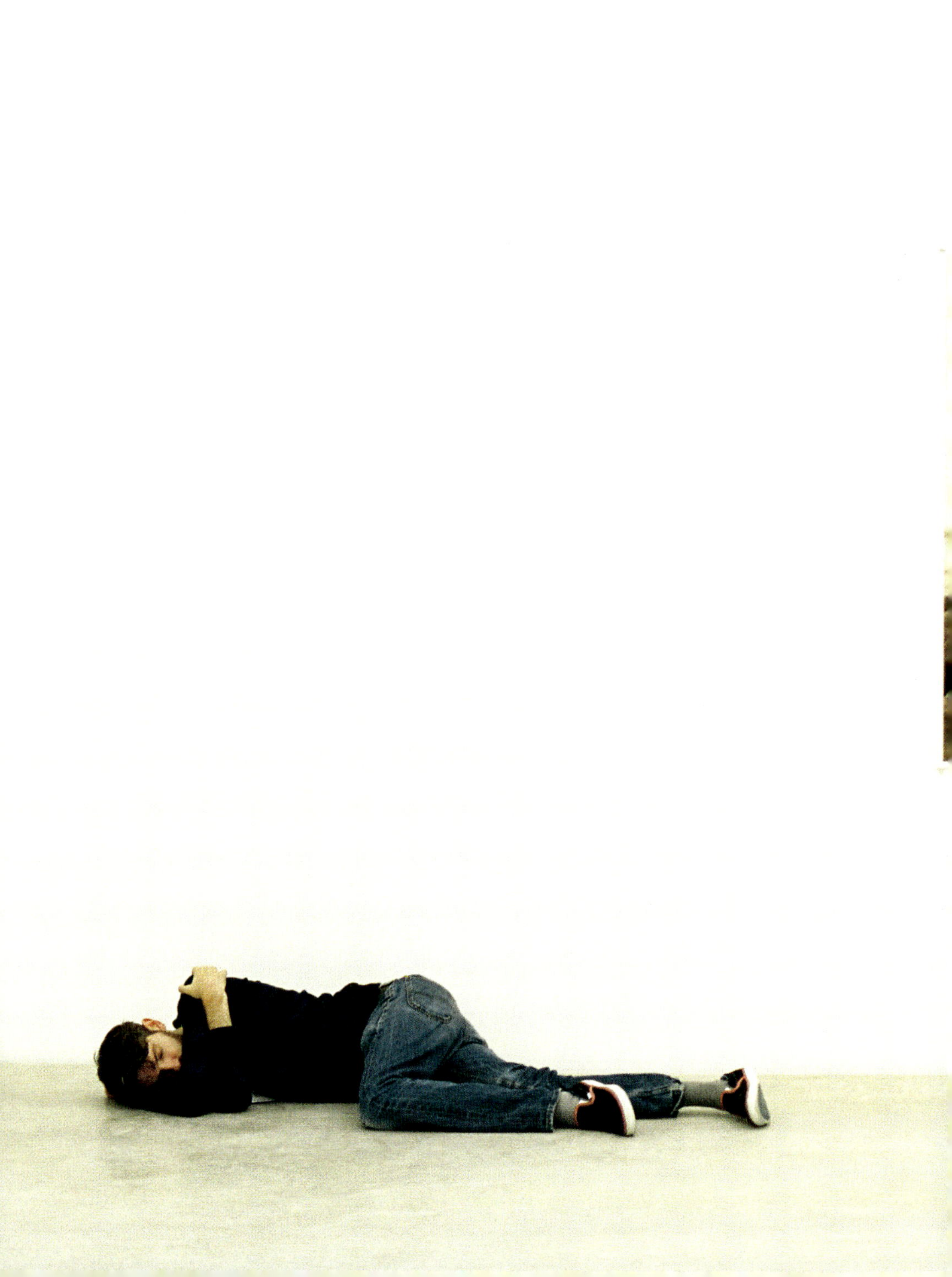

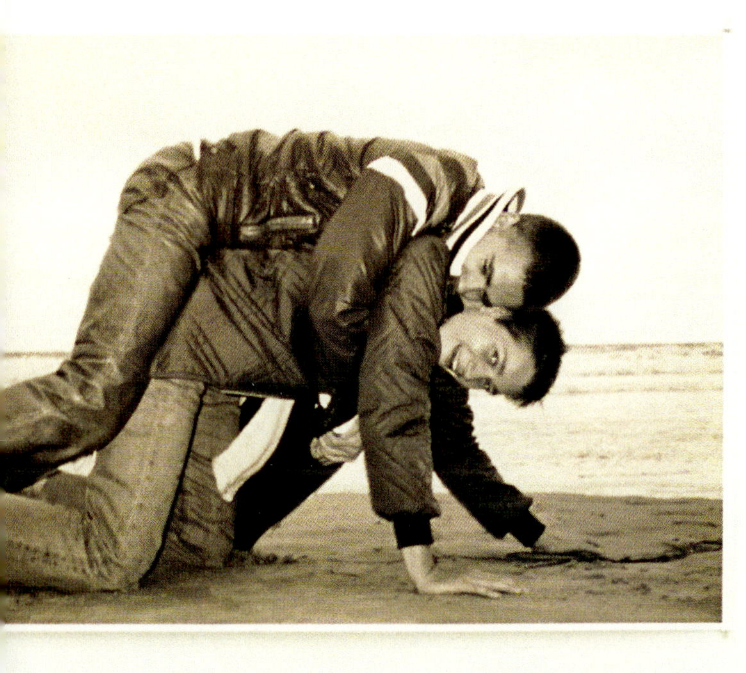

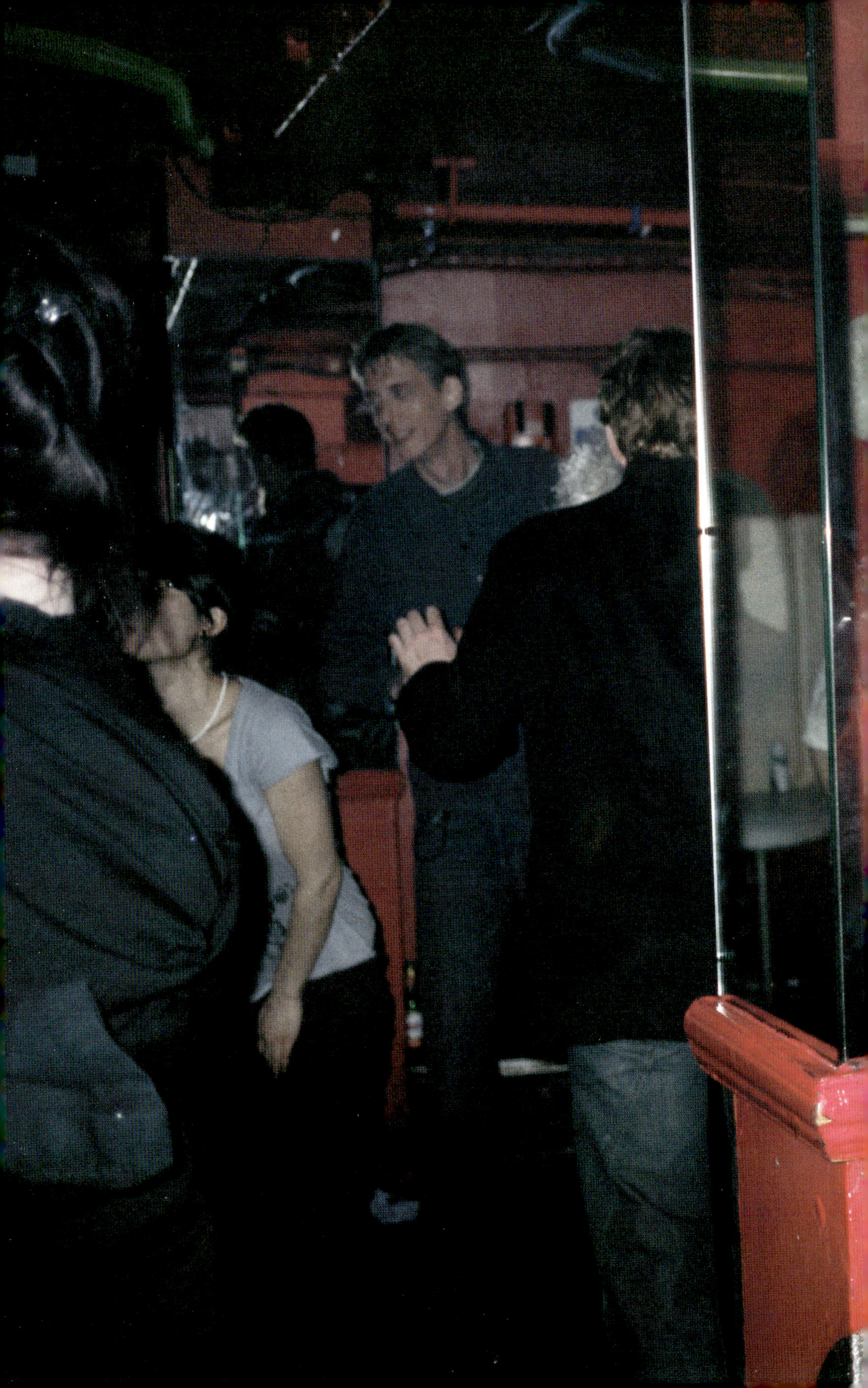

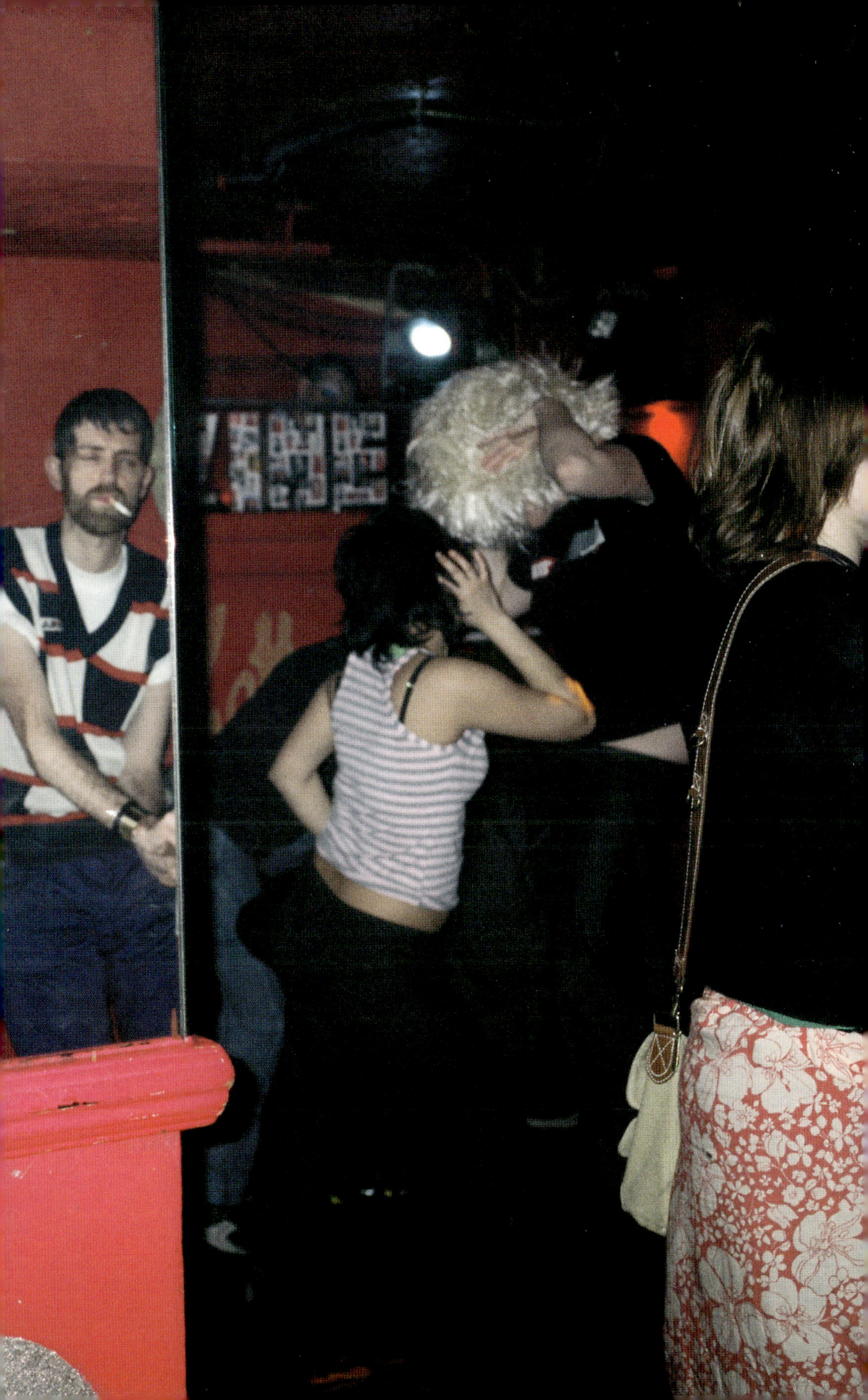

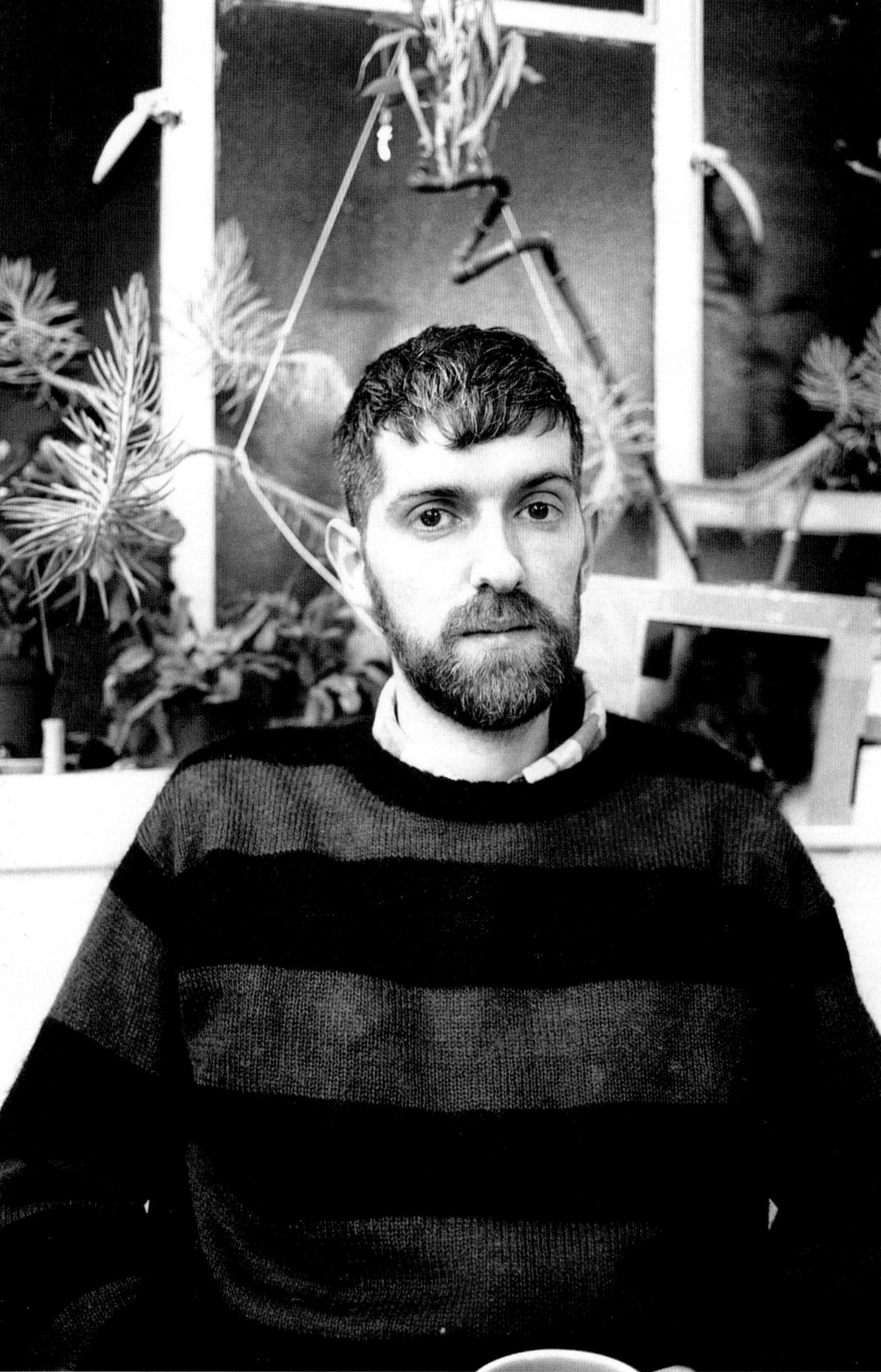

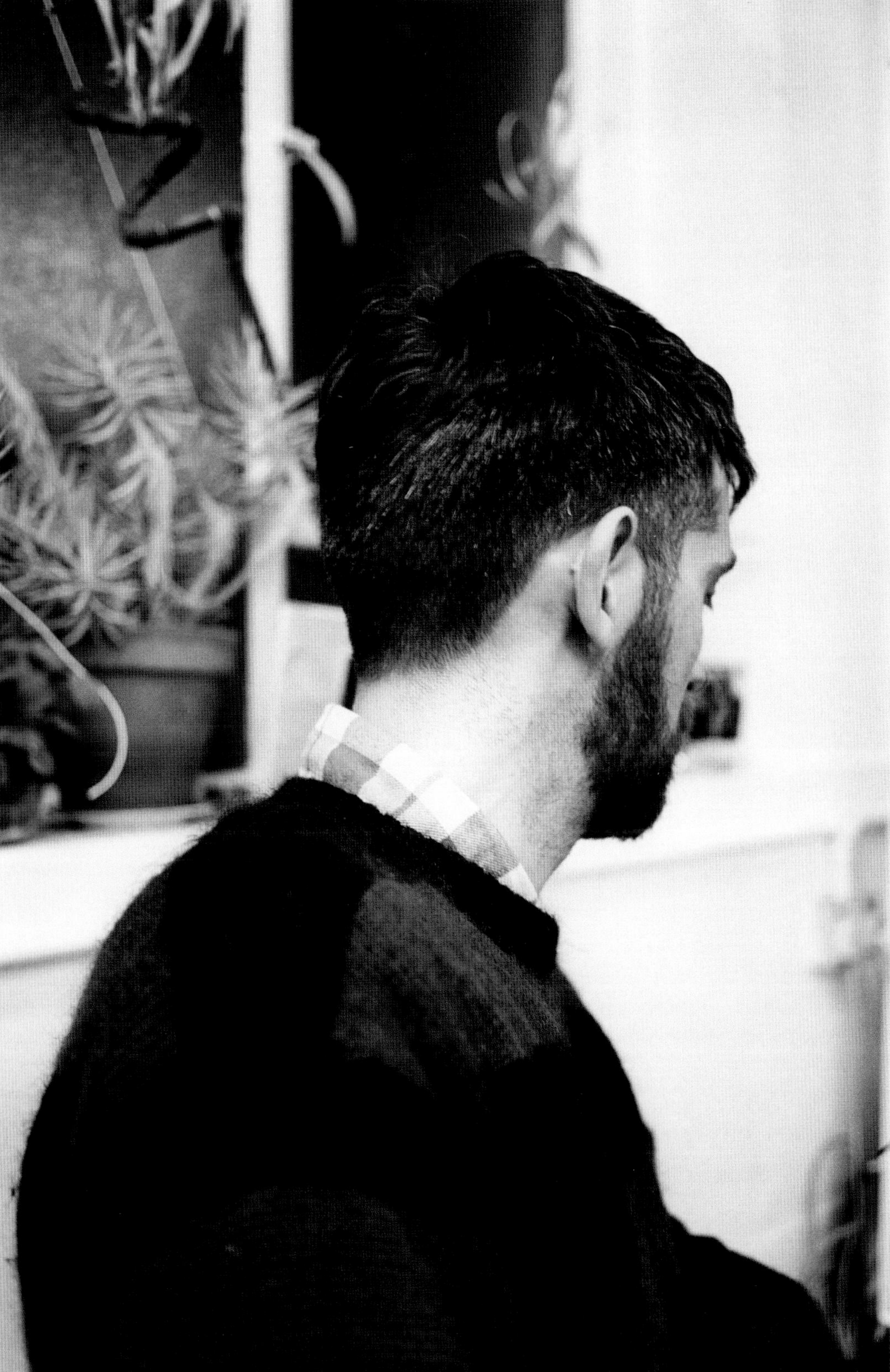

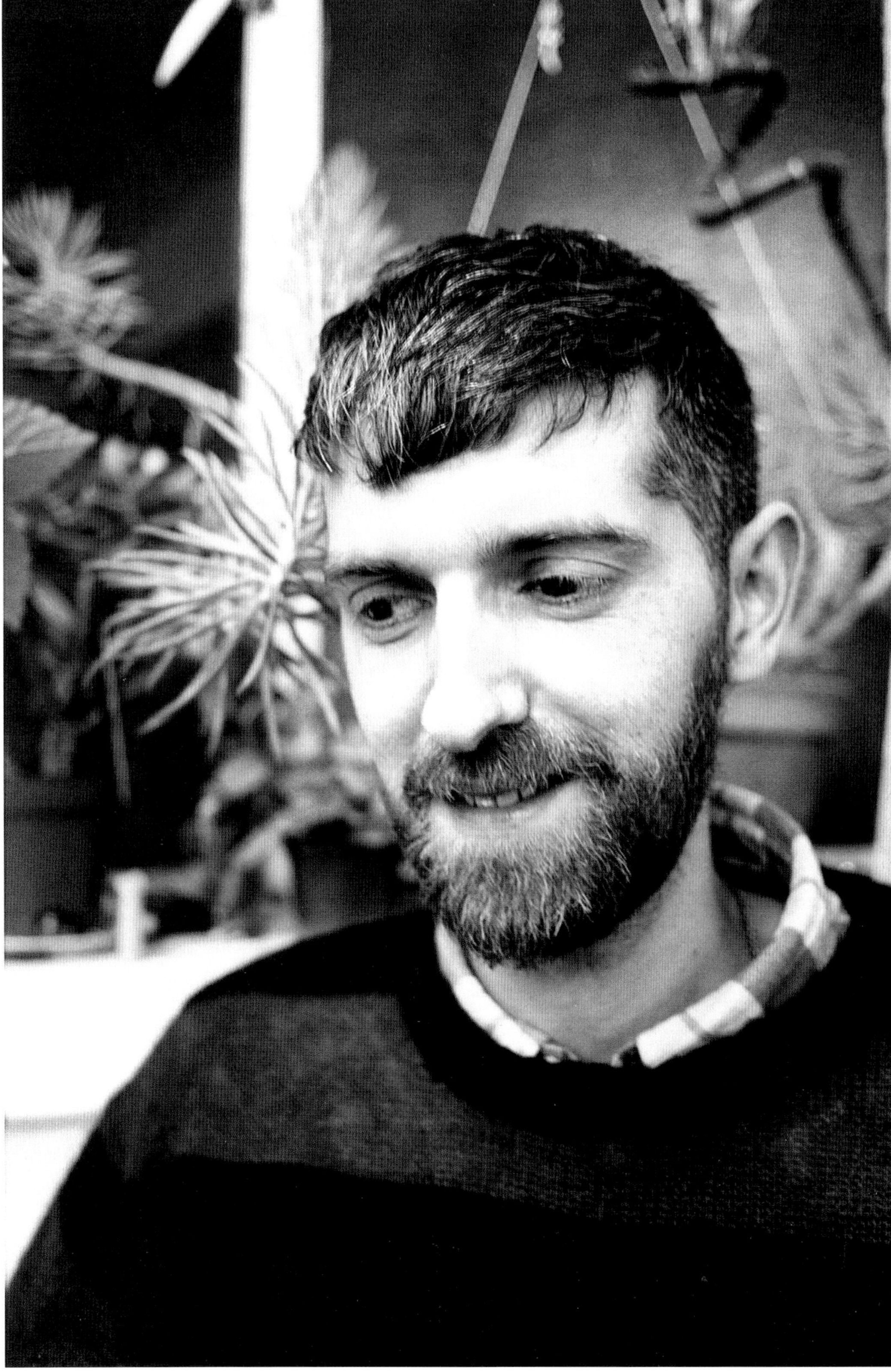

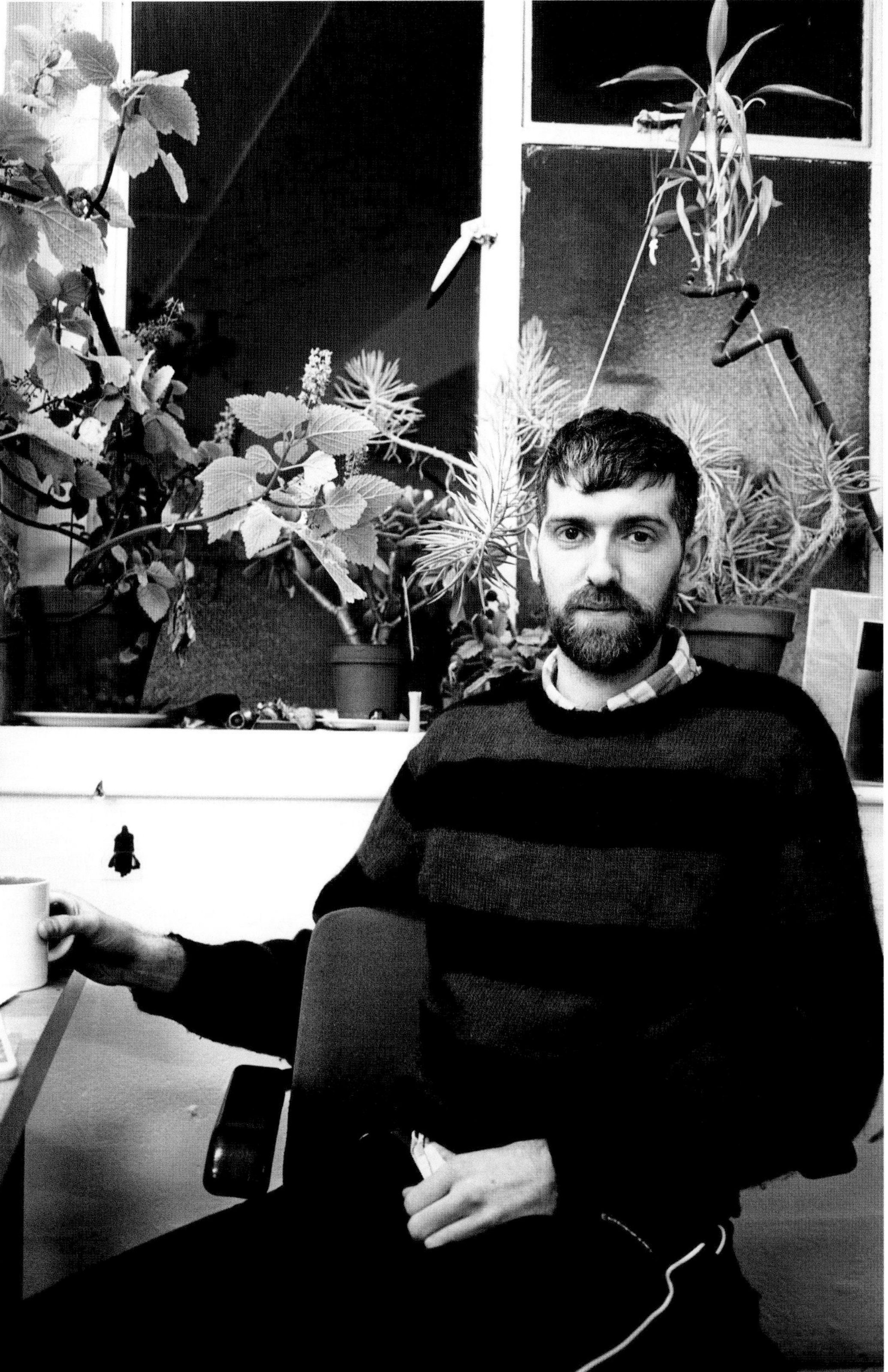

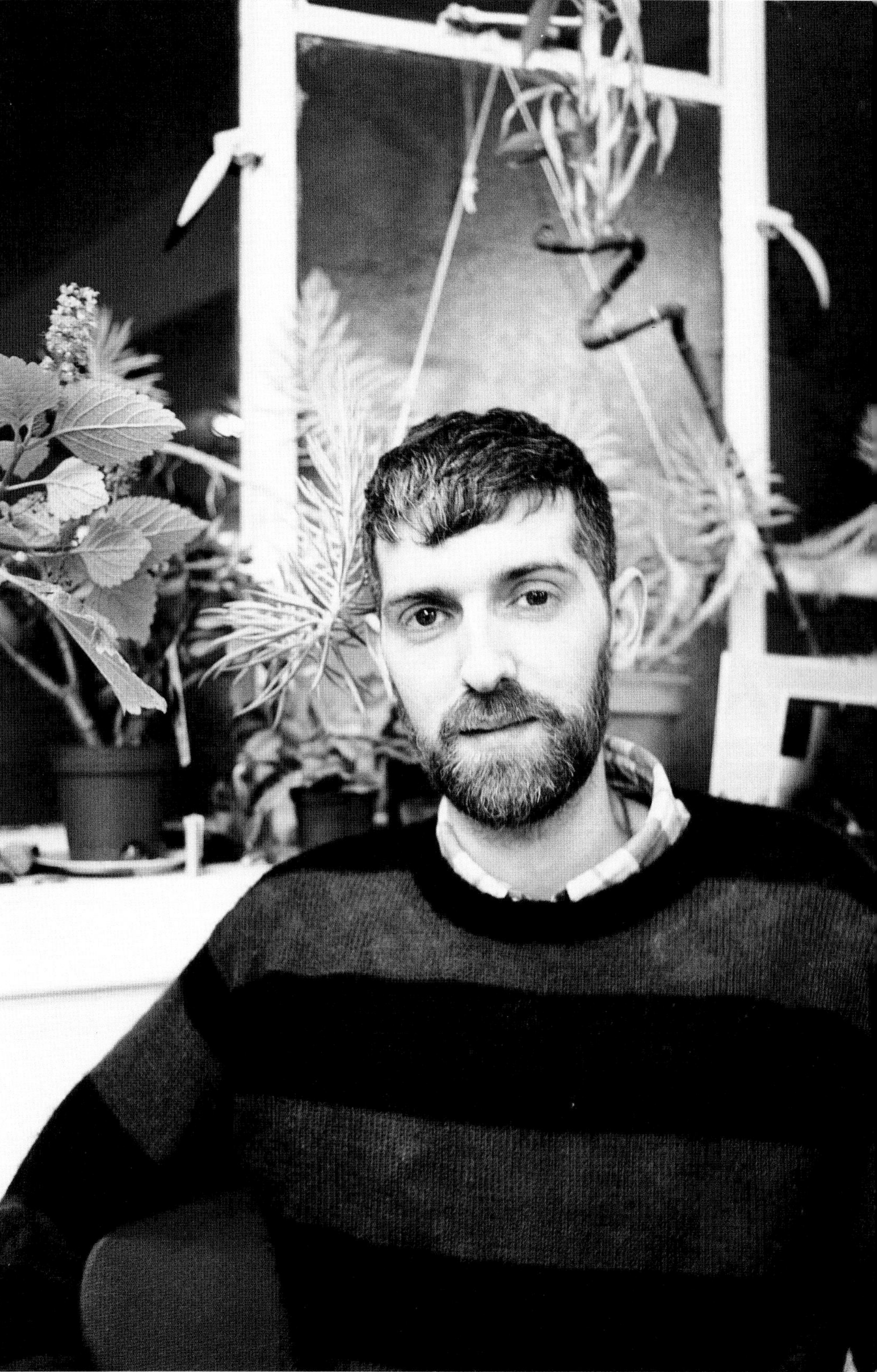

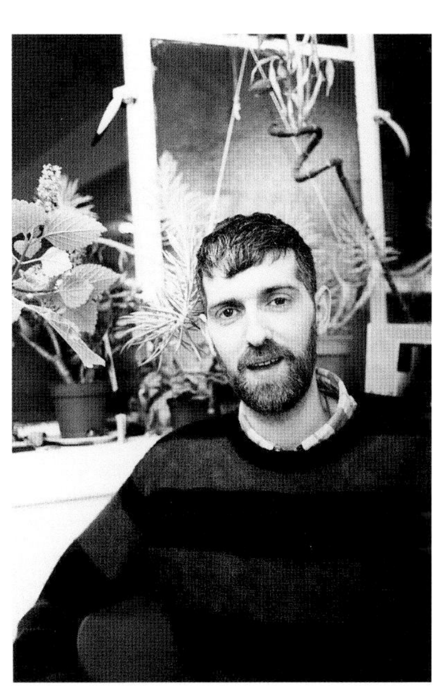

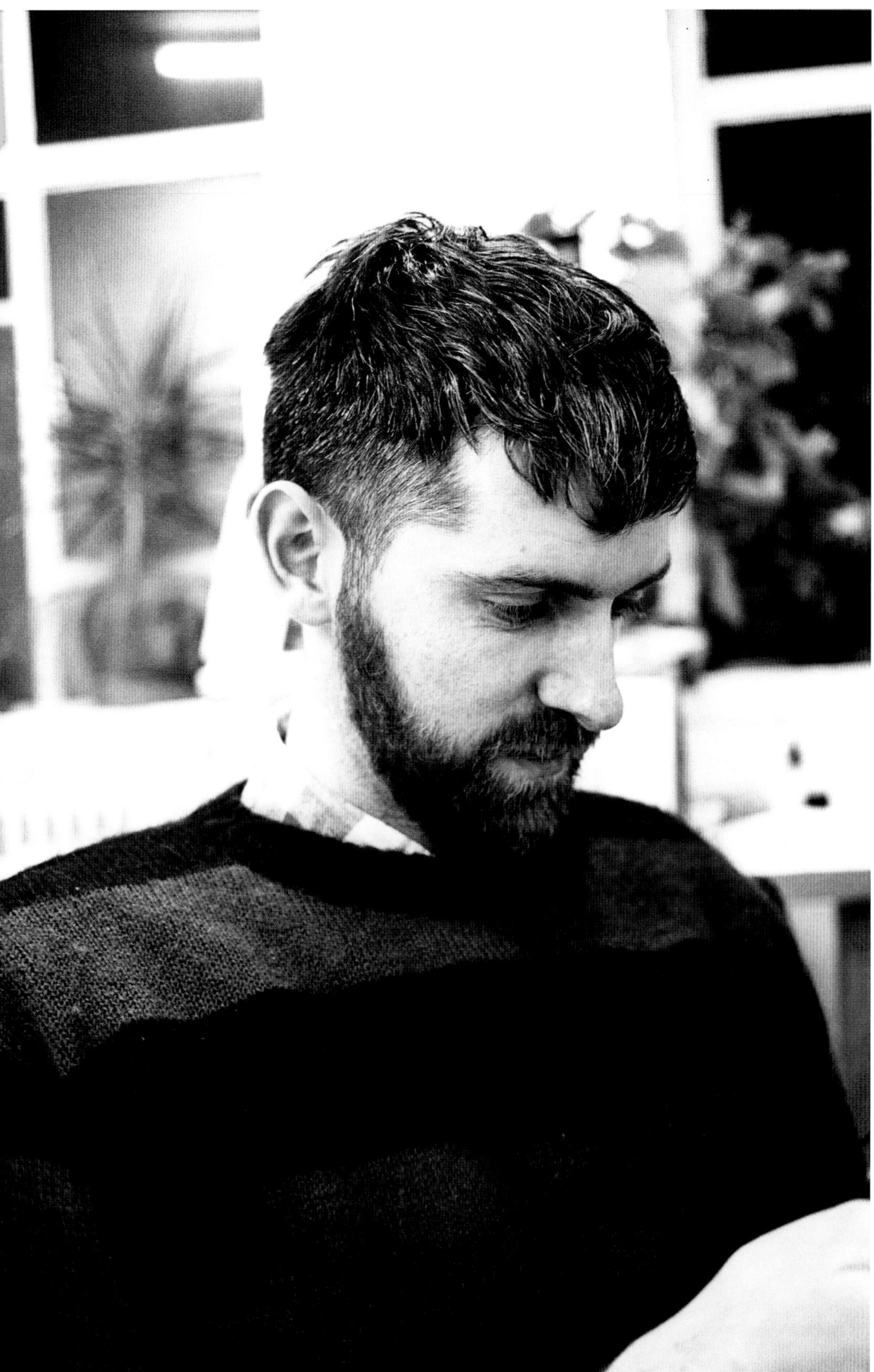

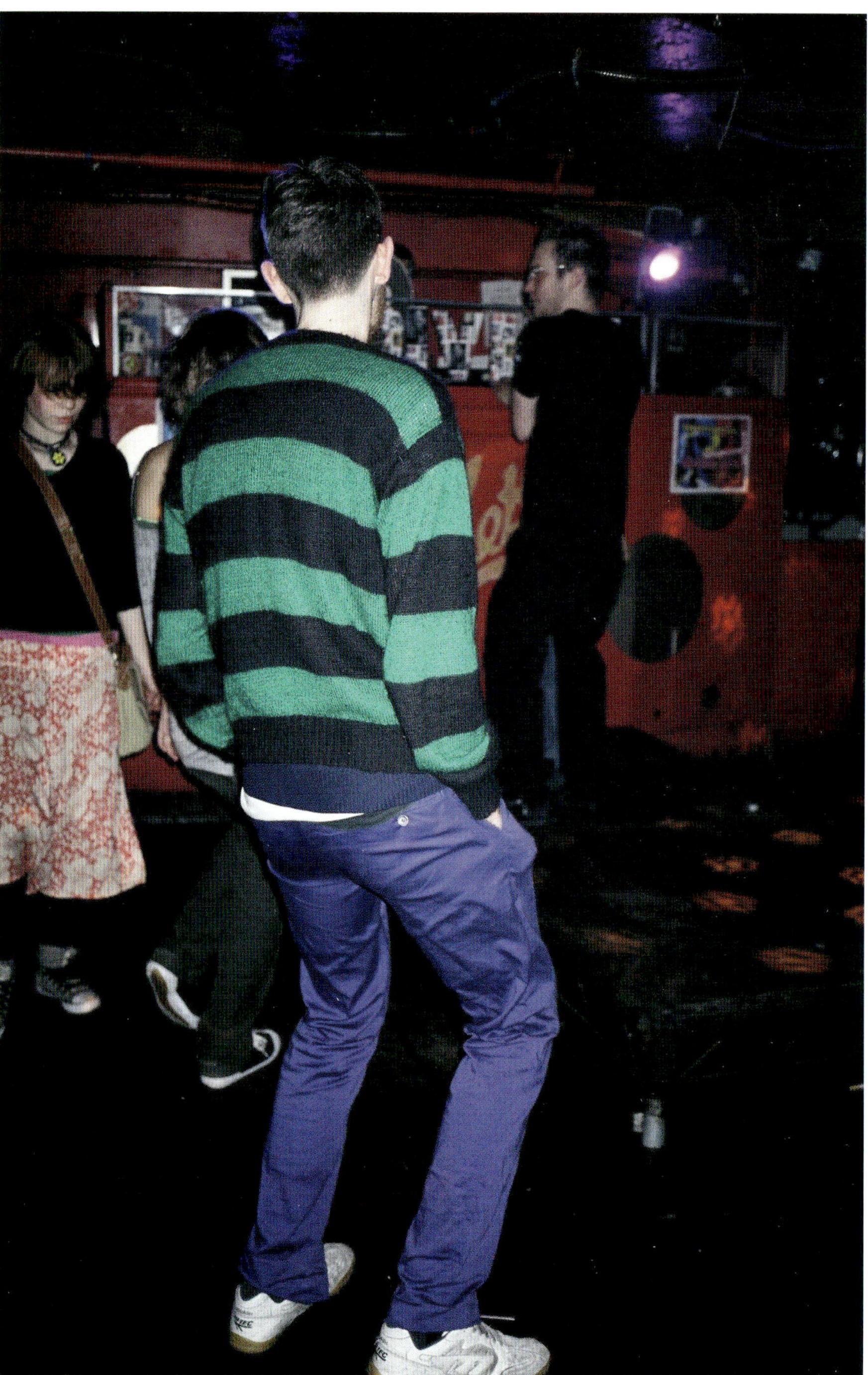

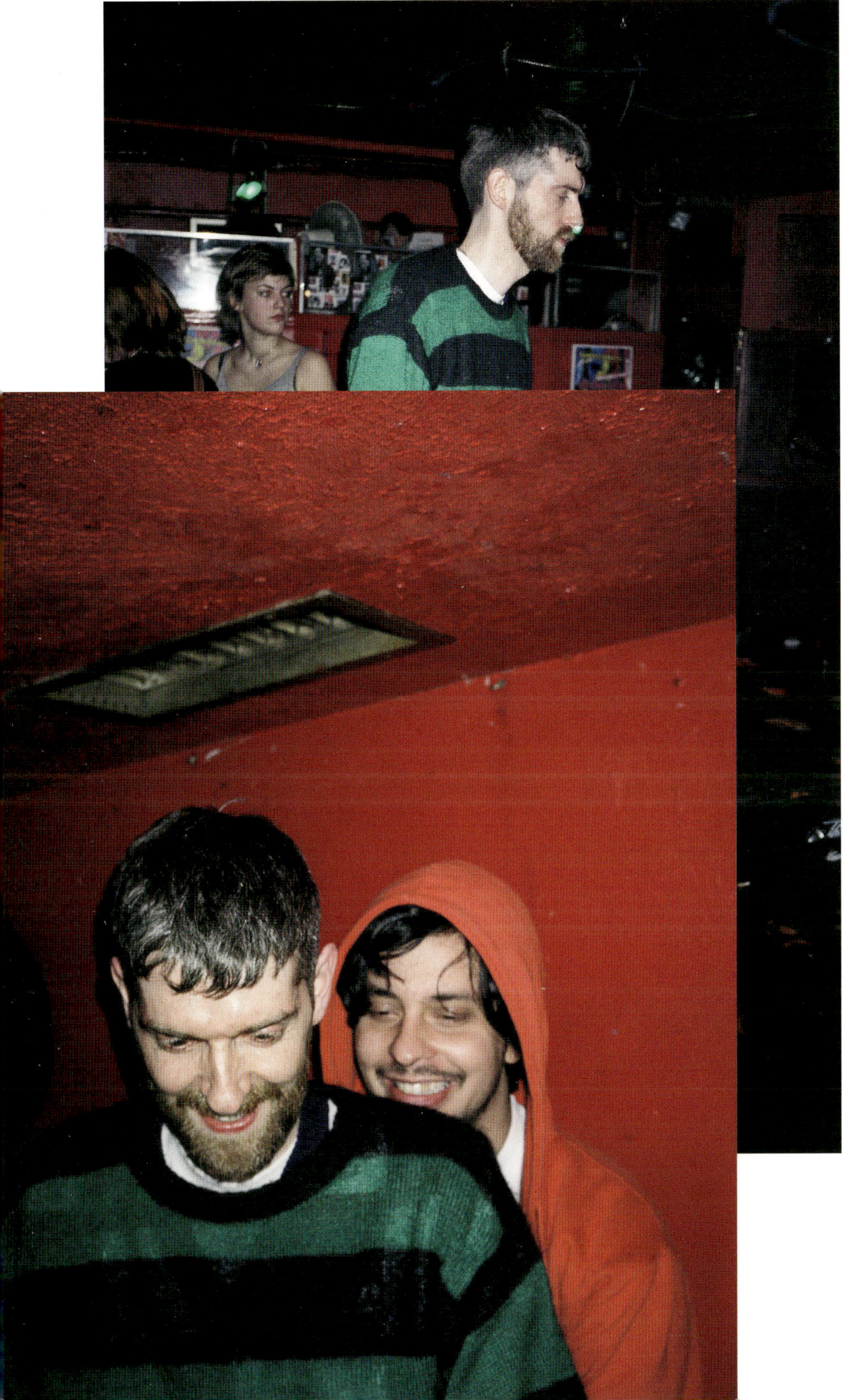

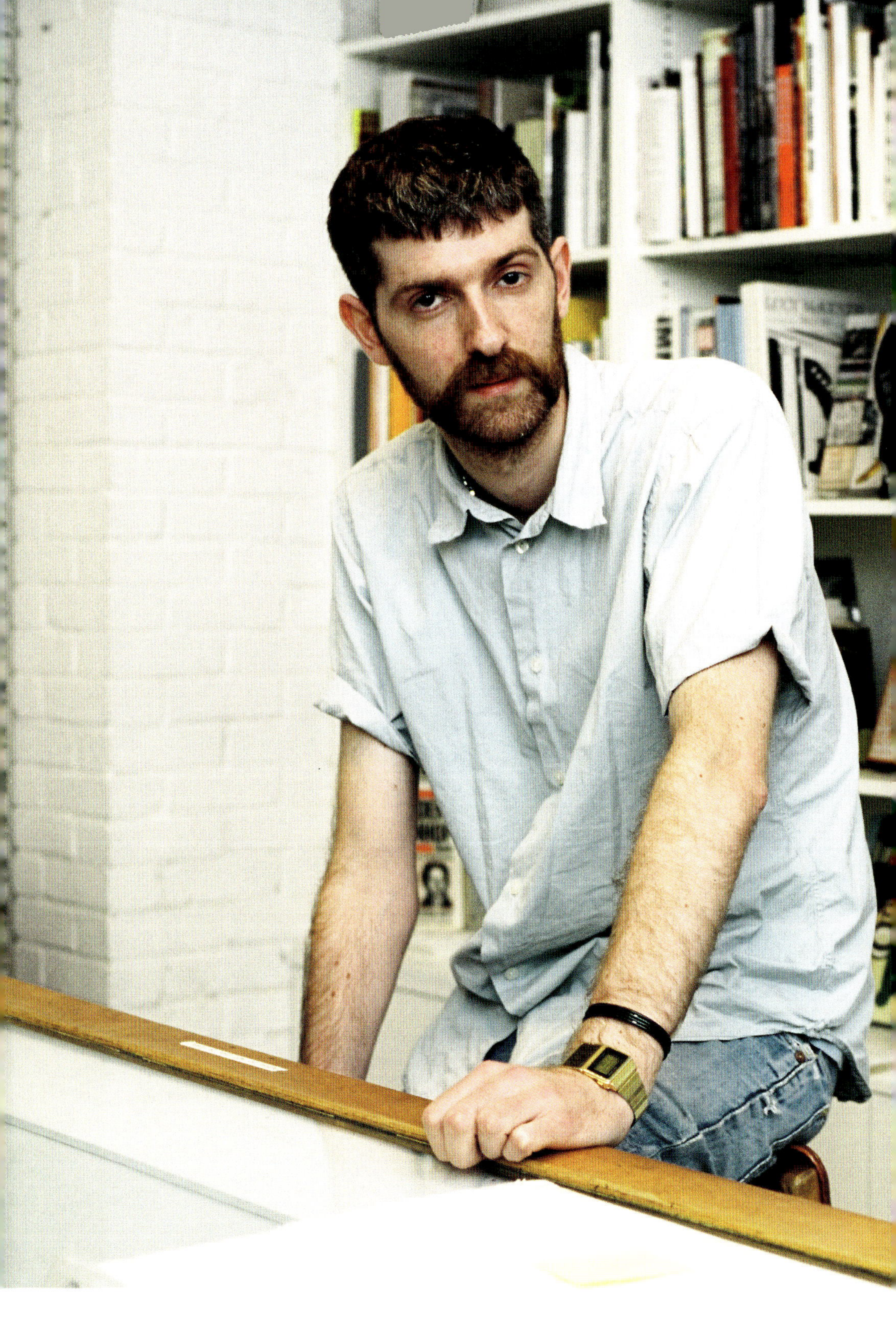

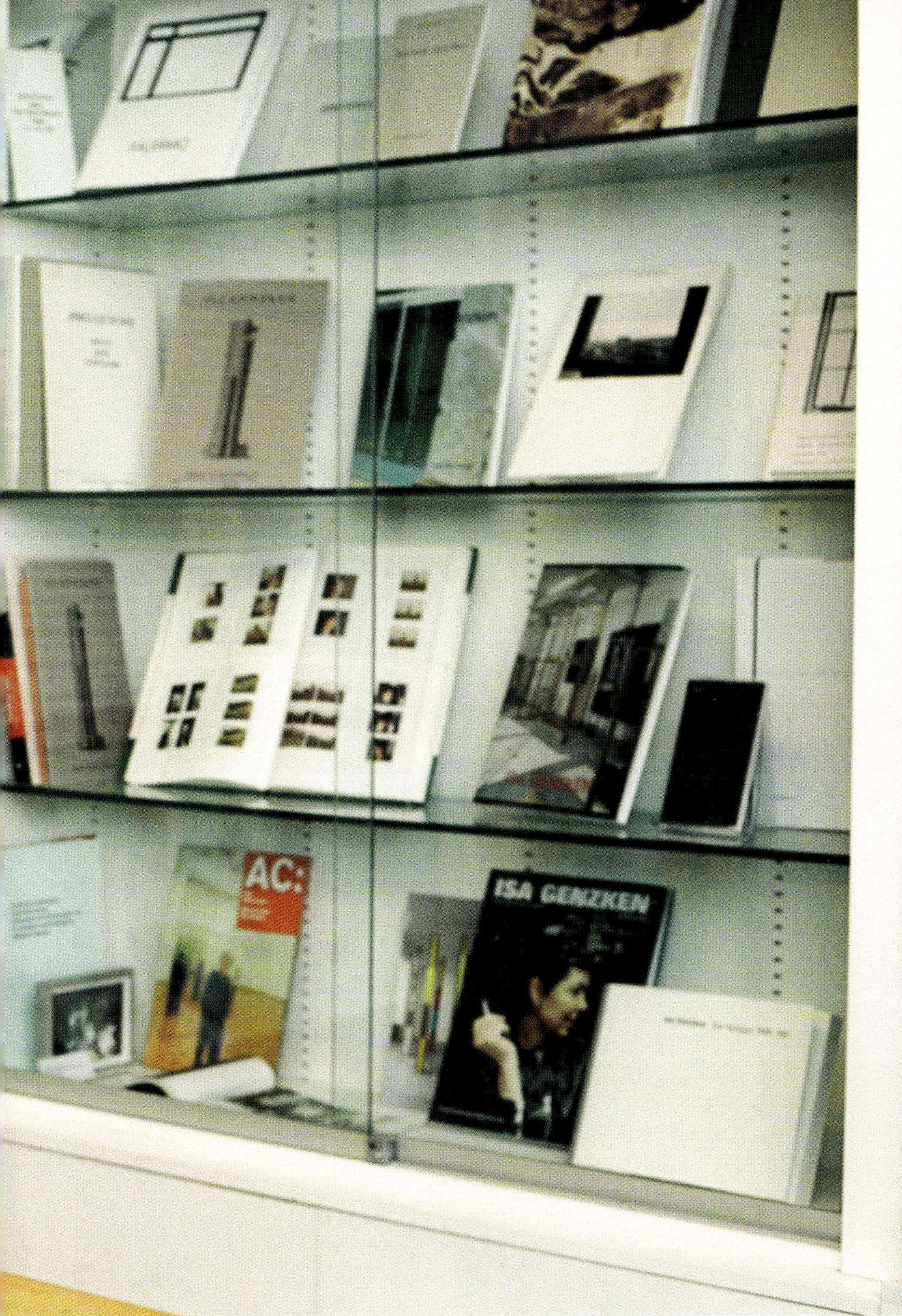
AC:
ISA GENZKEN

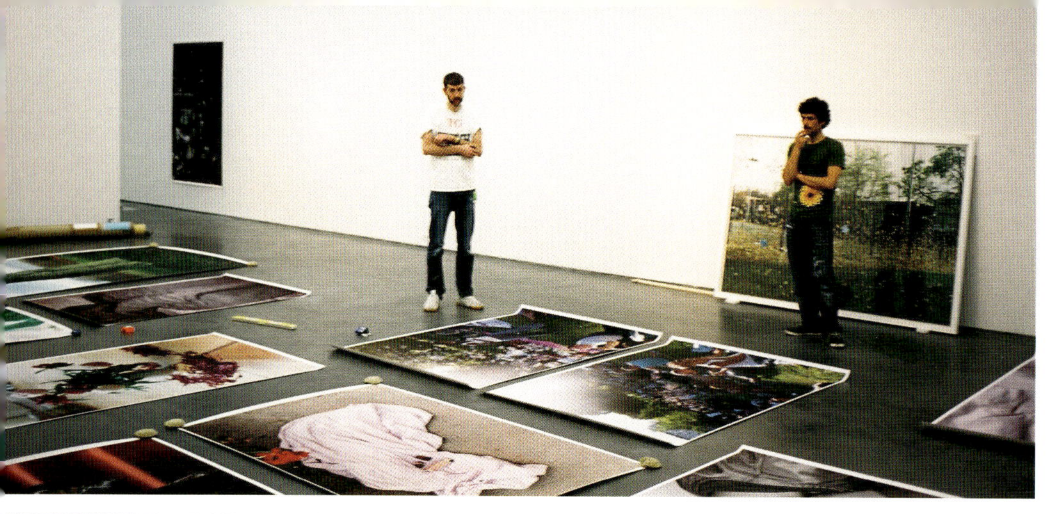

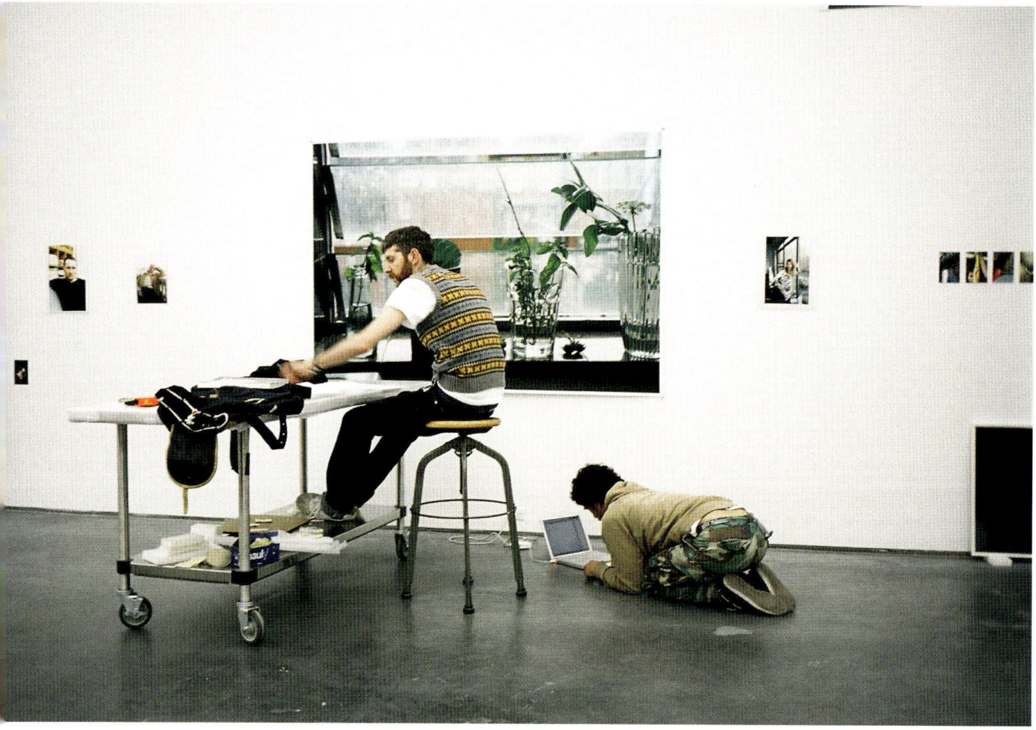

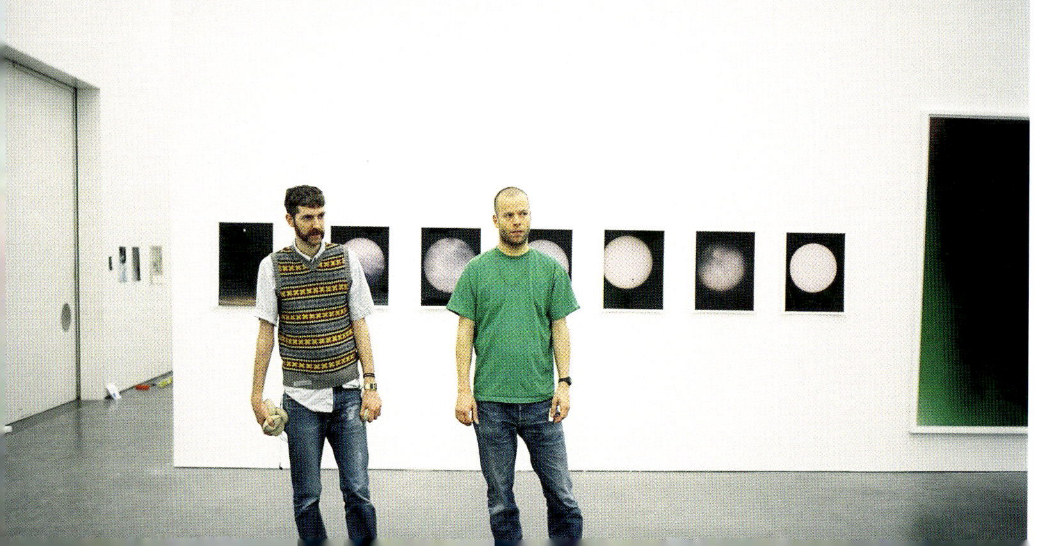

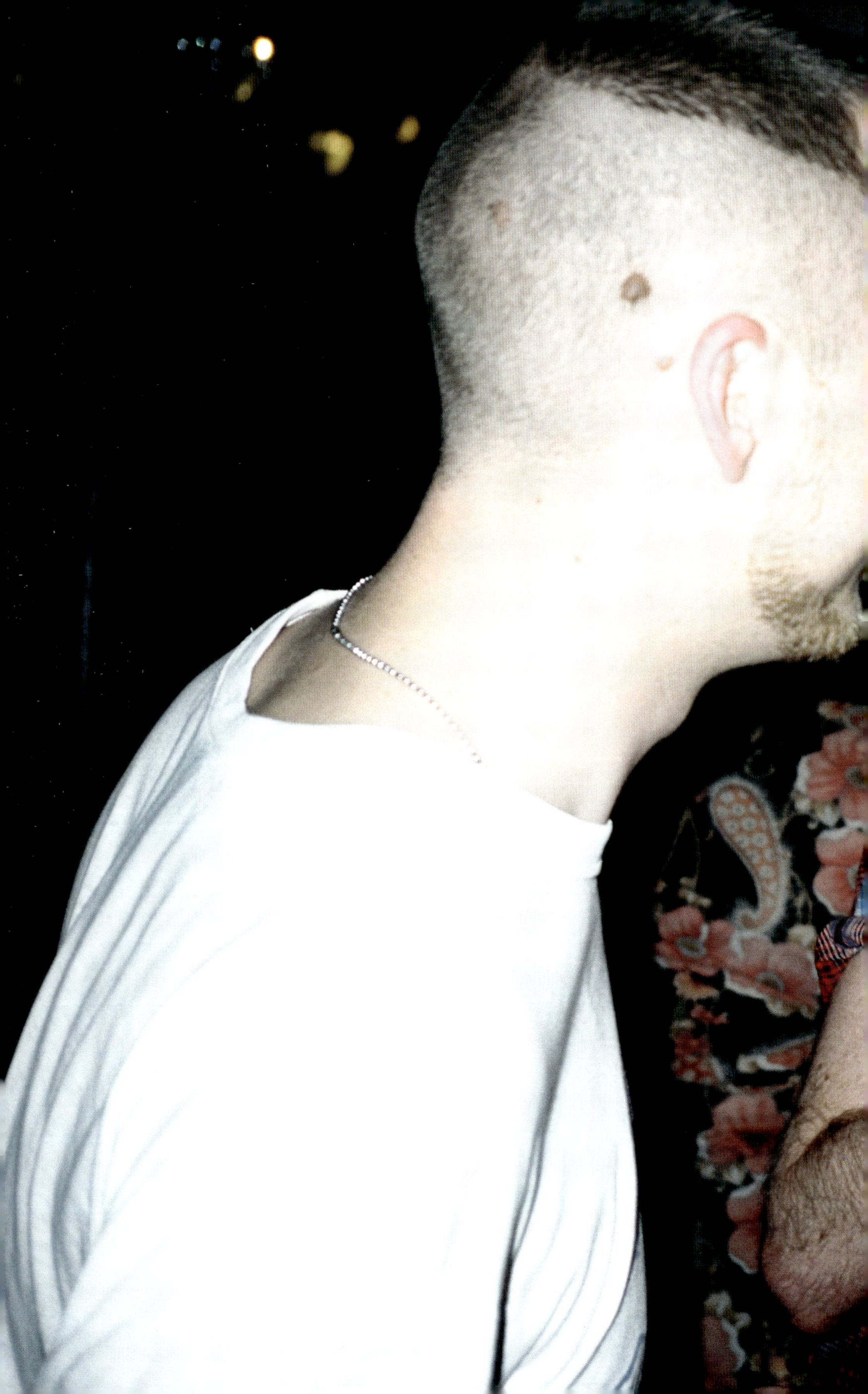

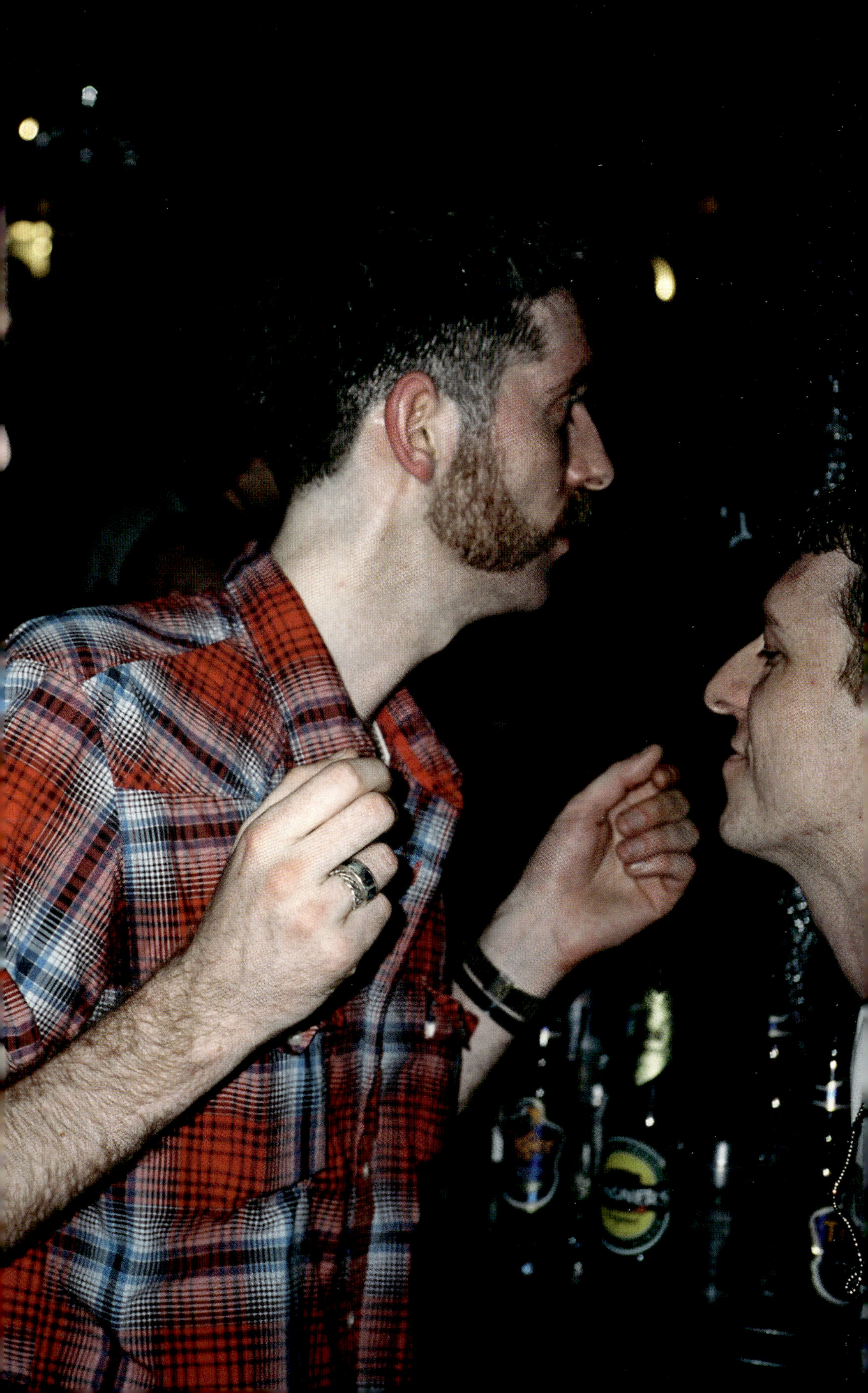

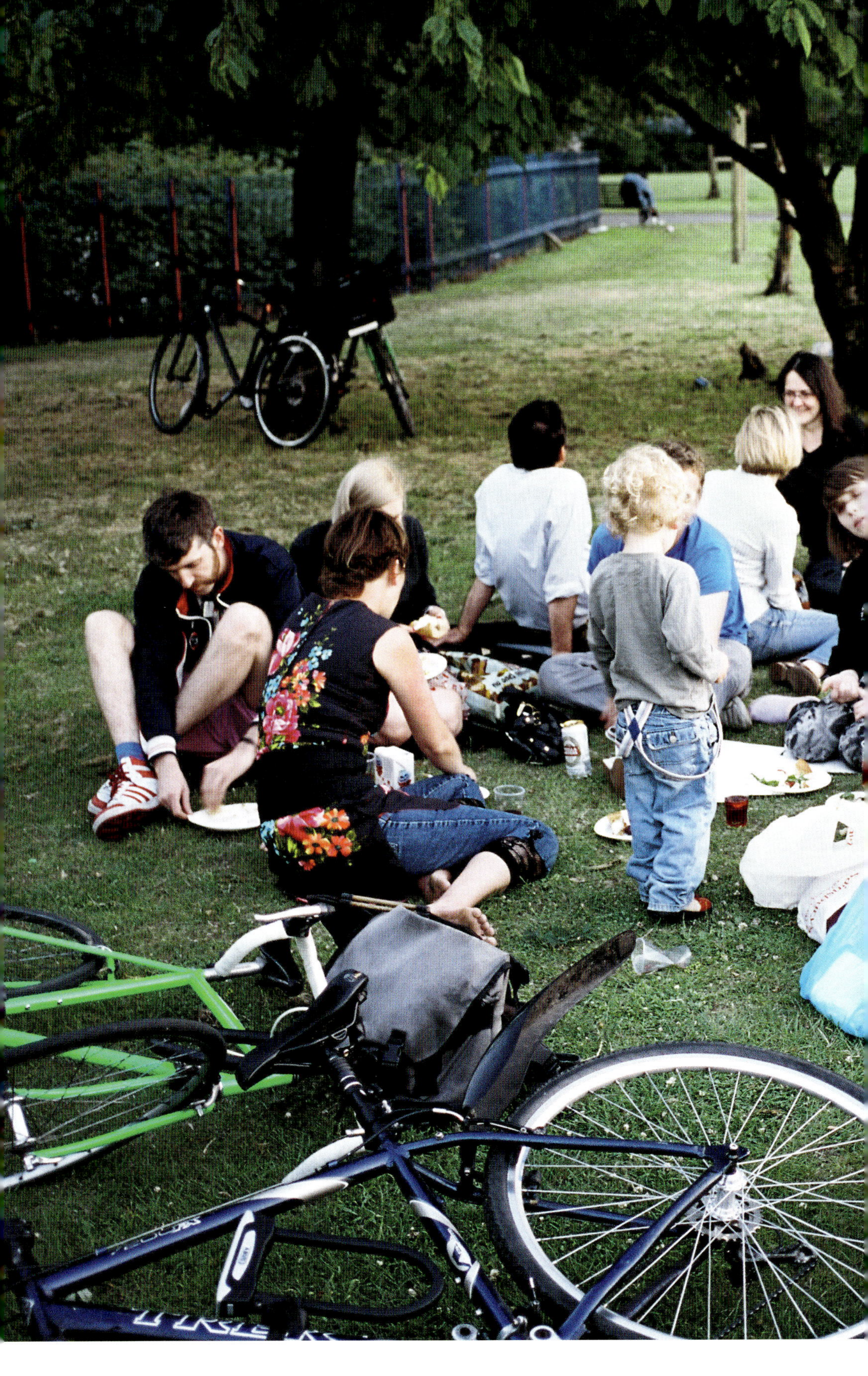

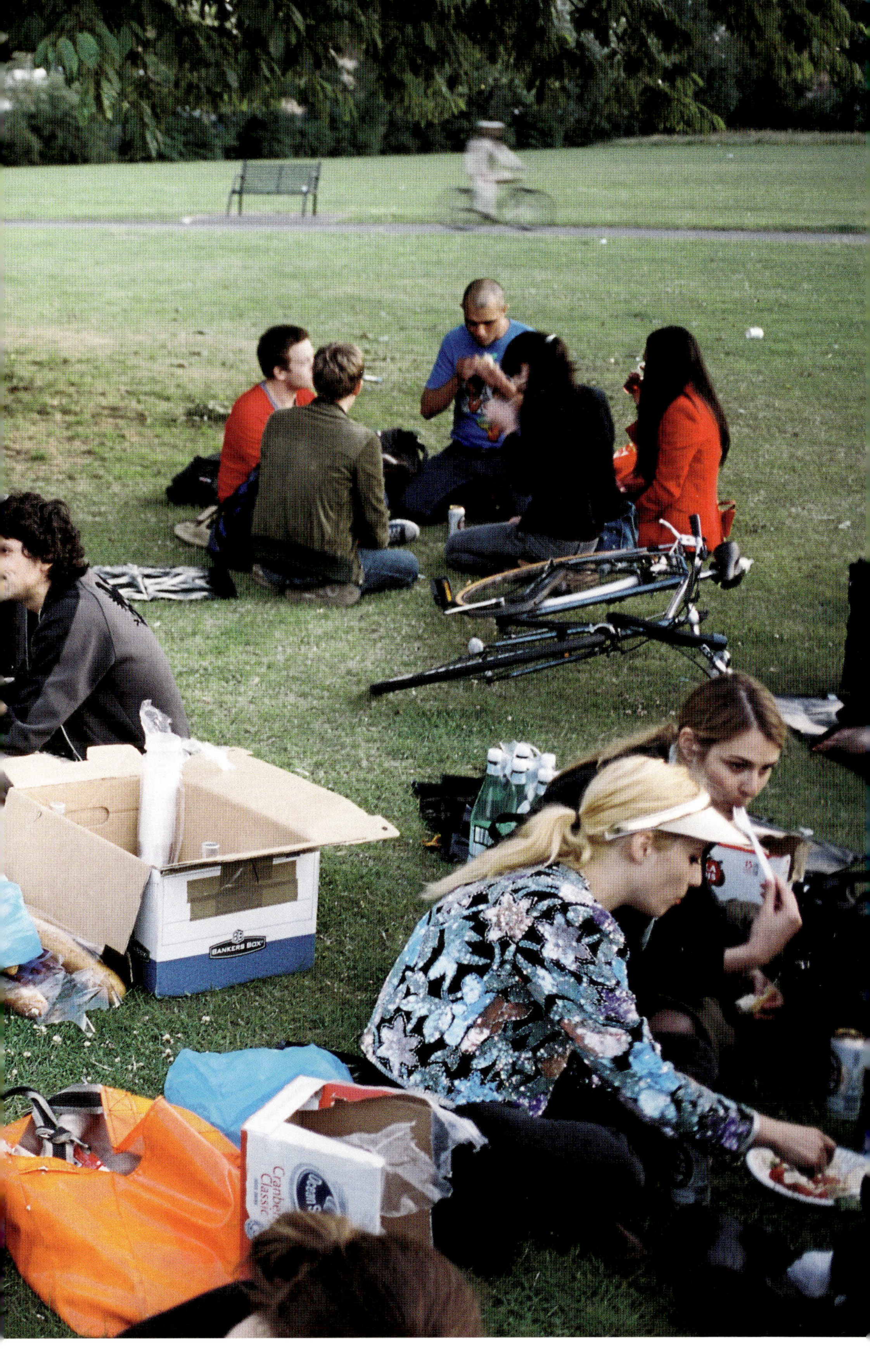
BANKERS BOX

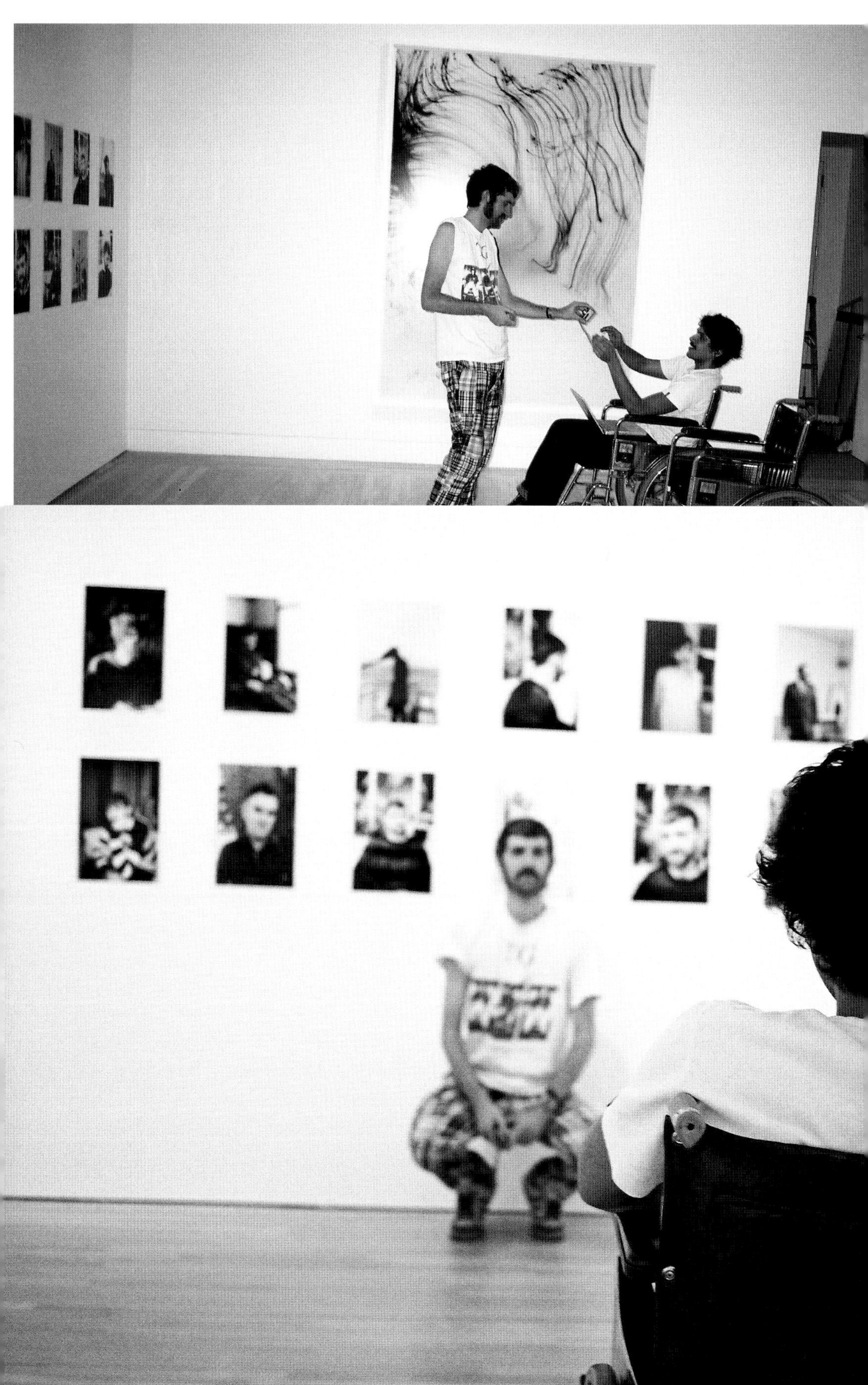

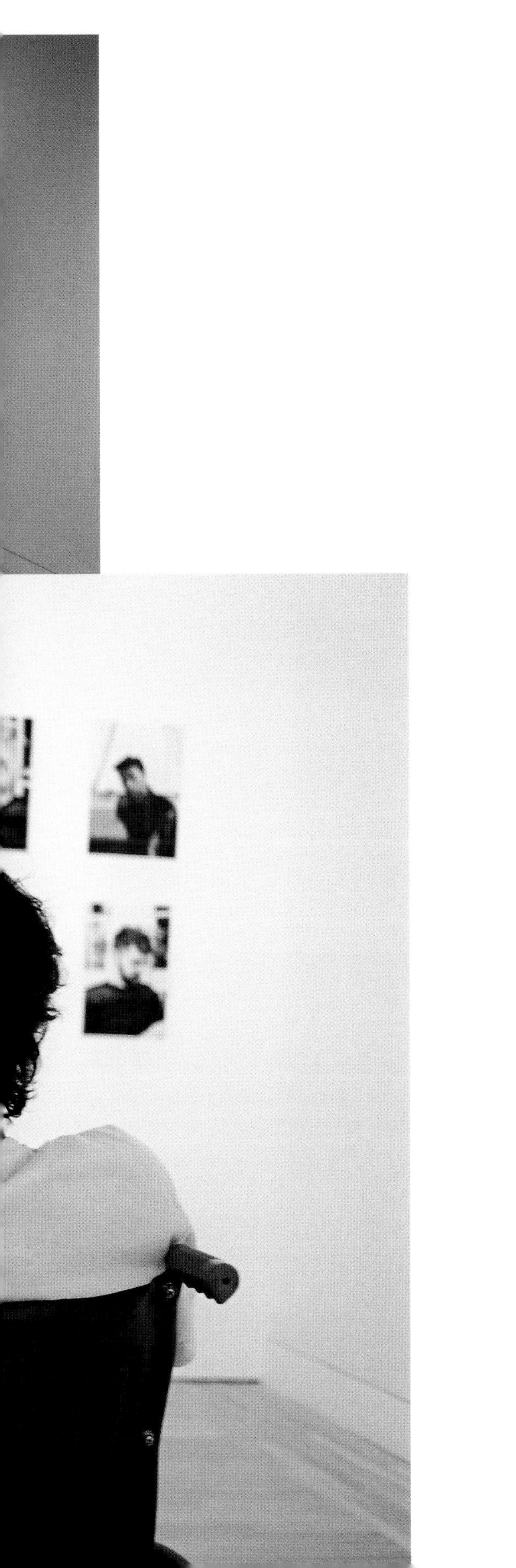

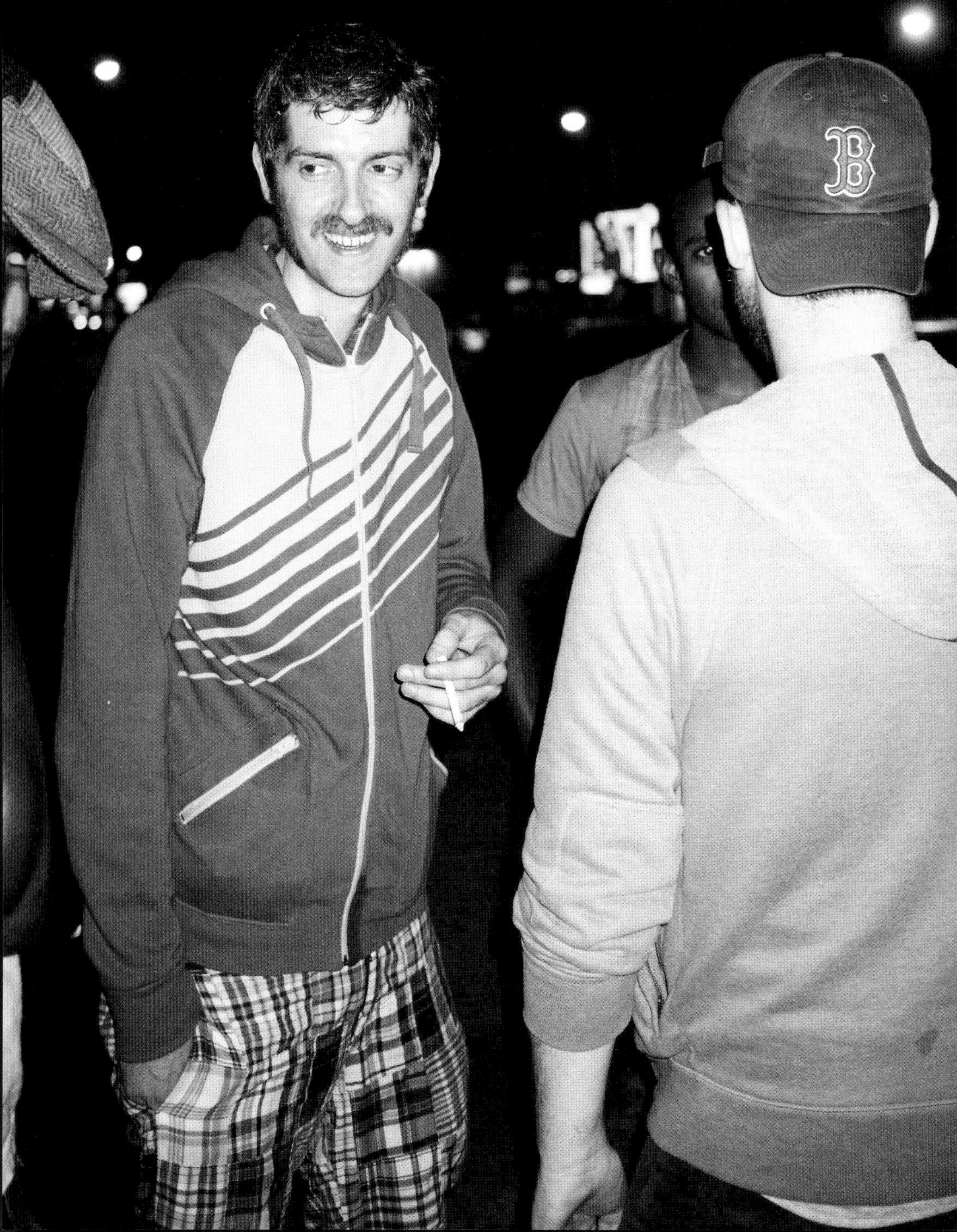

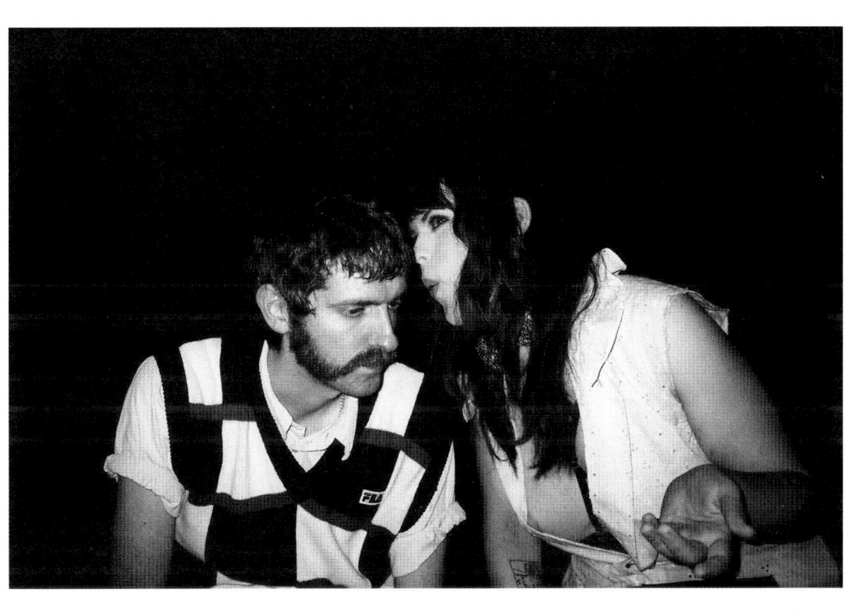

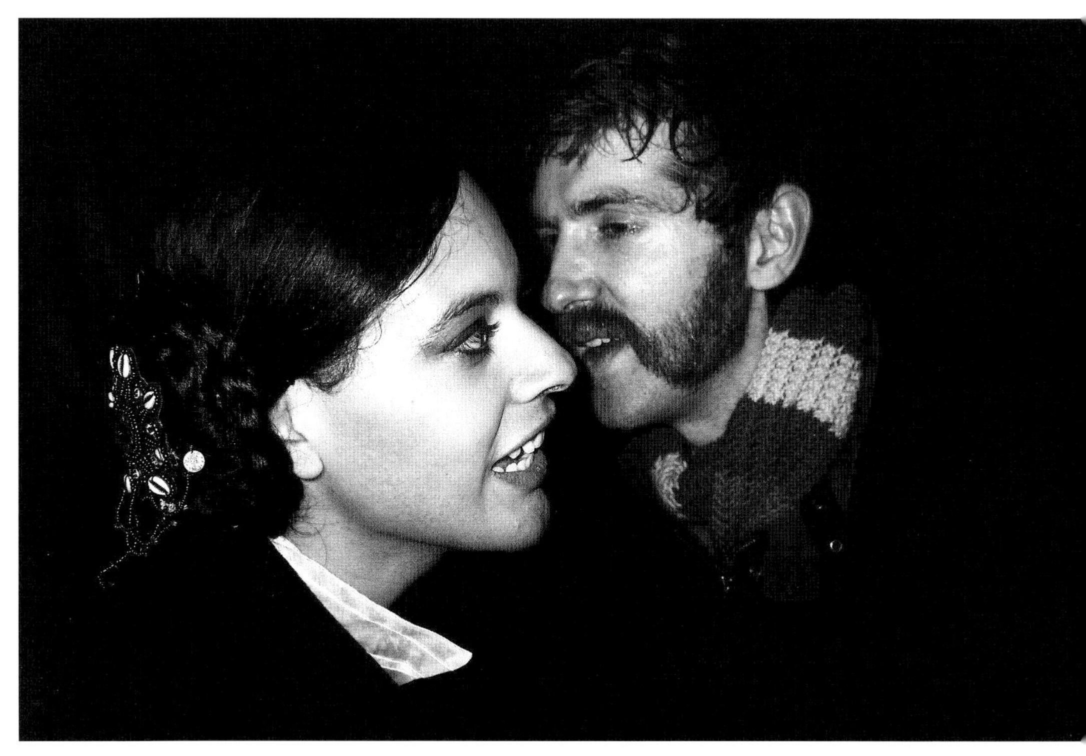

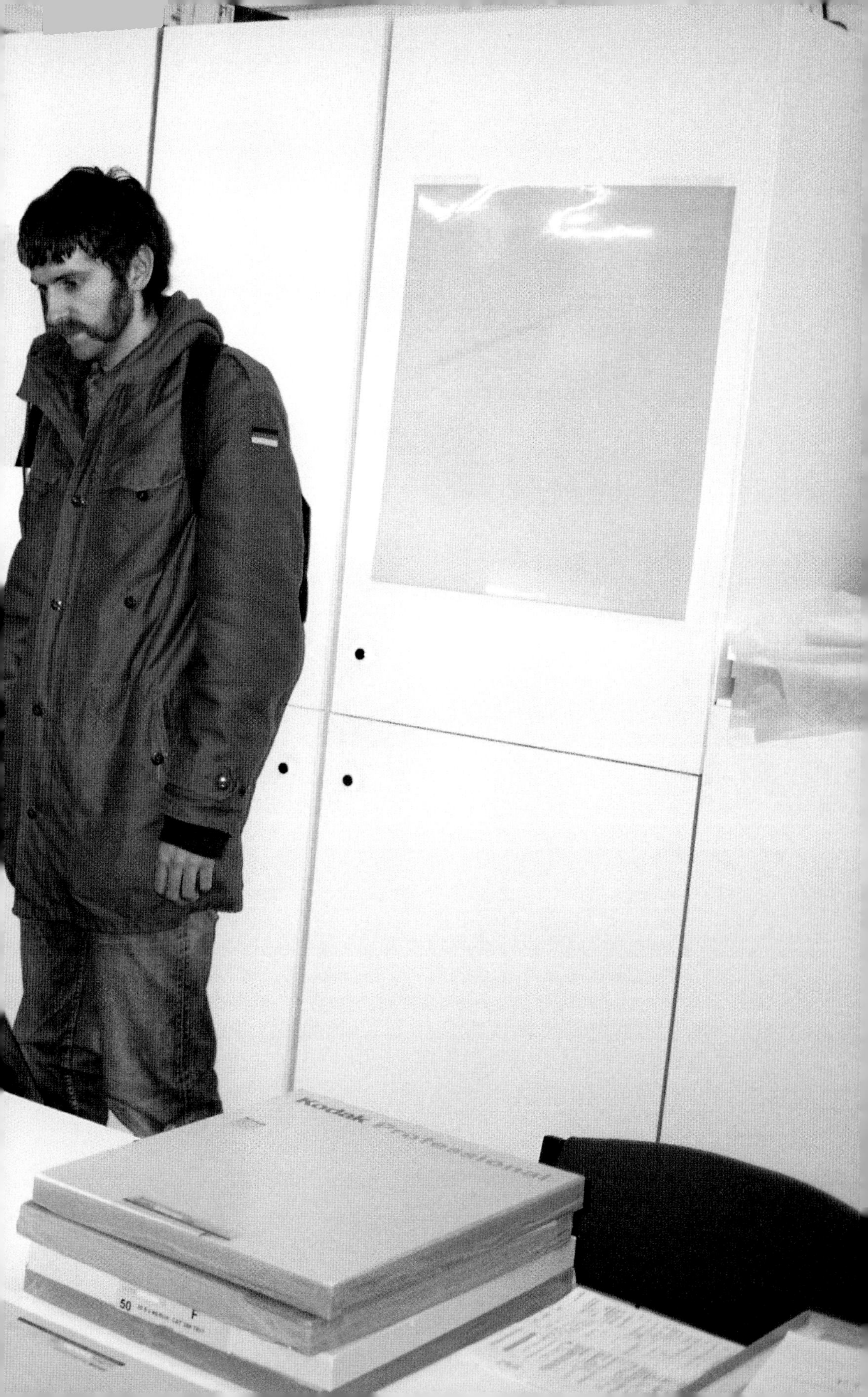
Kodak Professional
50
F

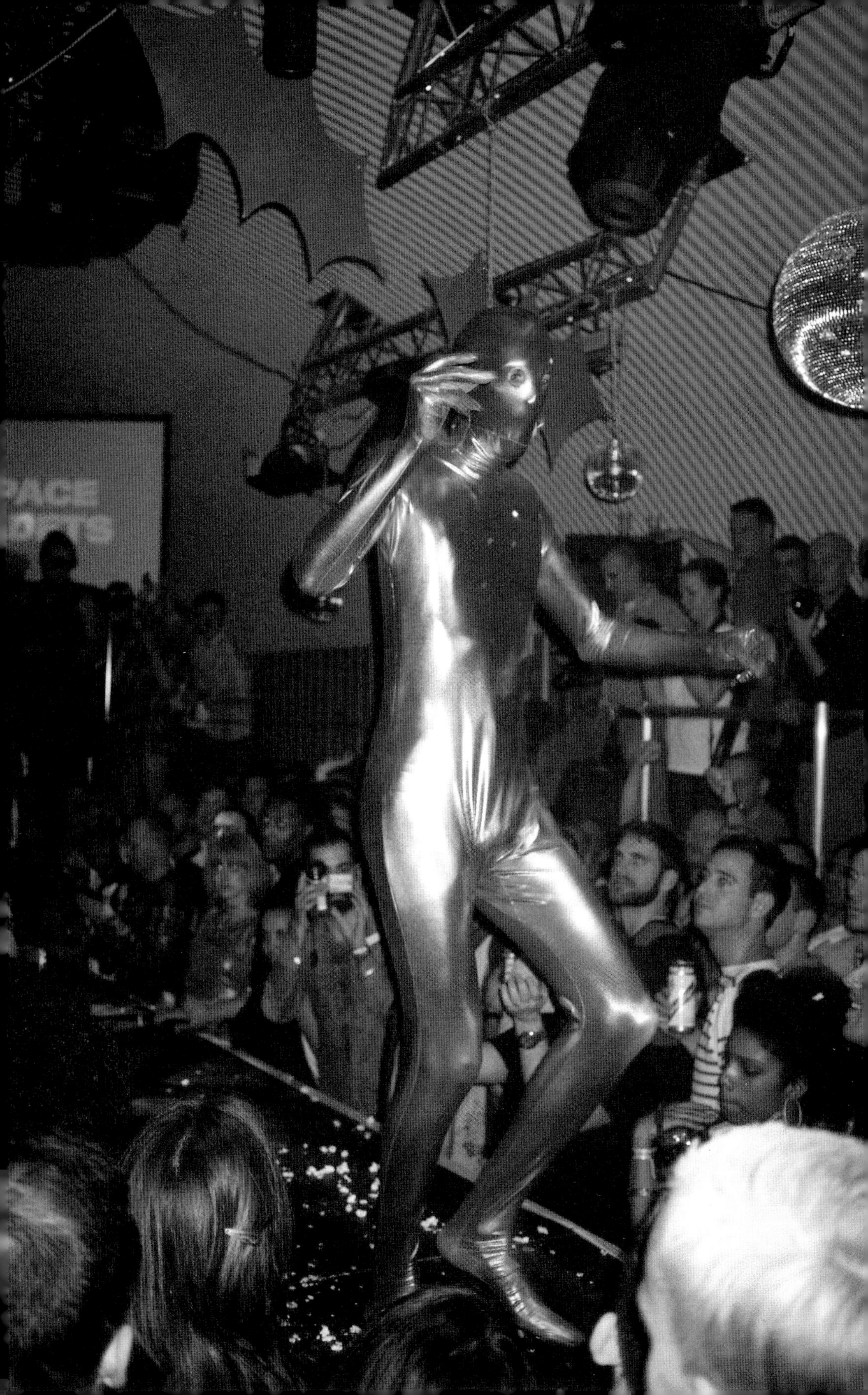

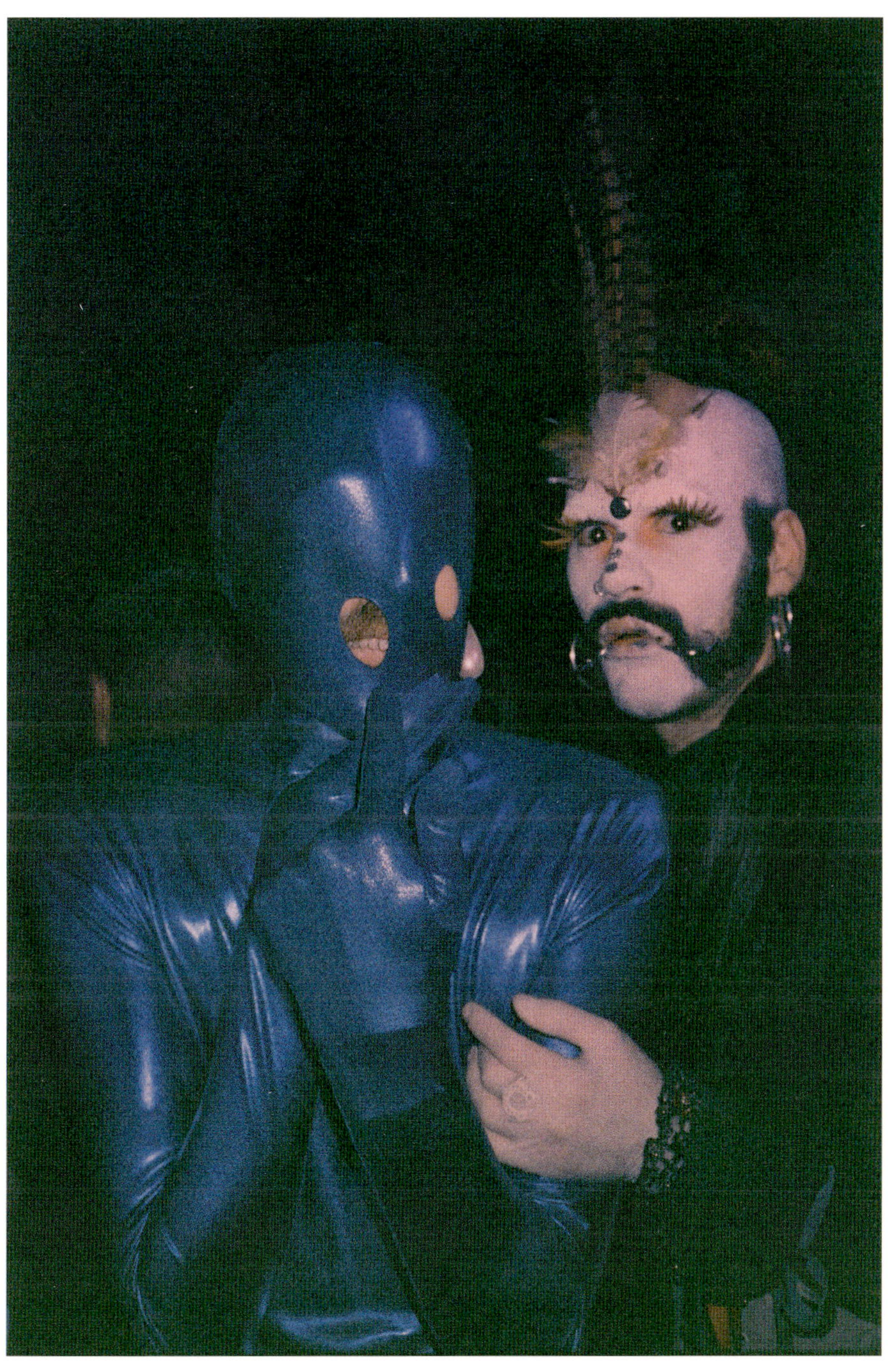

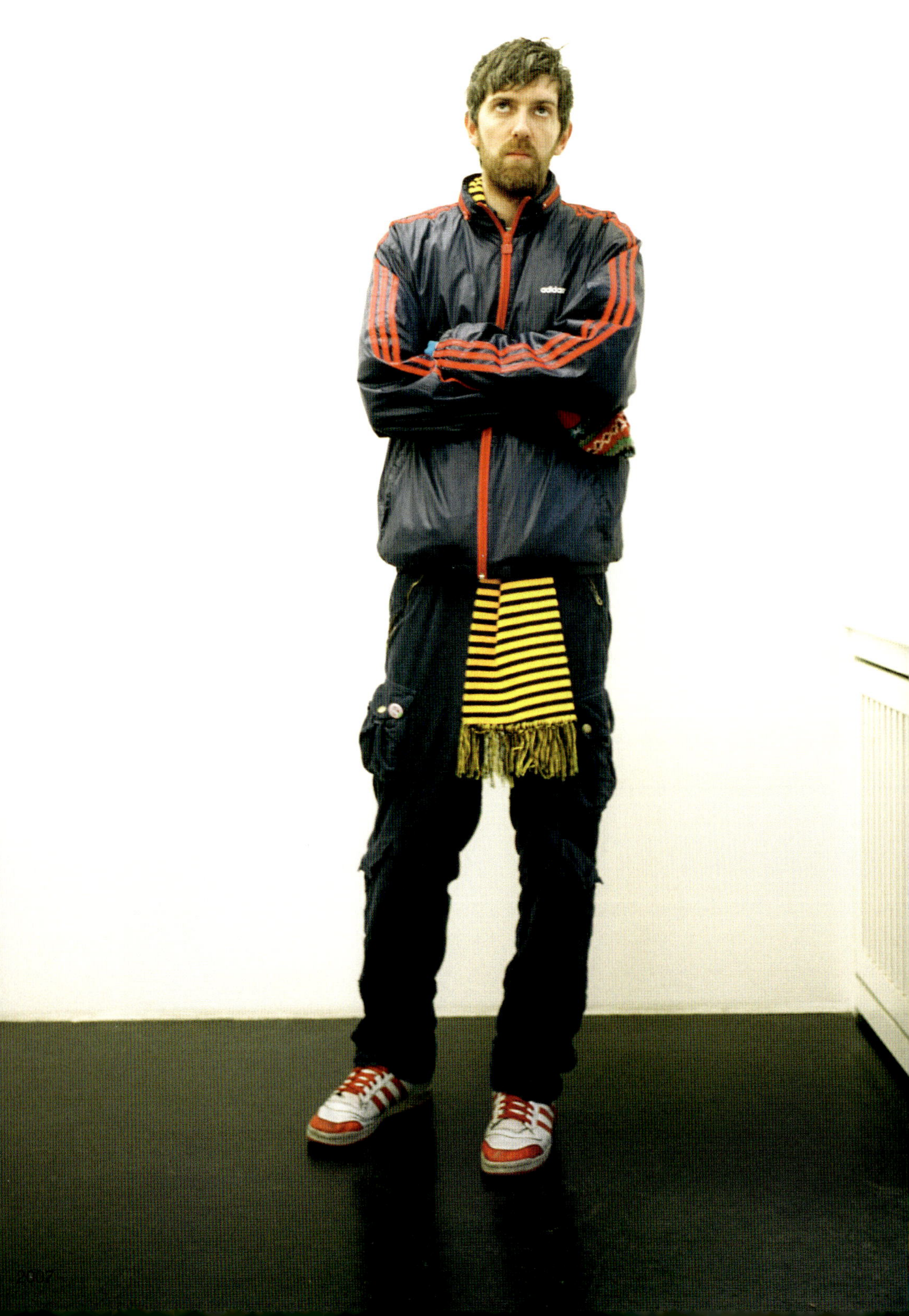

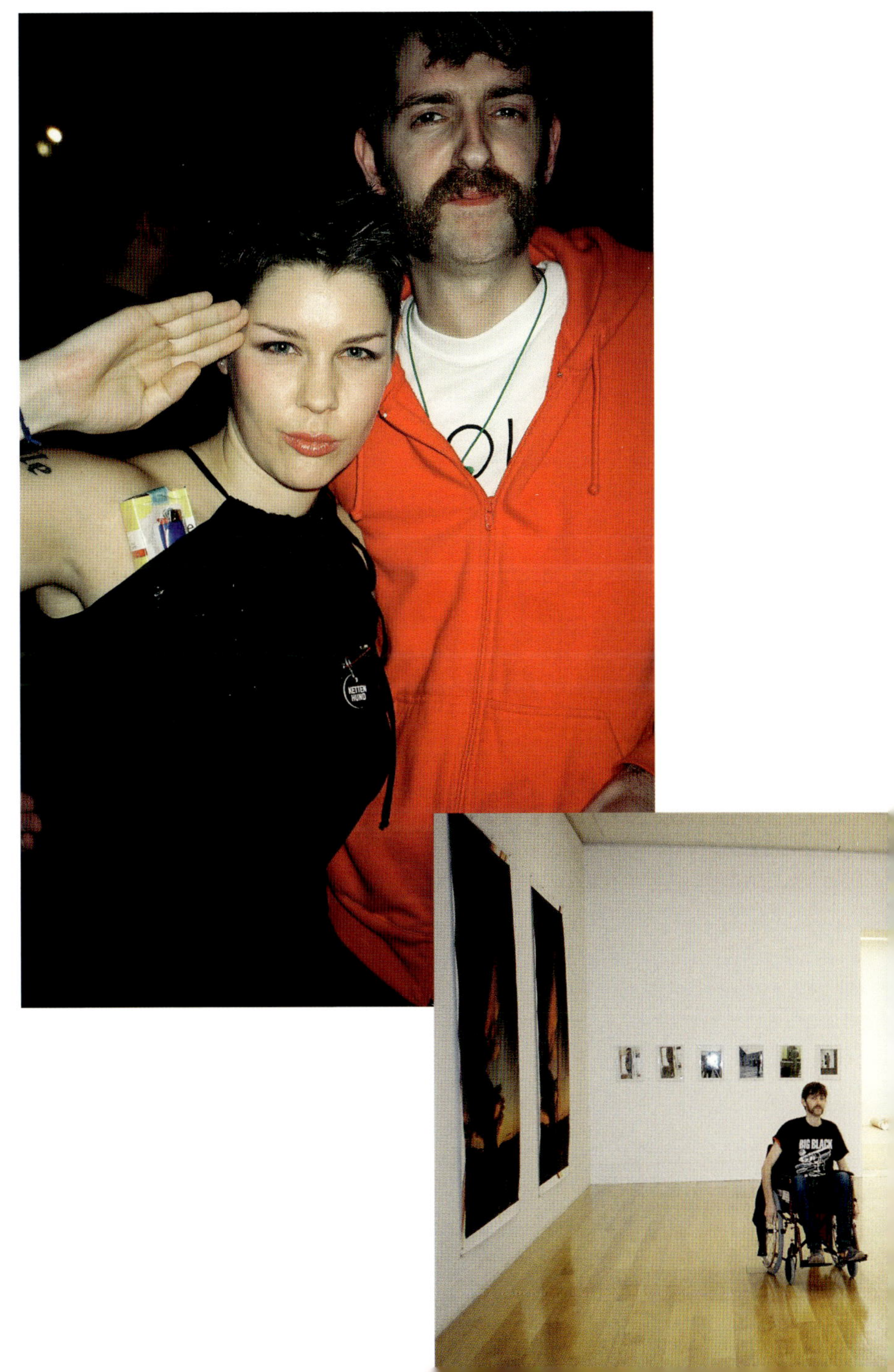
KETTEN
HUND
BIG BLACK

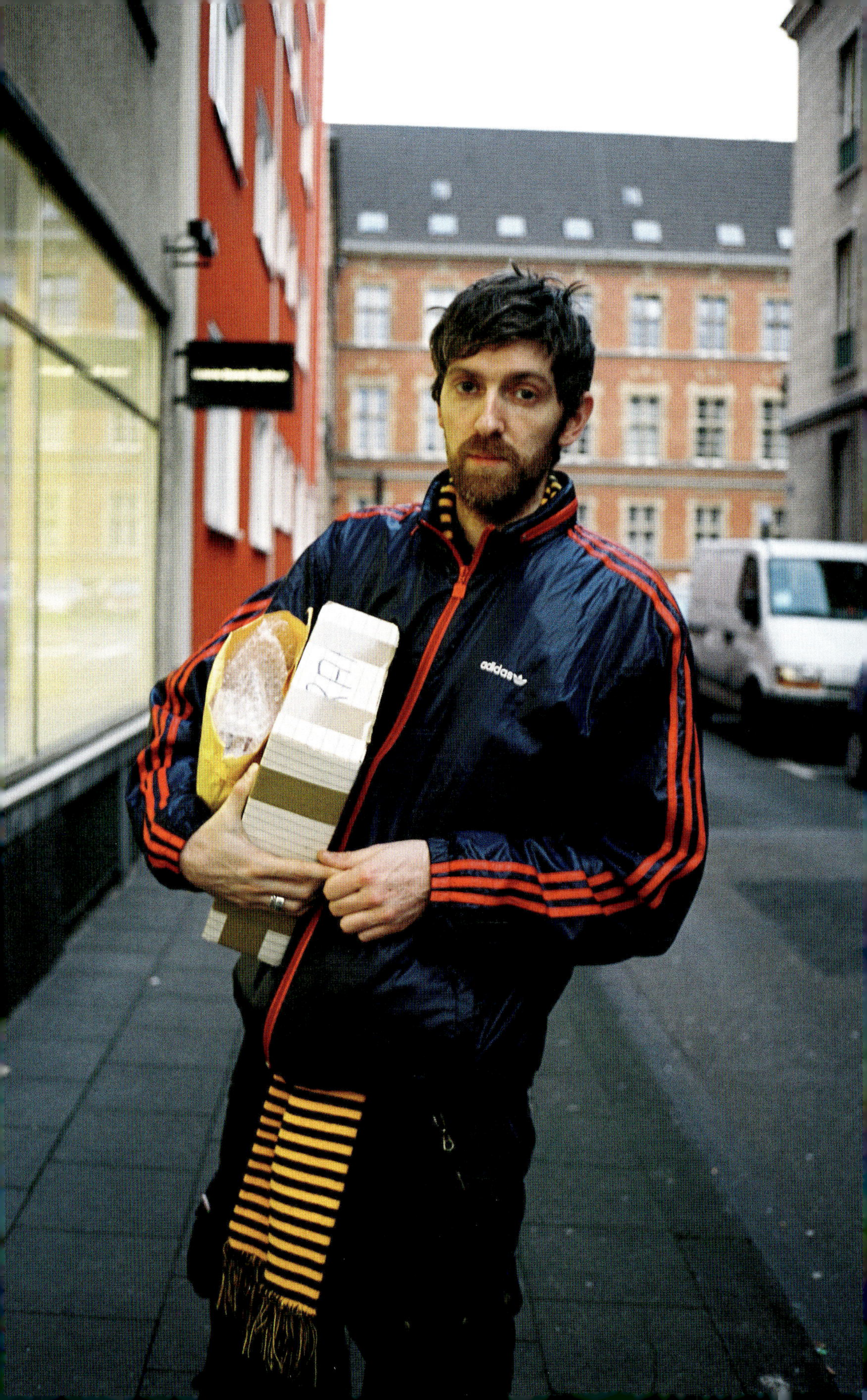
adidas

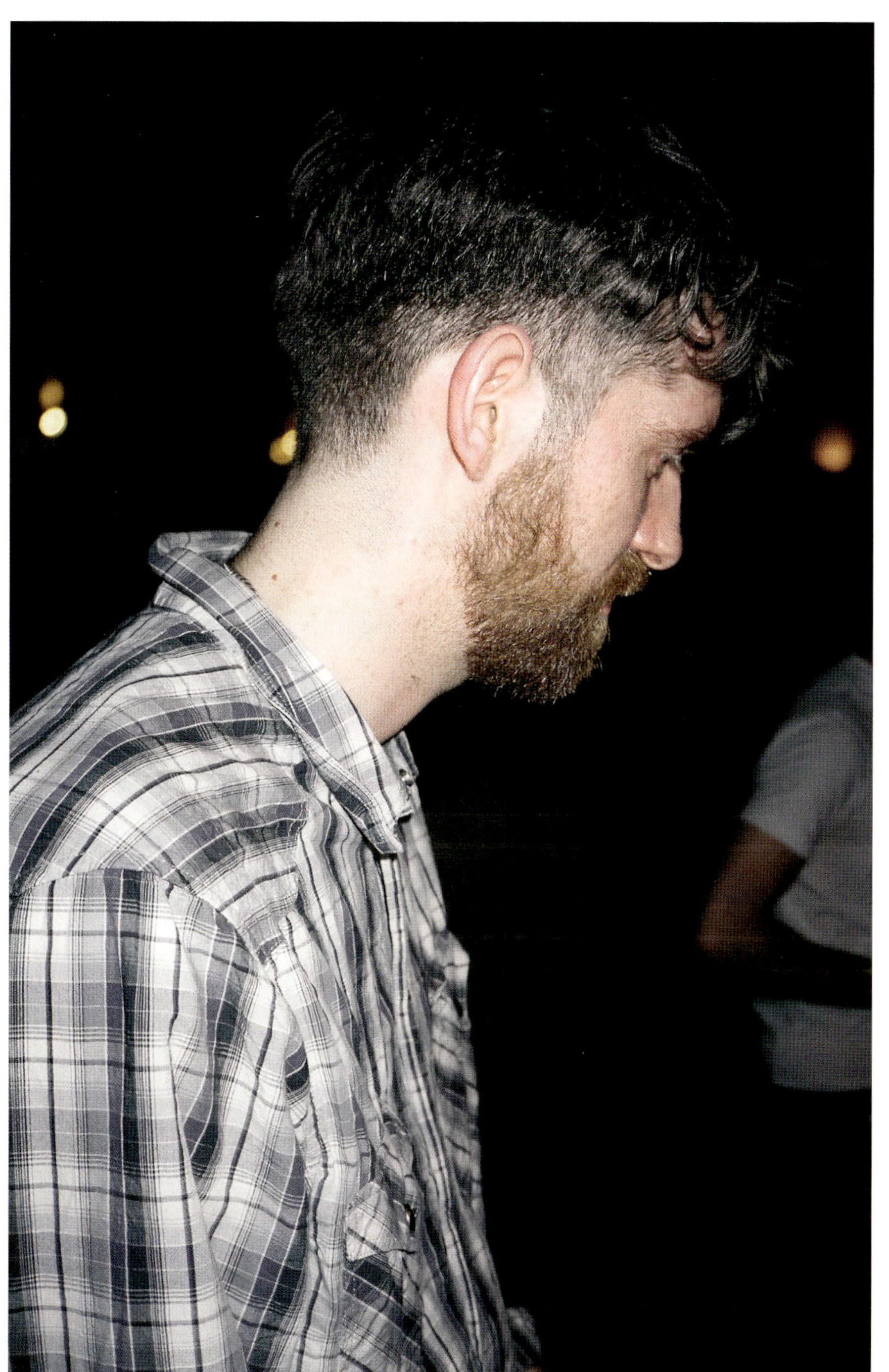

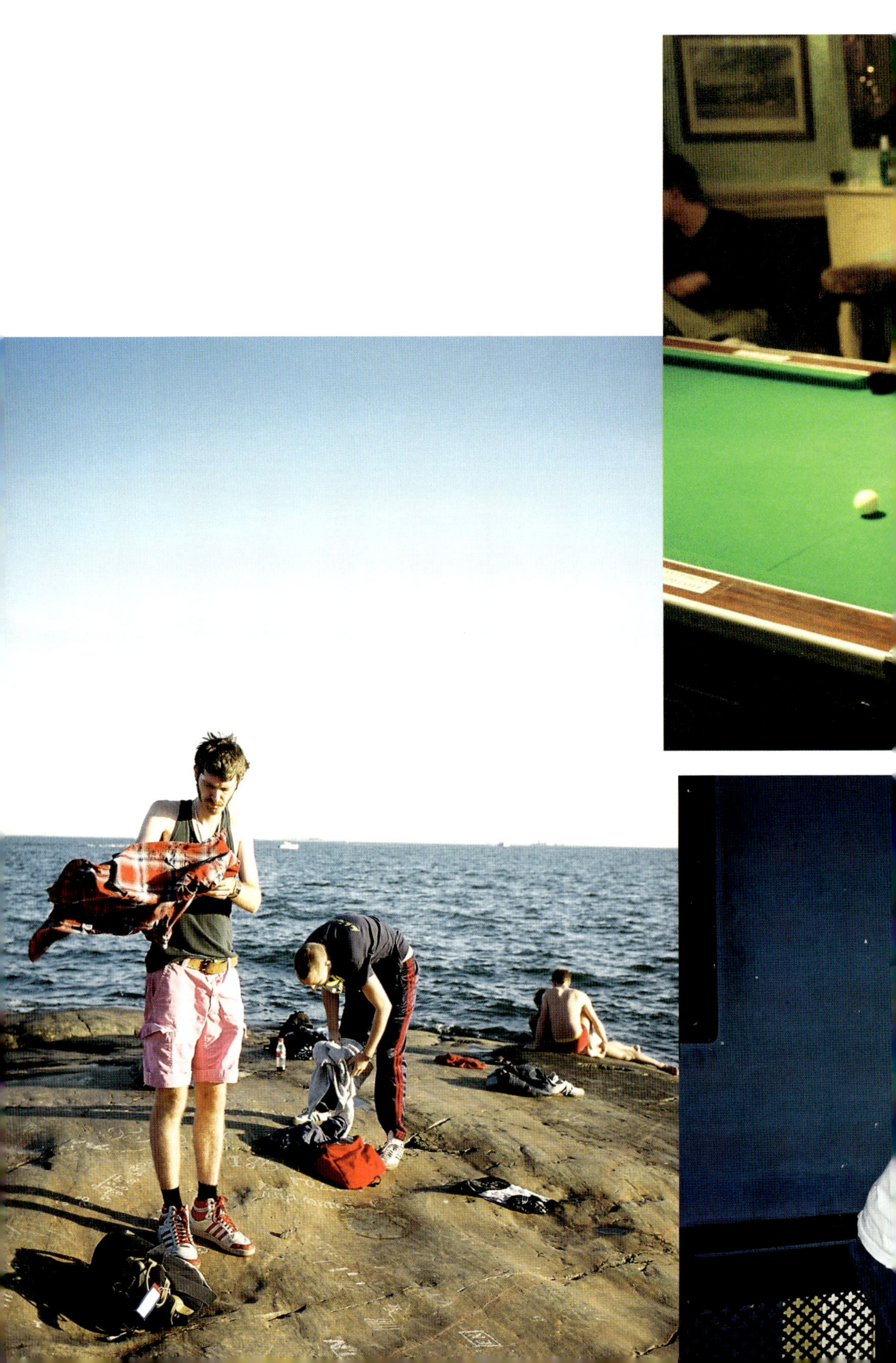

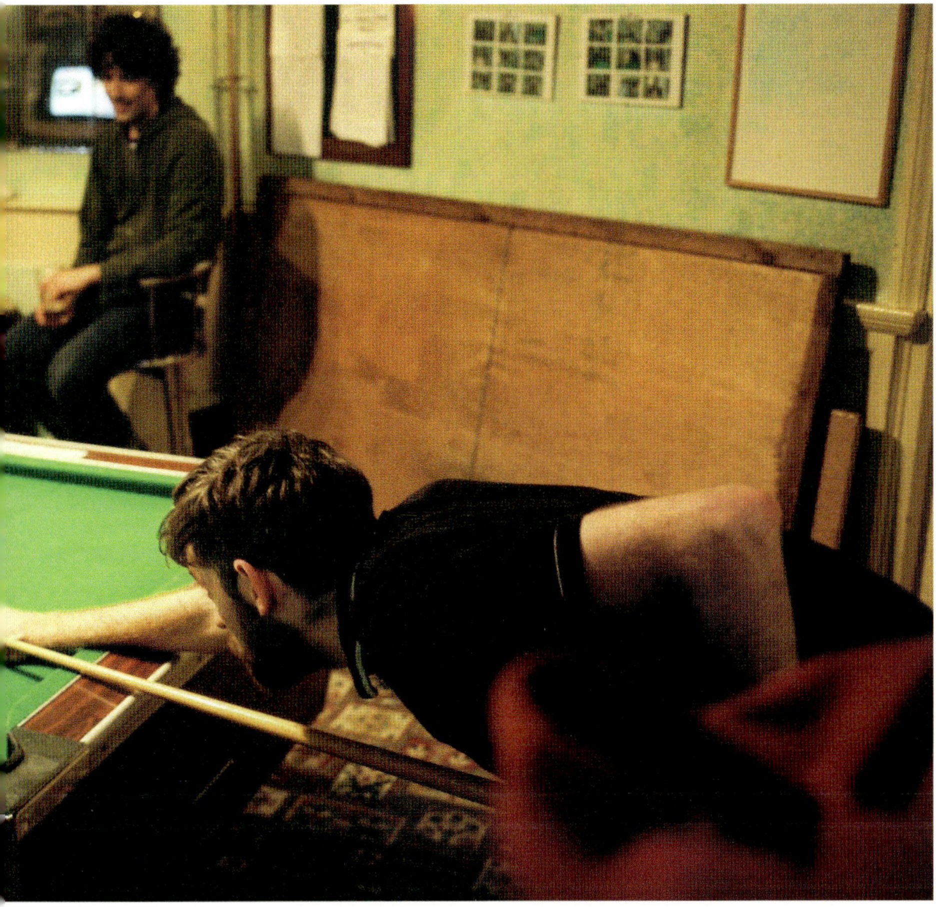

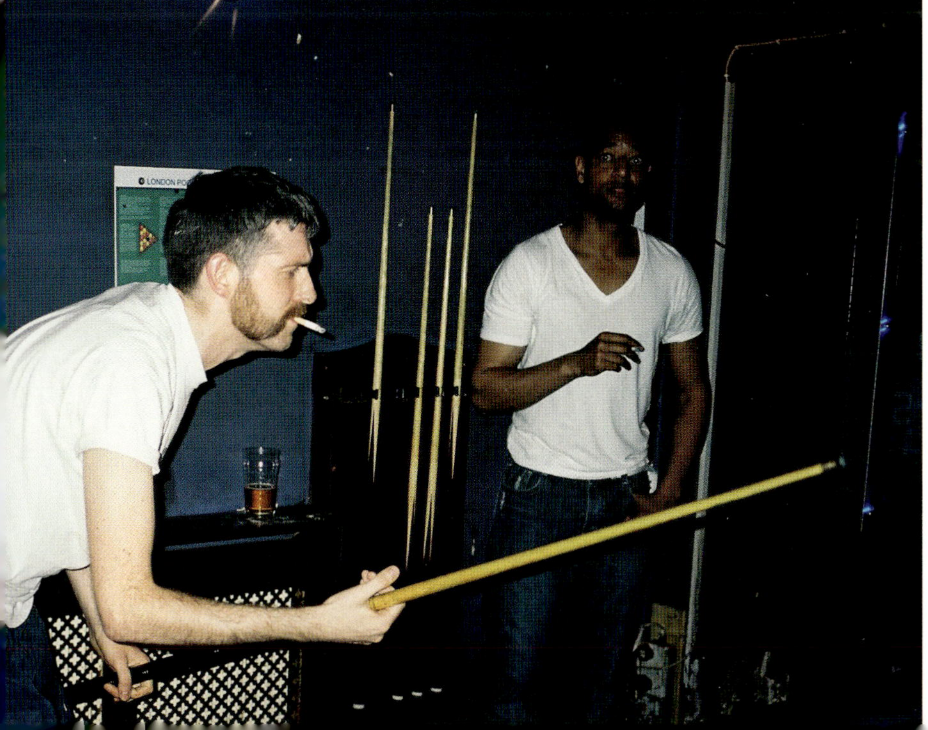

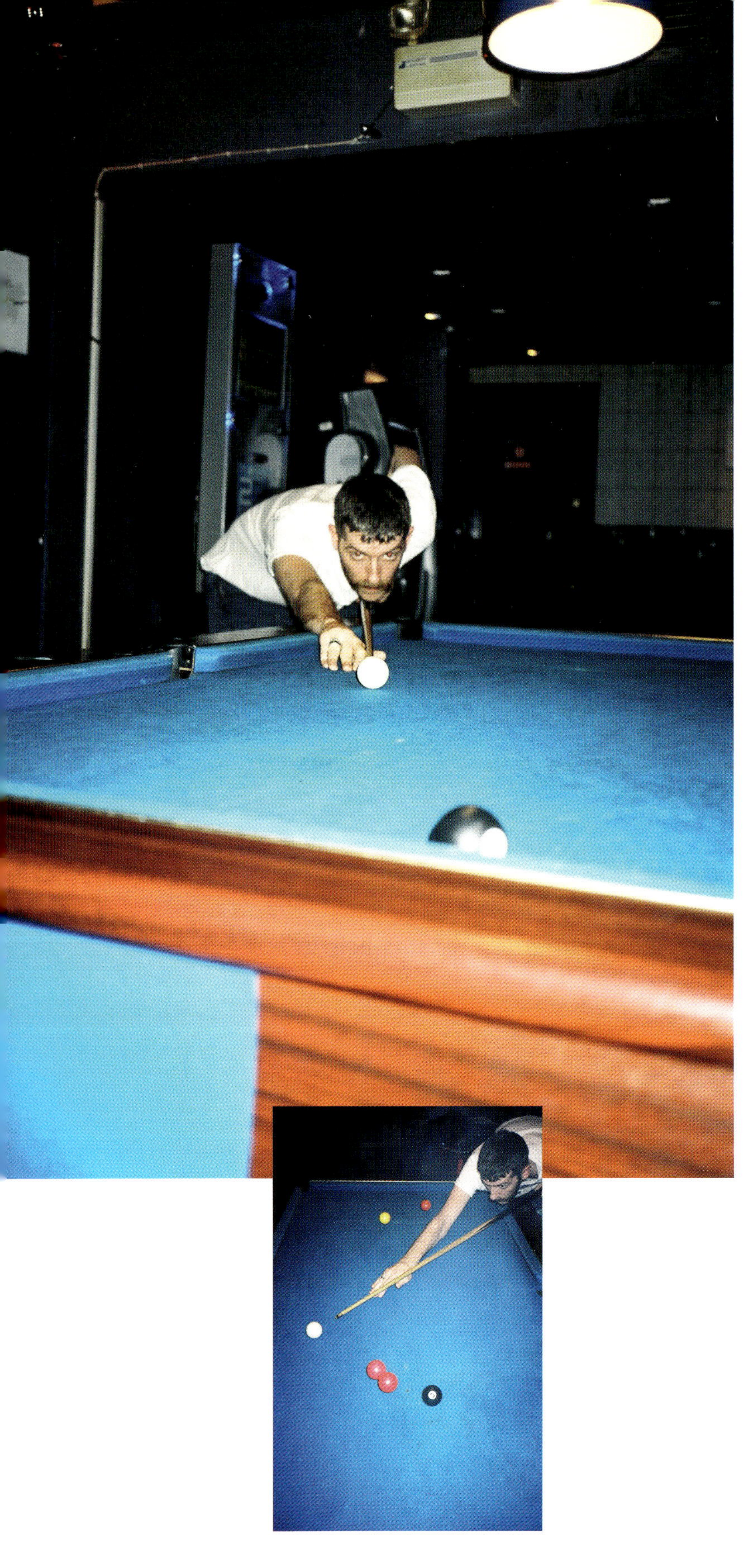

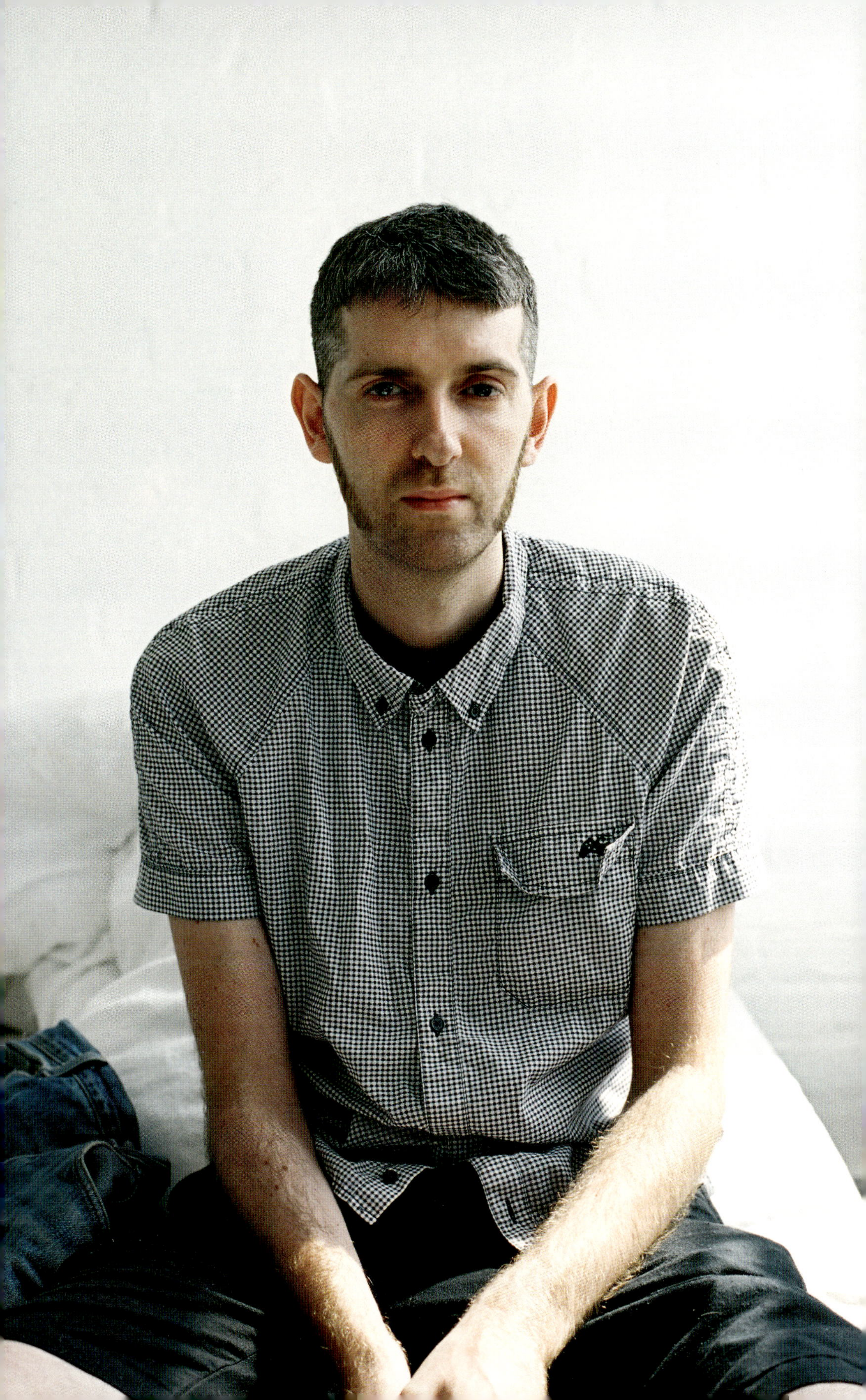

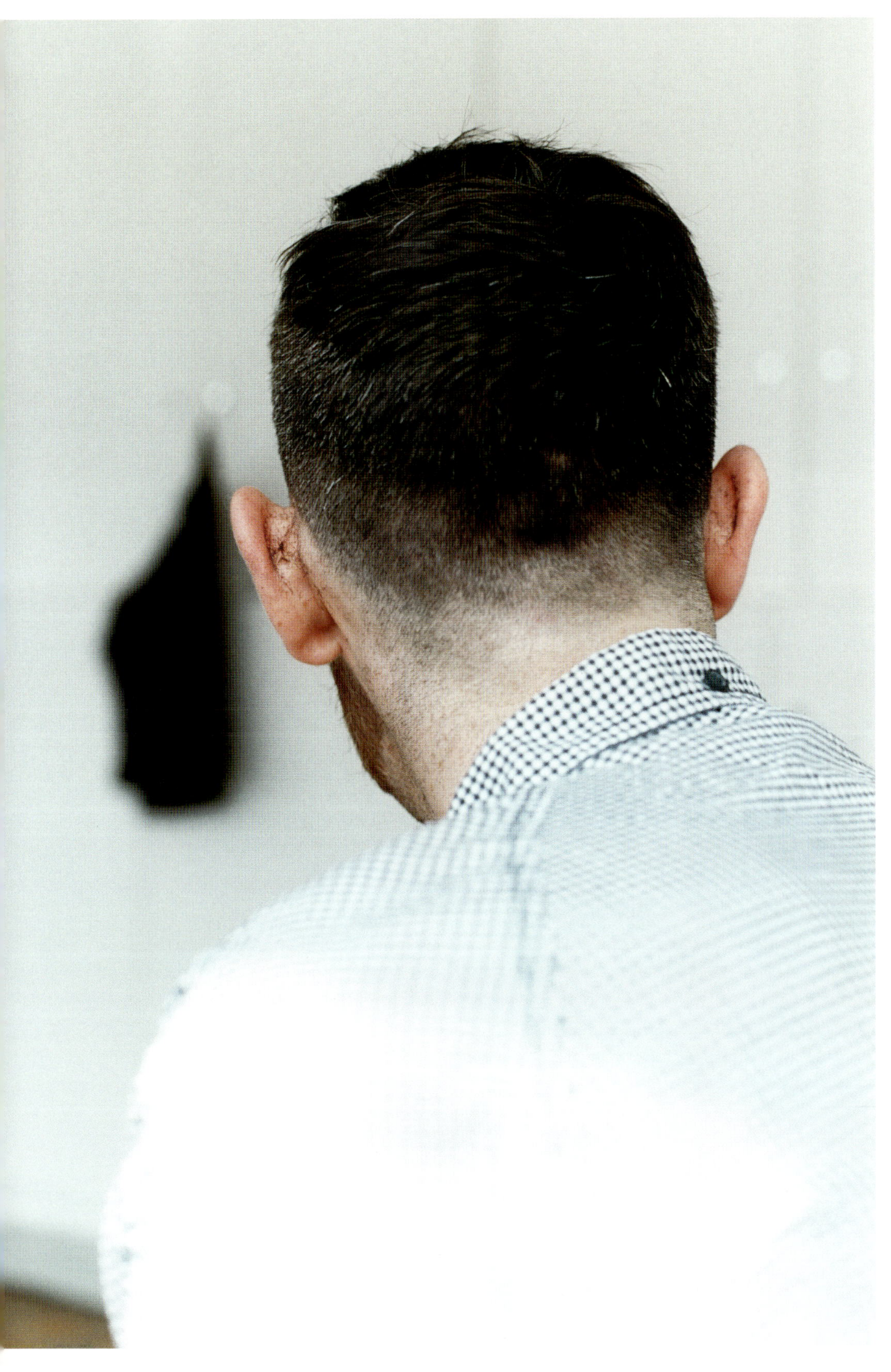

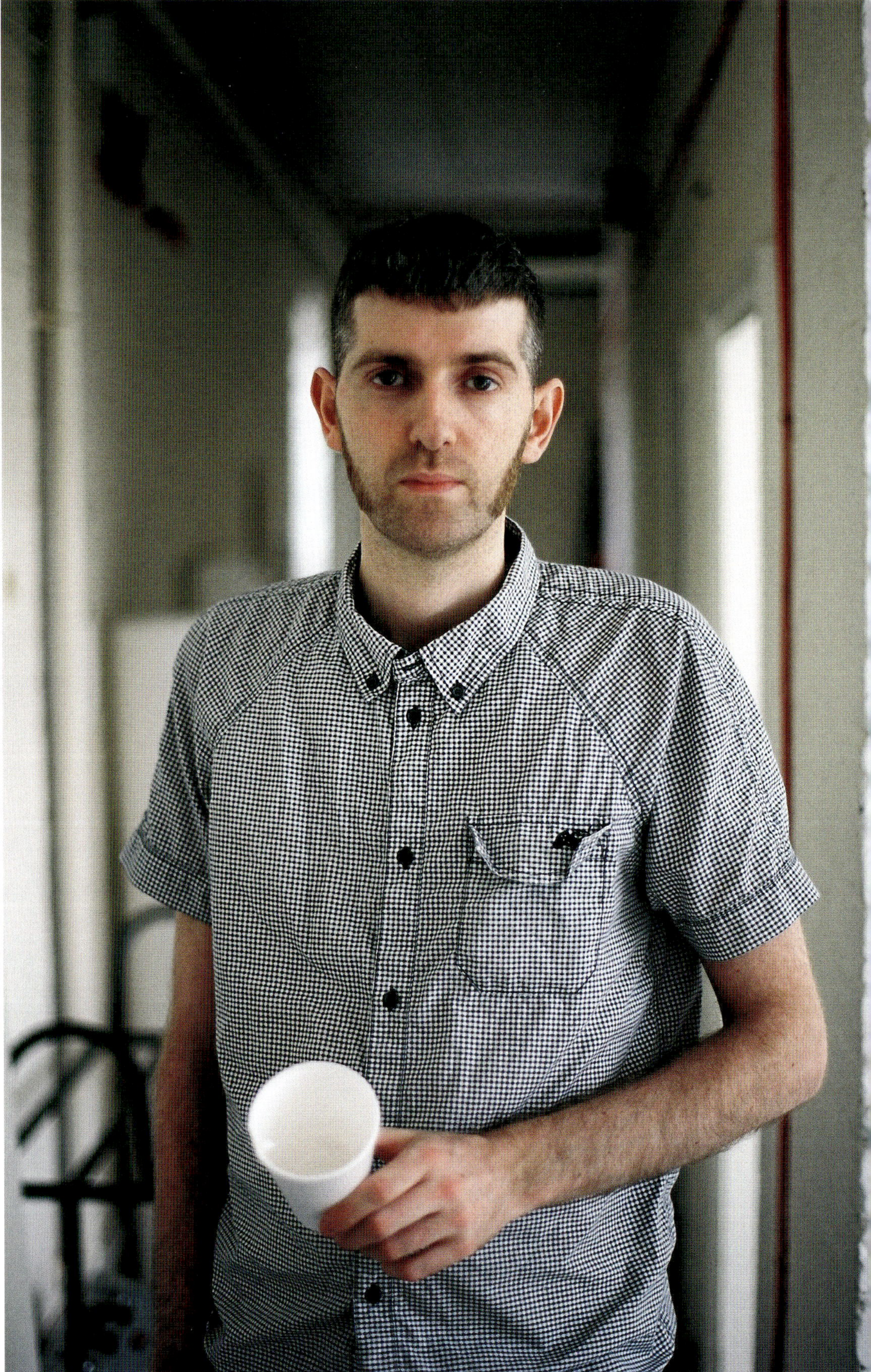

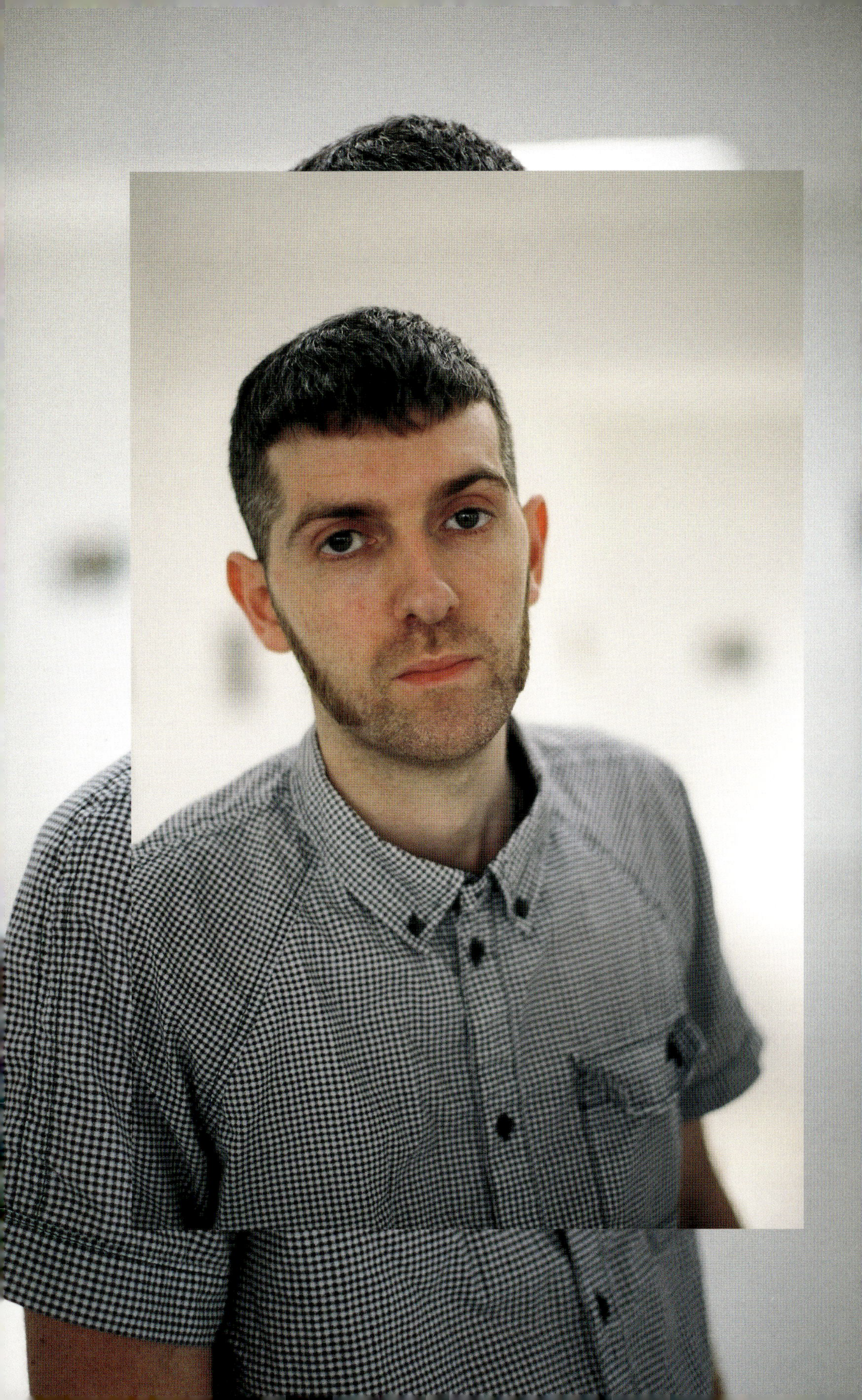

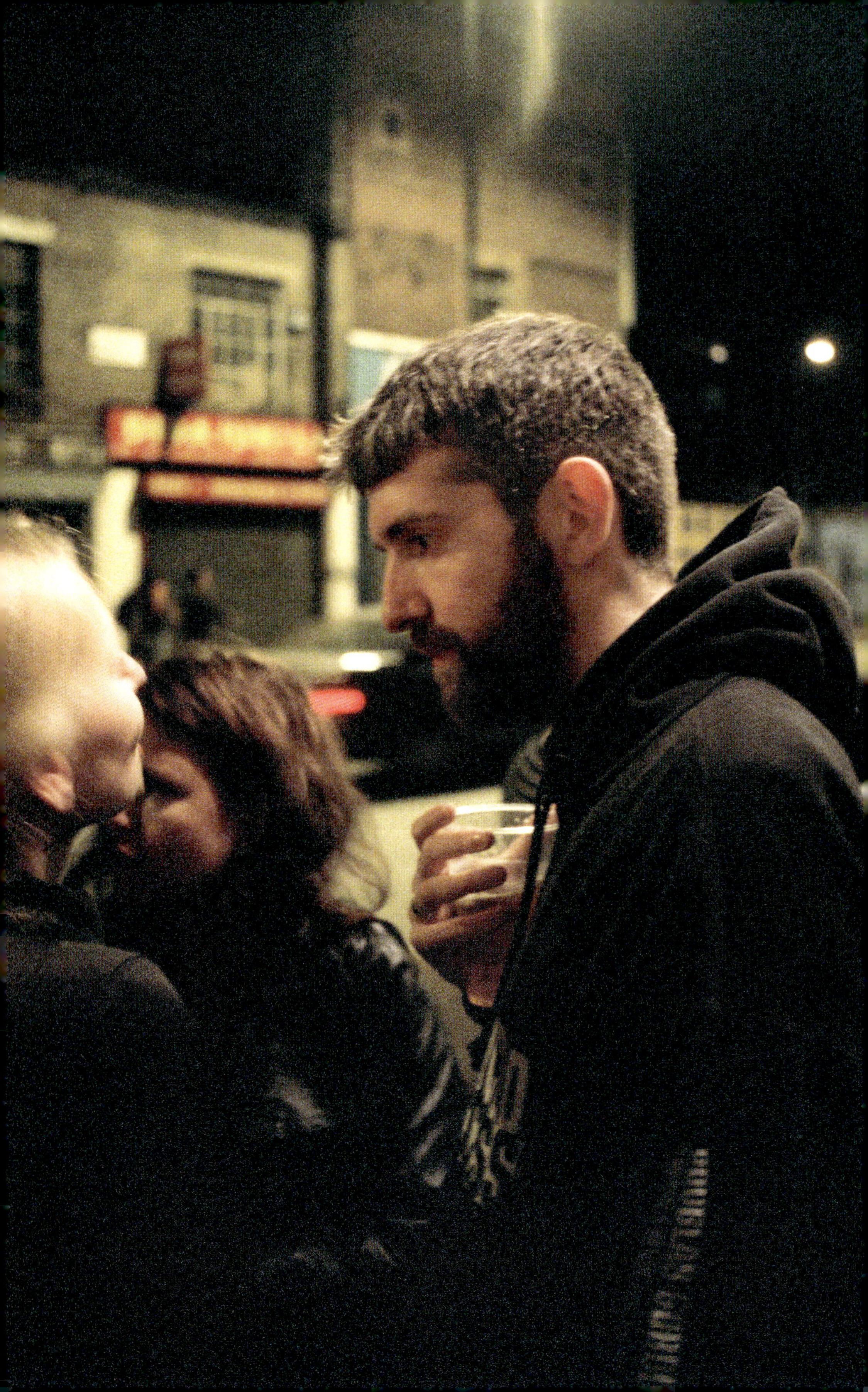

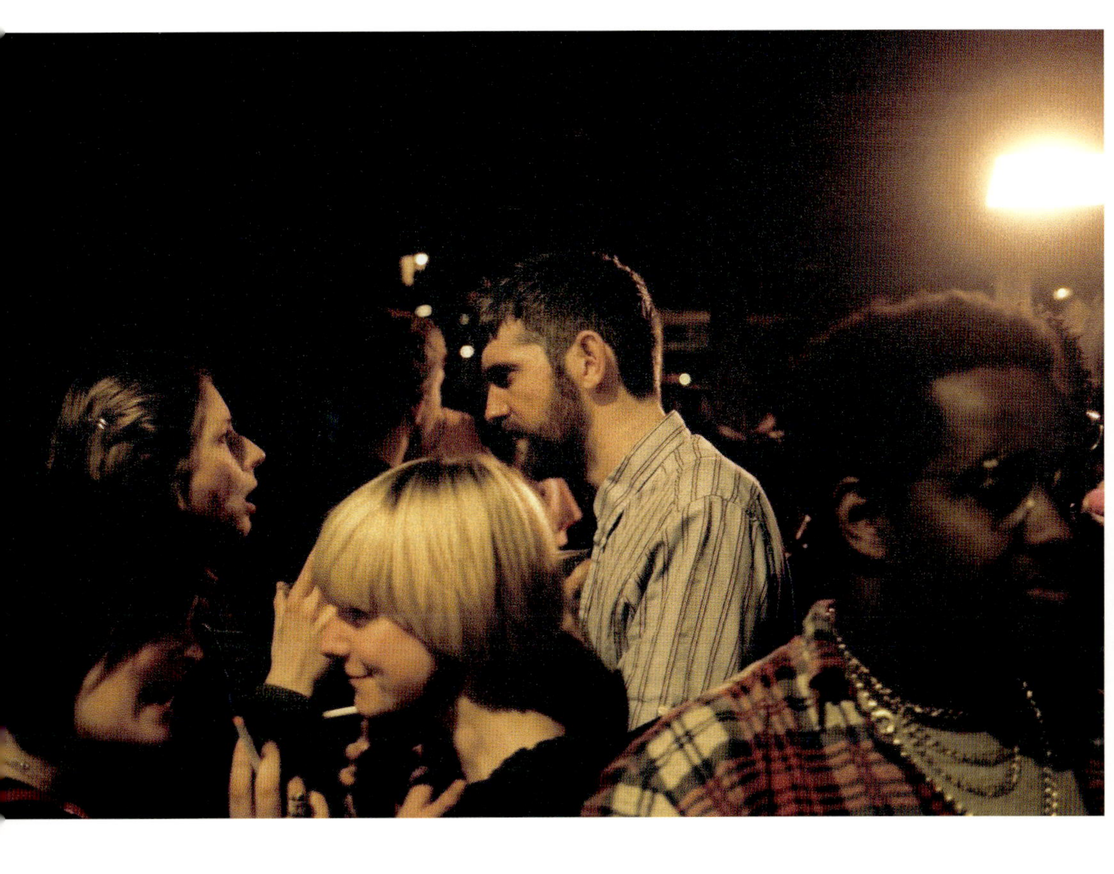

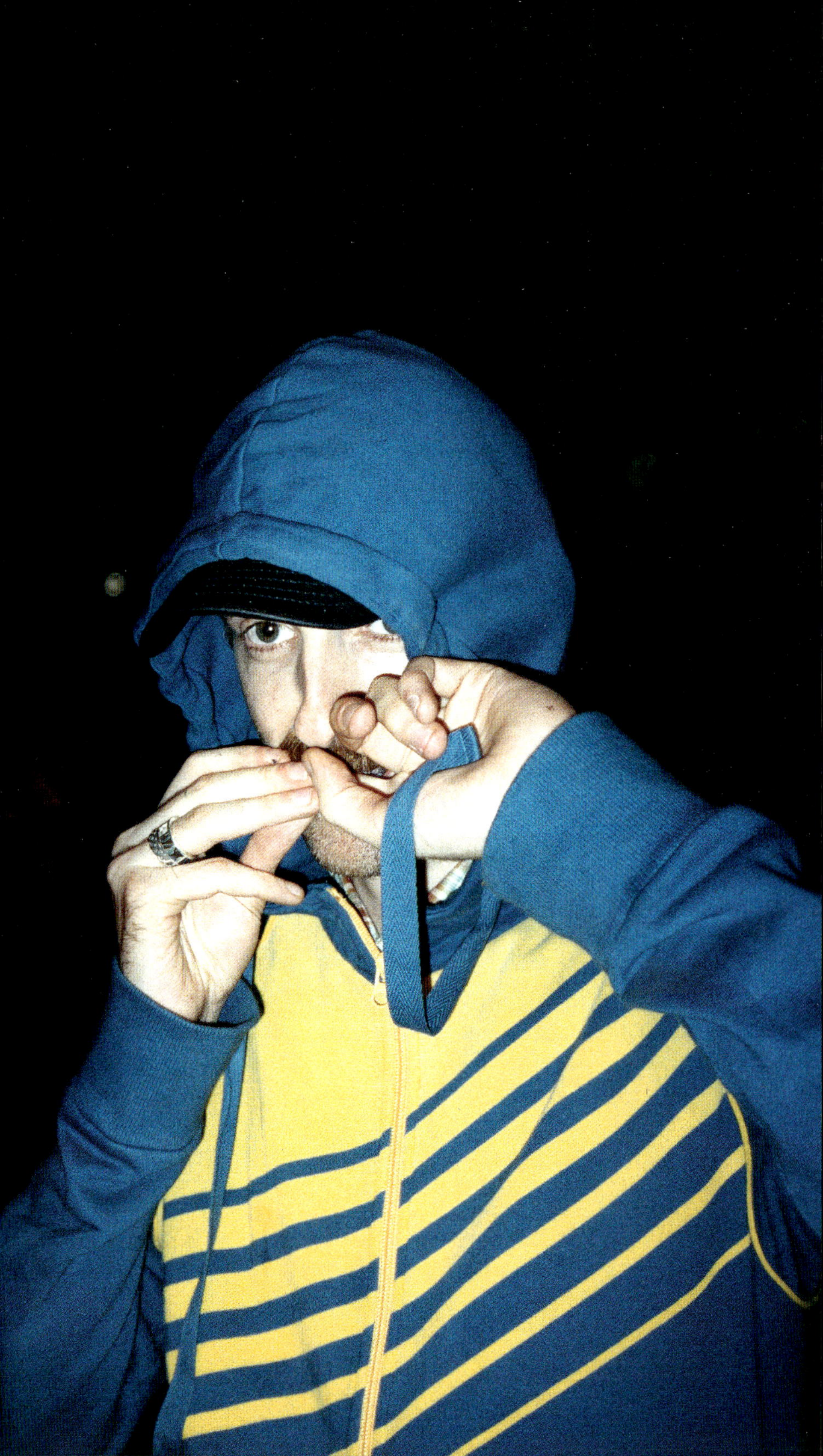

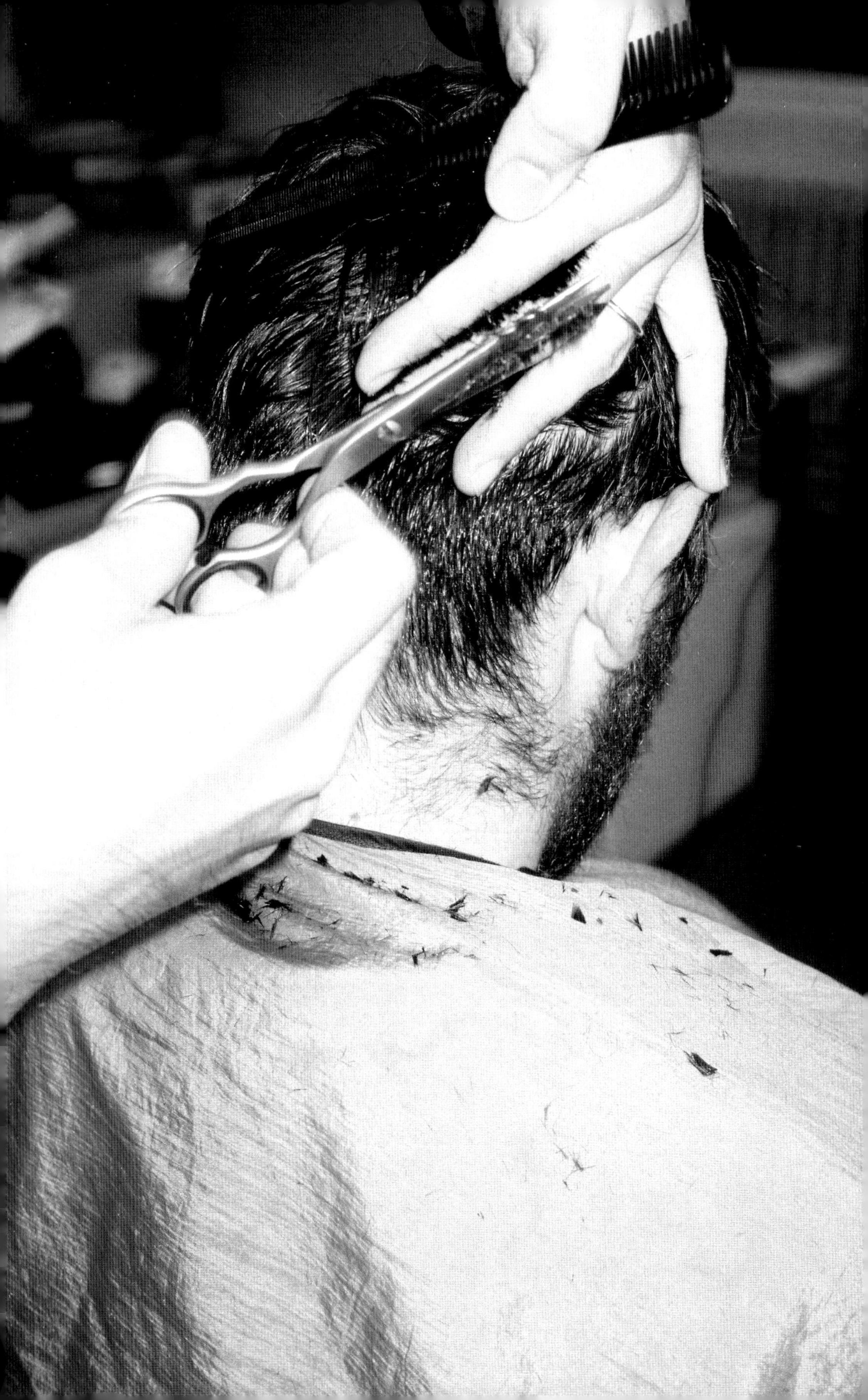

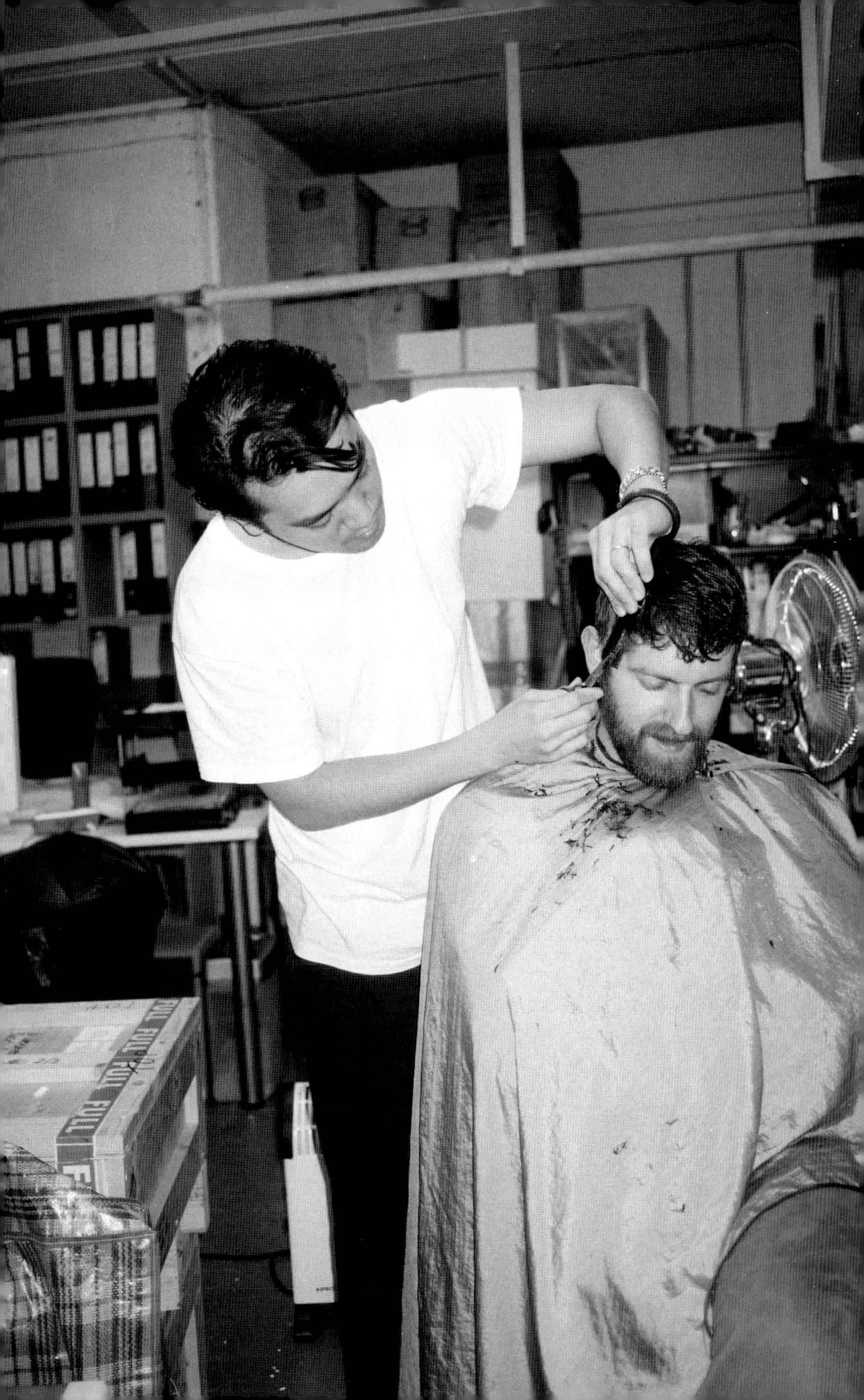
FULL

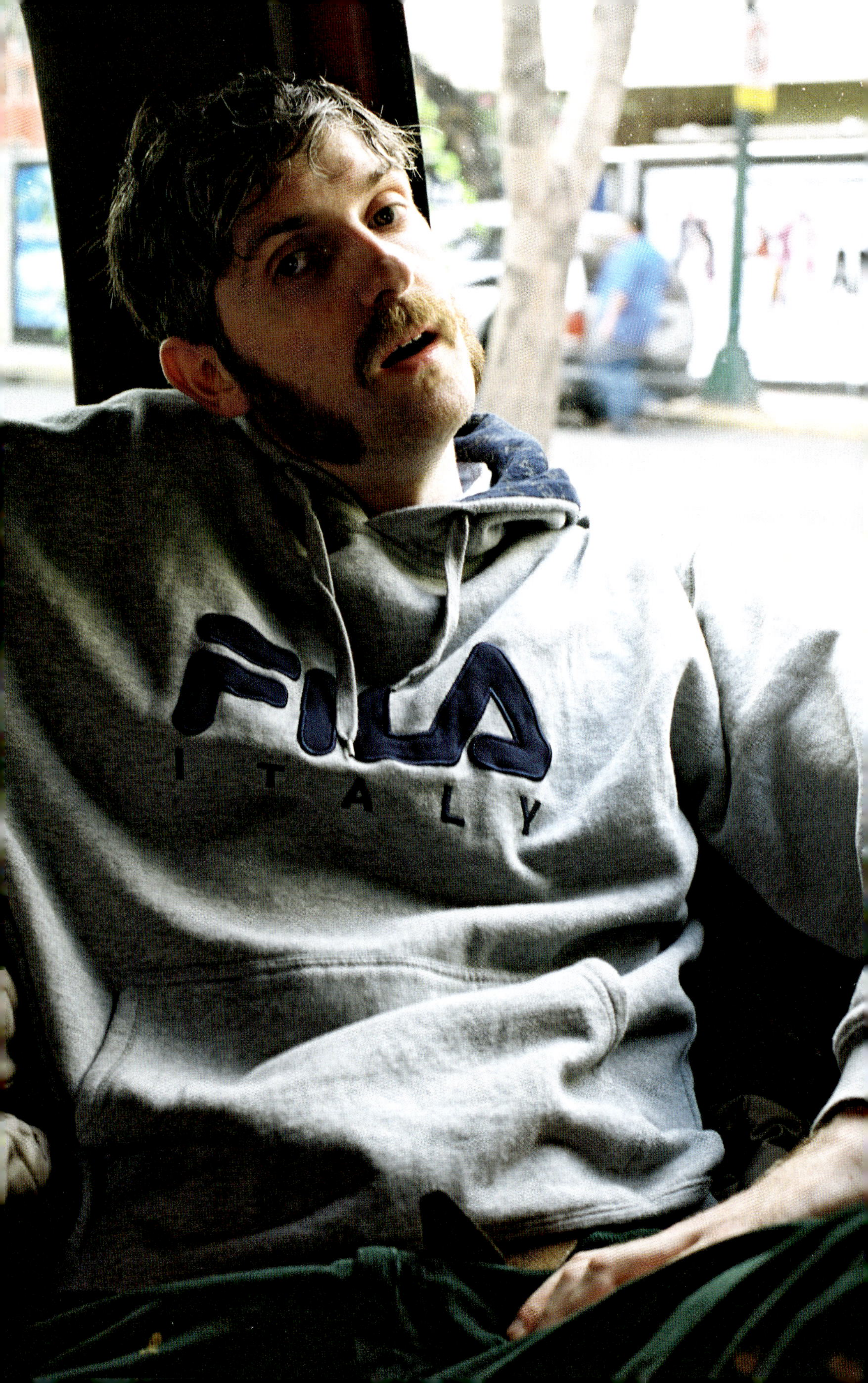
FILA
ITALY

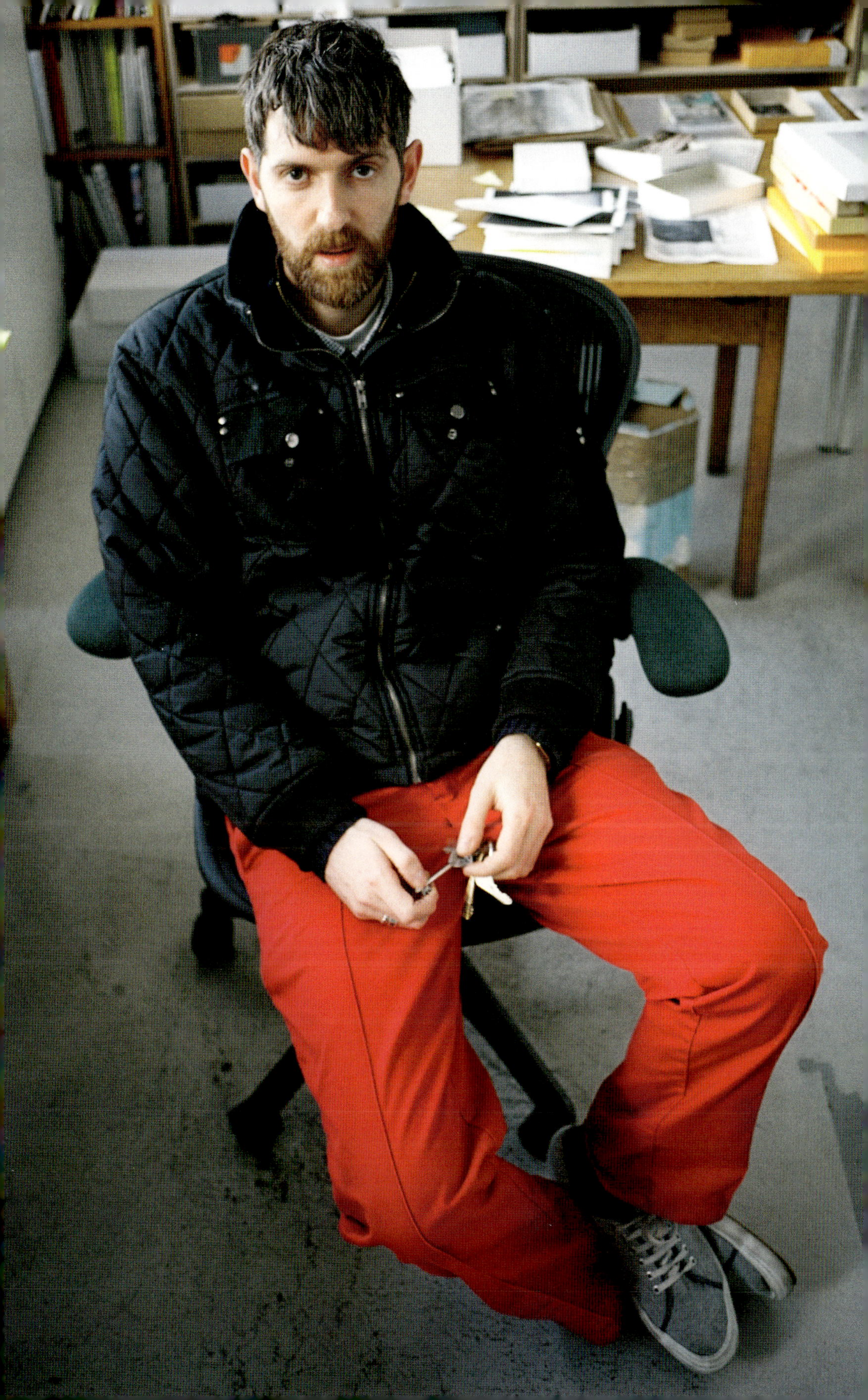

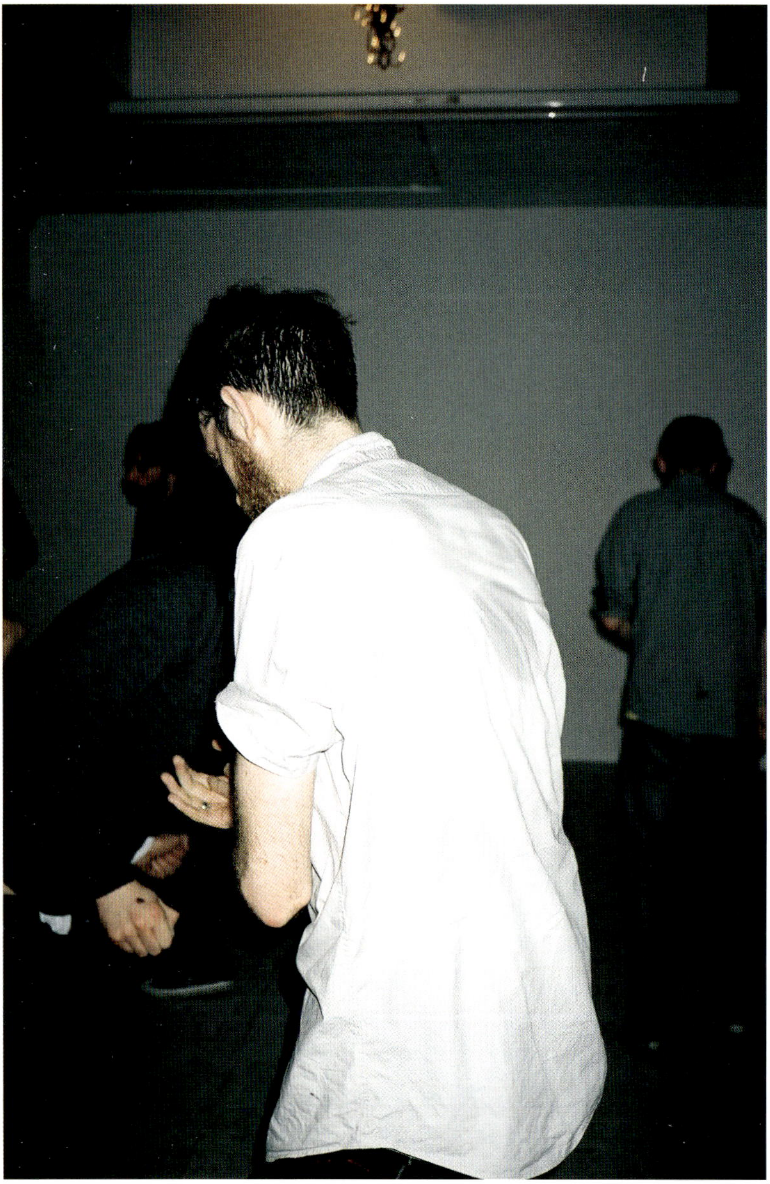

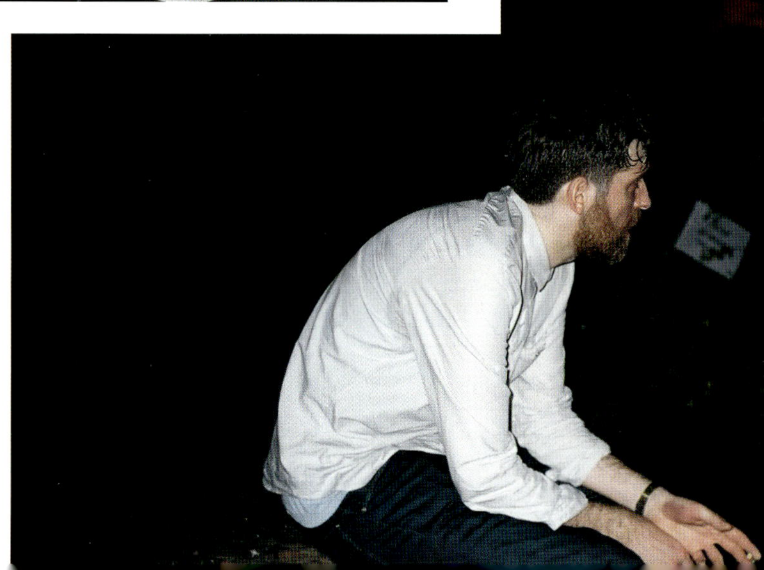

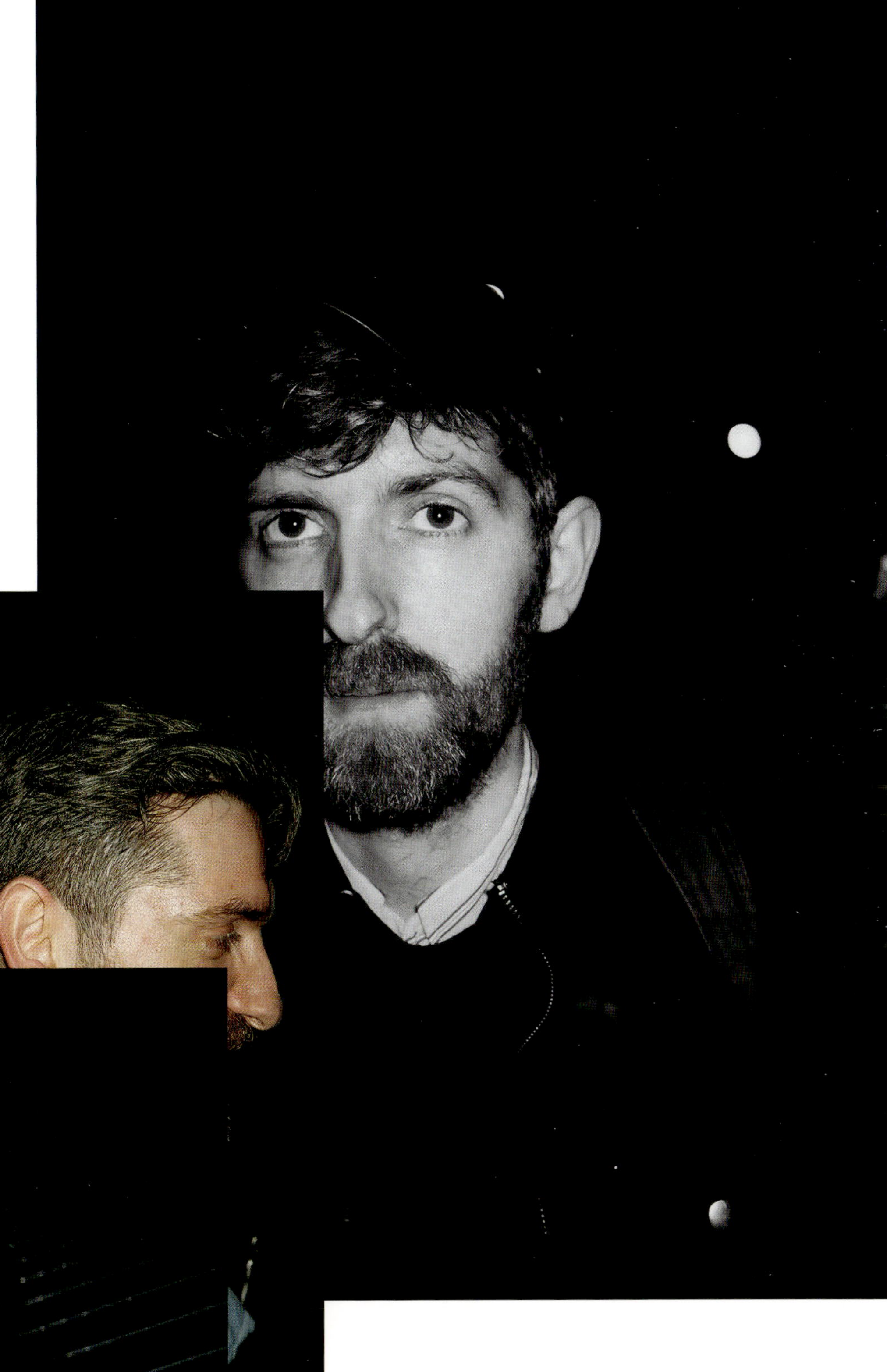

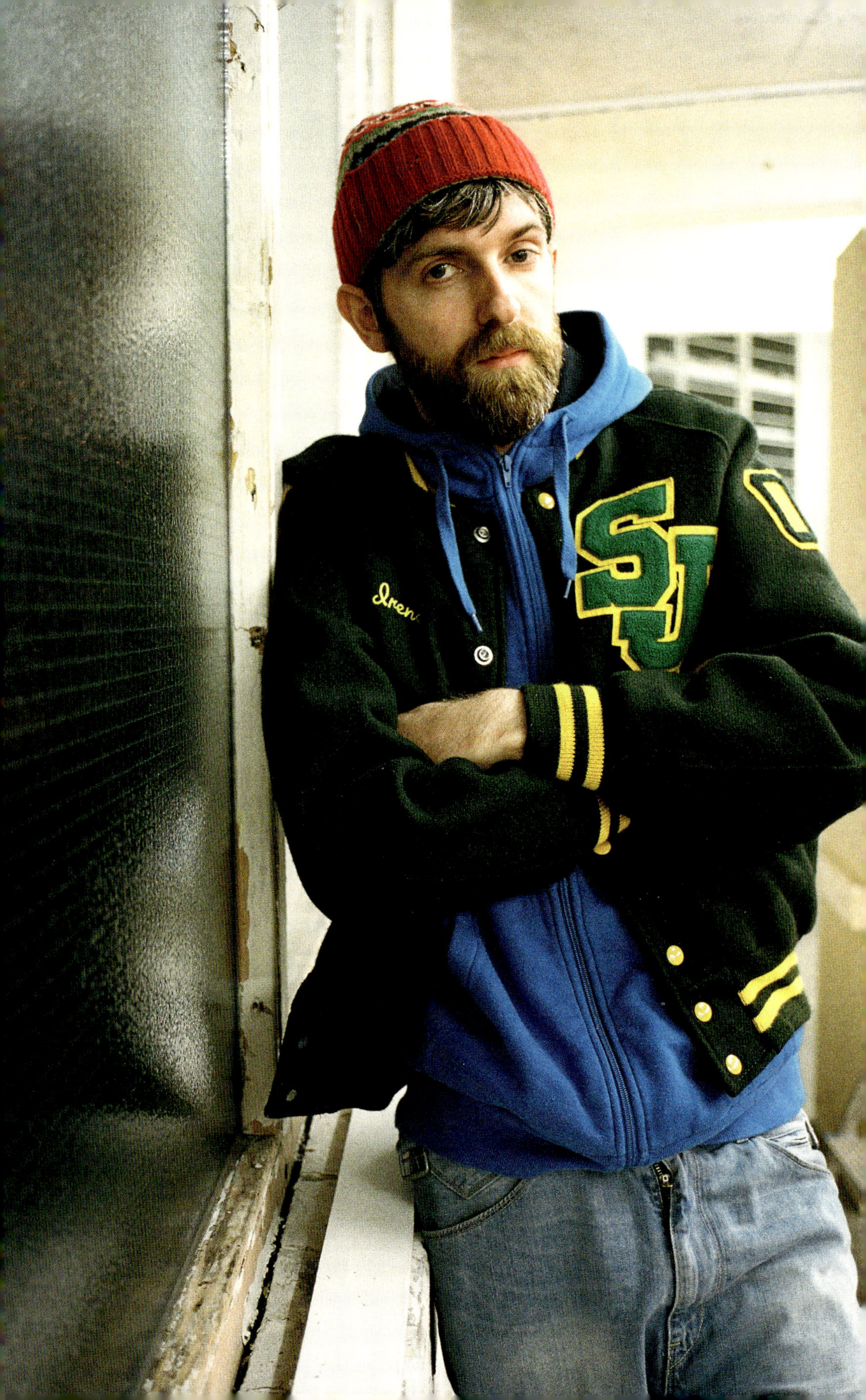

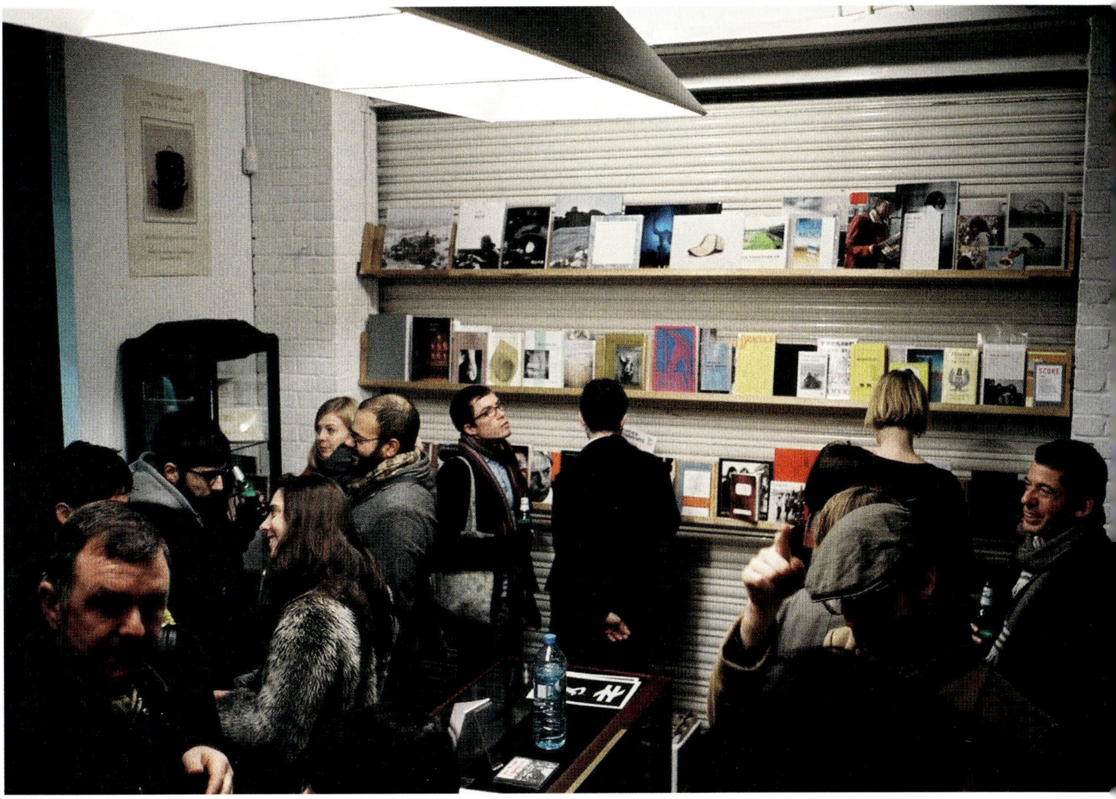

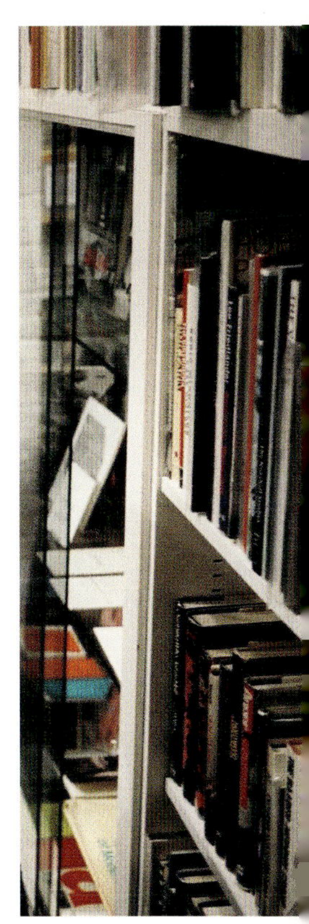

2008

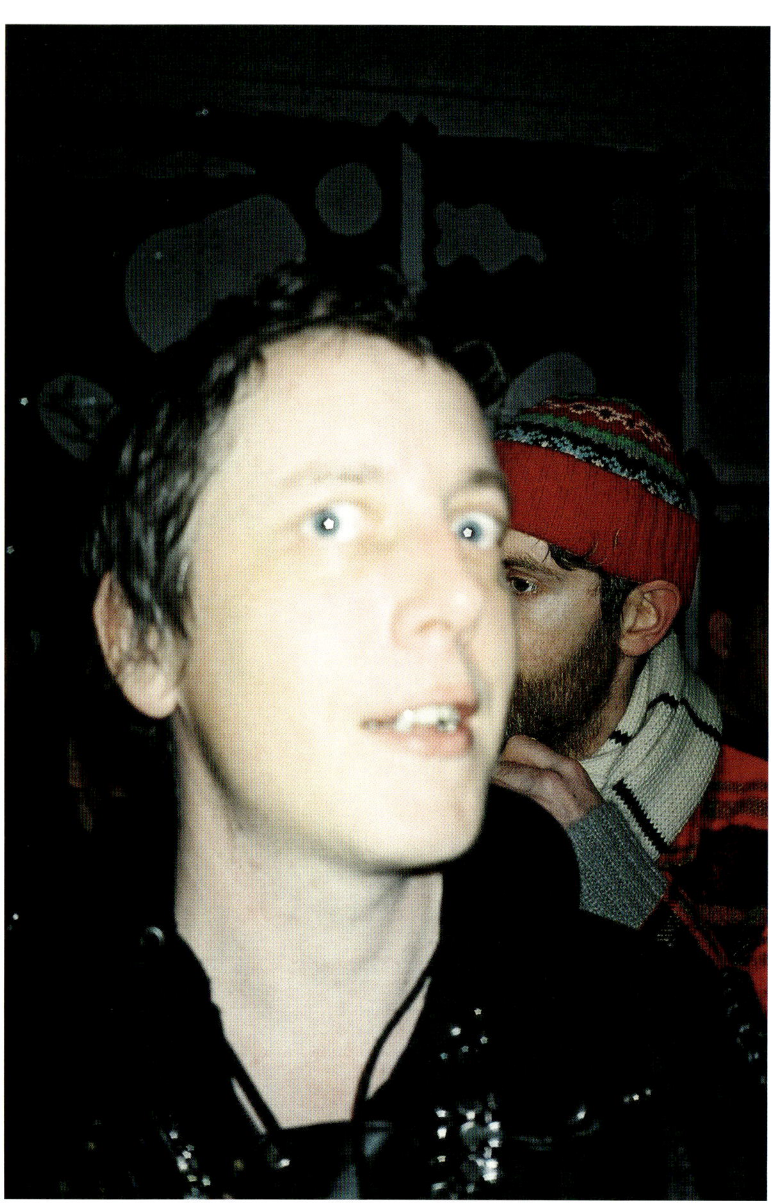

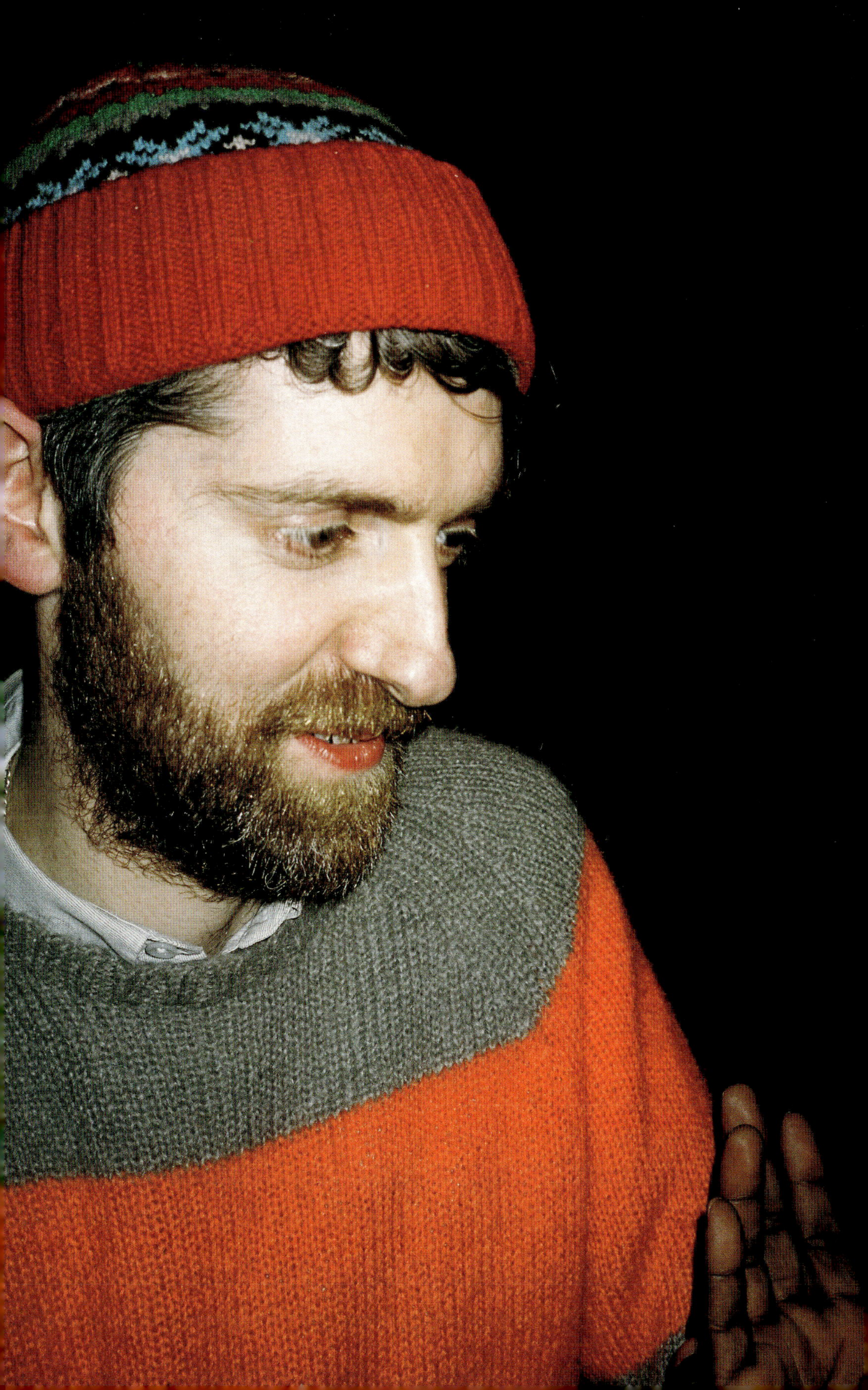

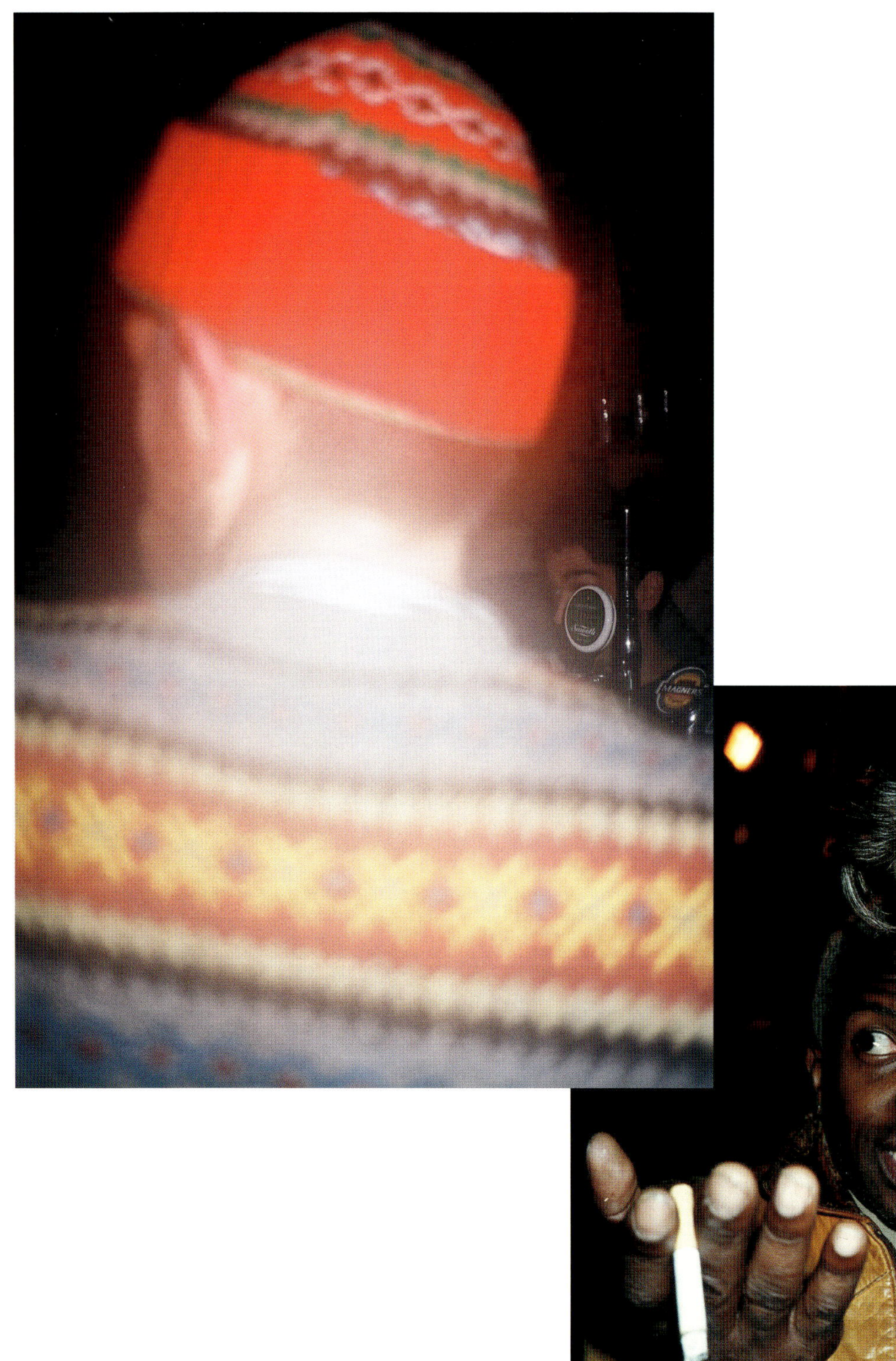

2009

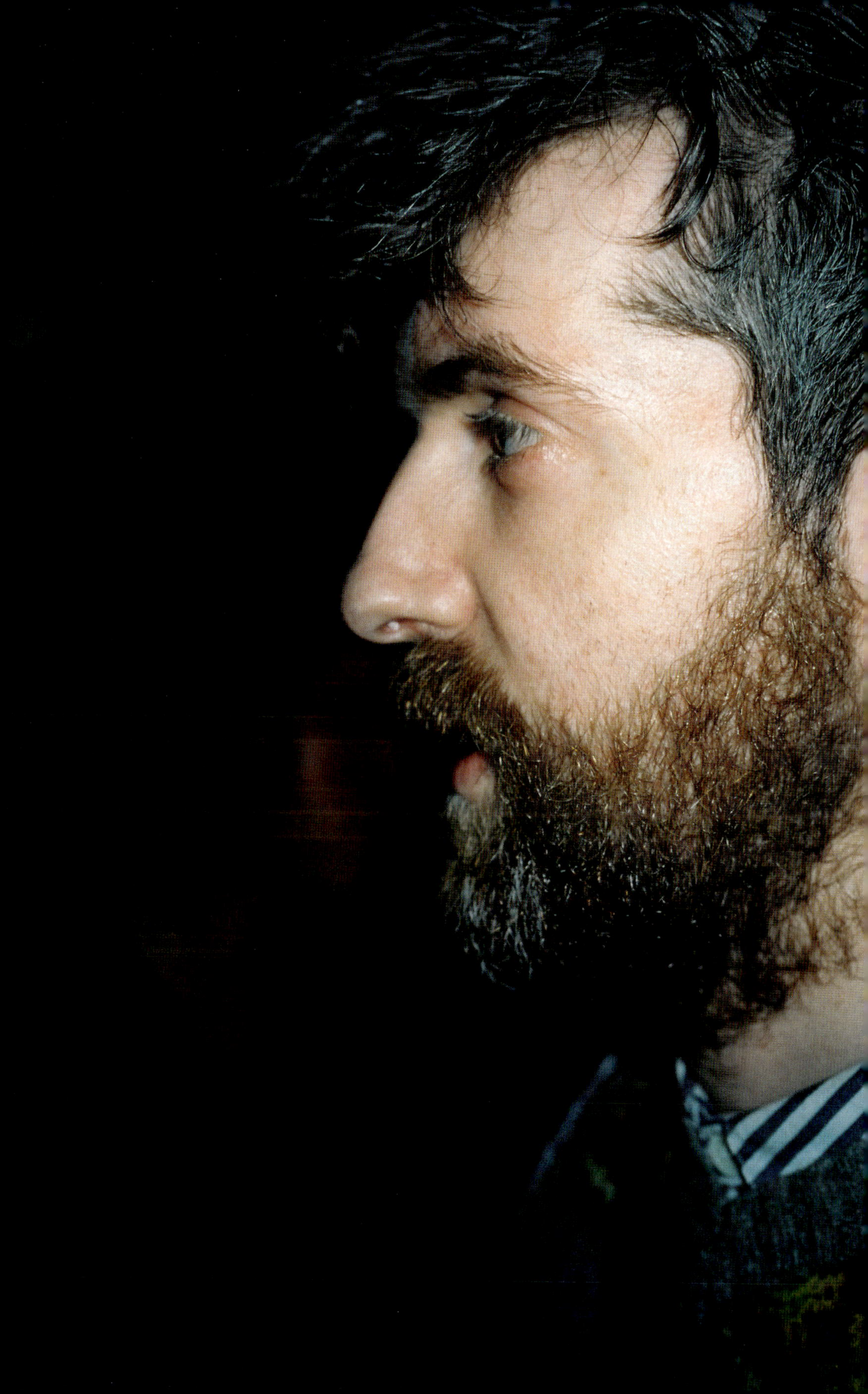

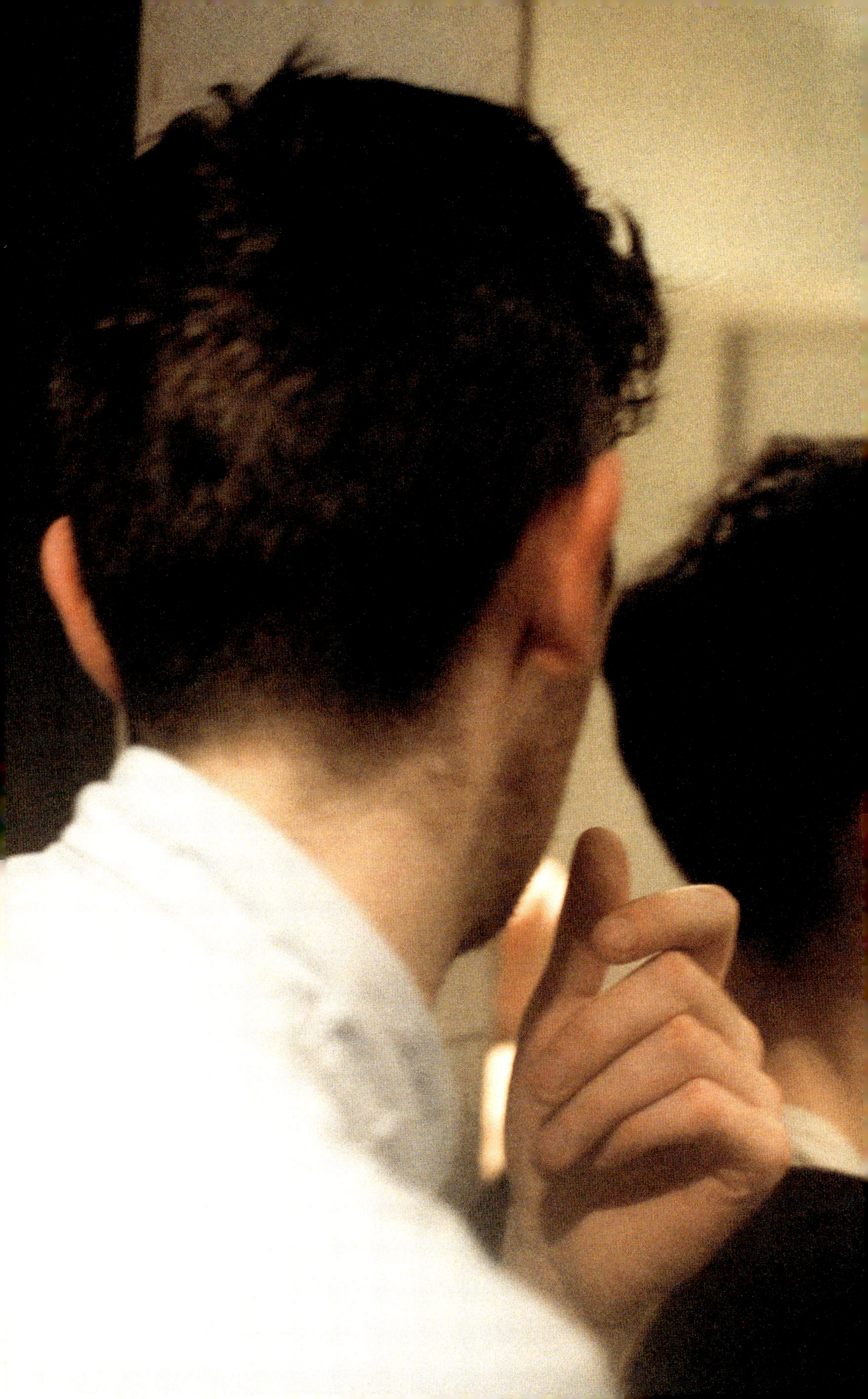

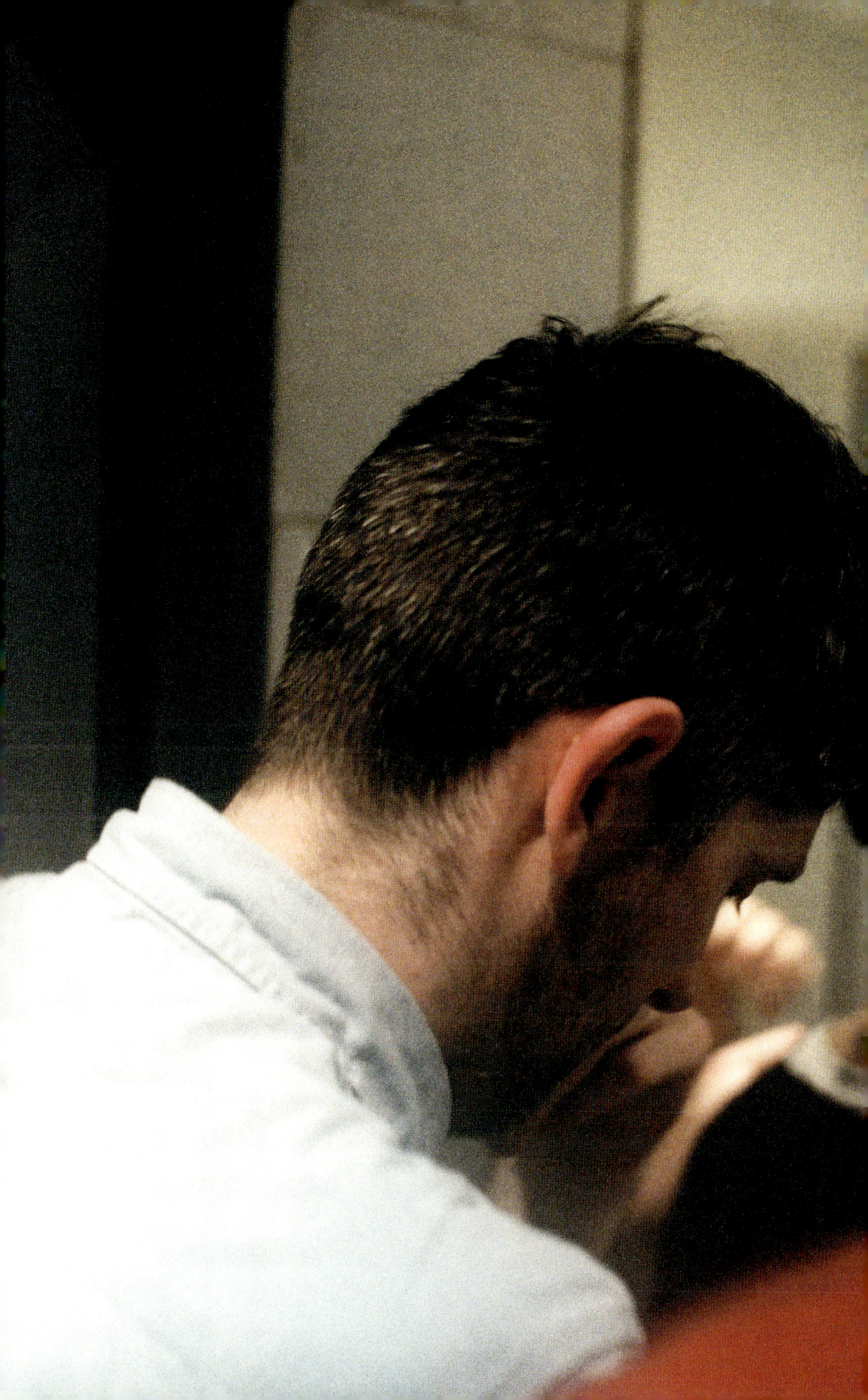

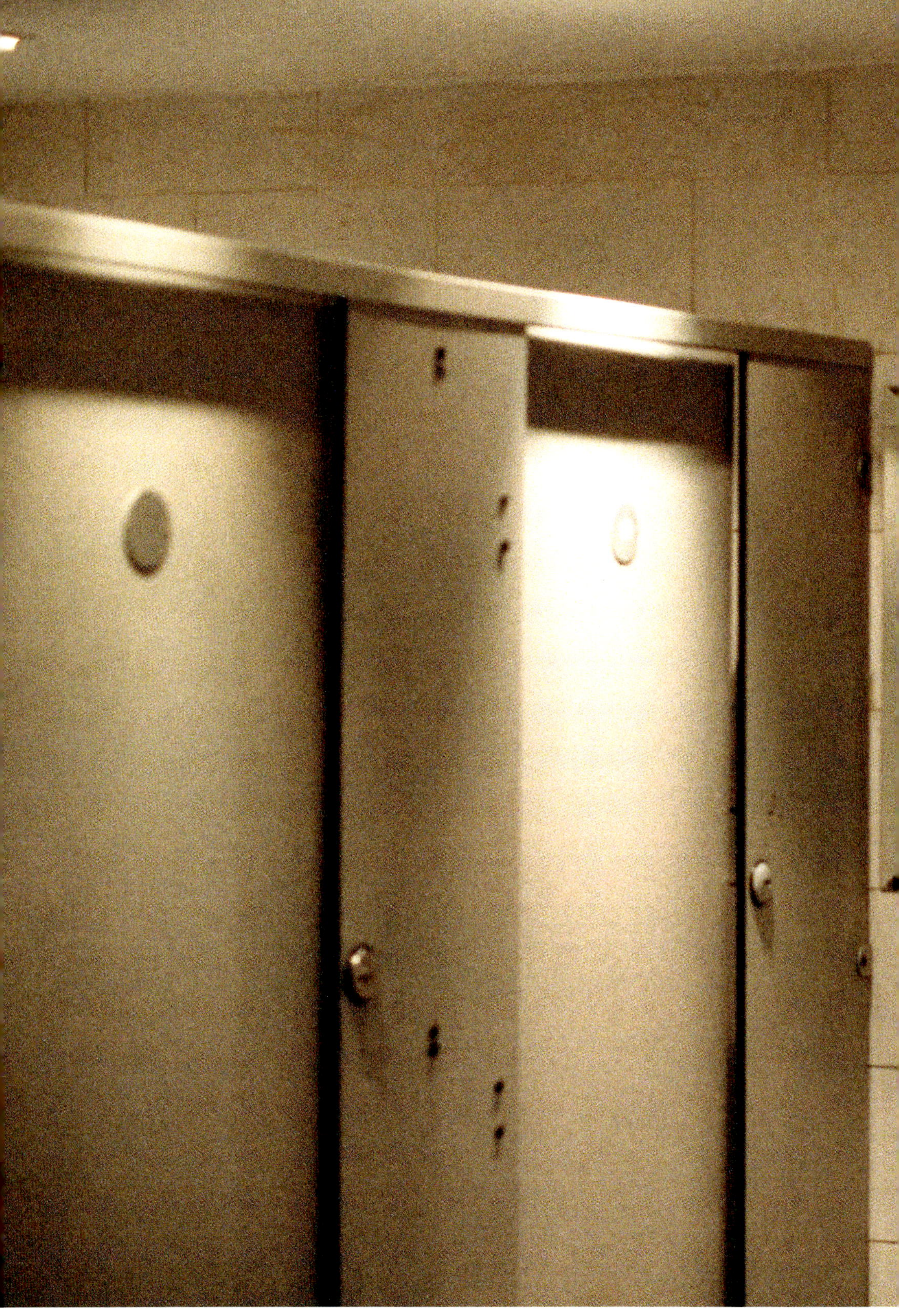

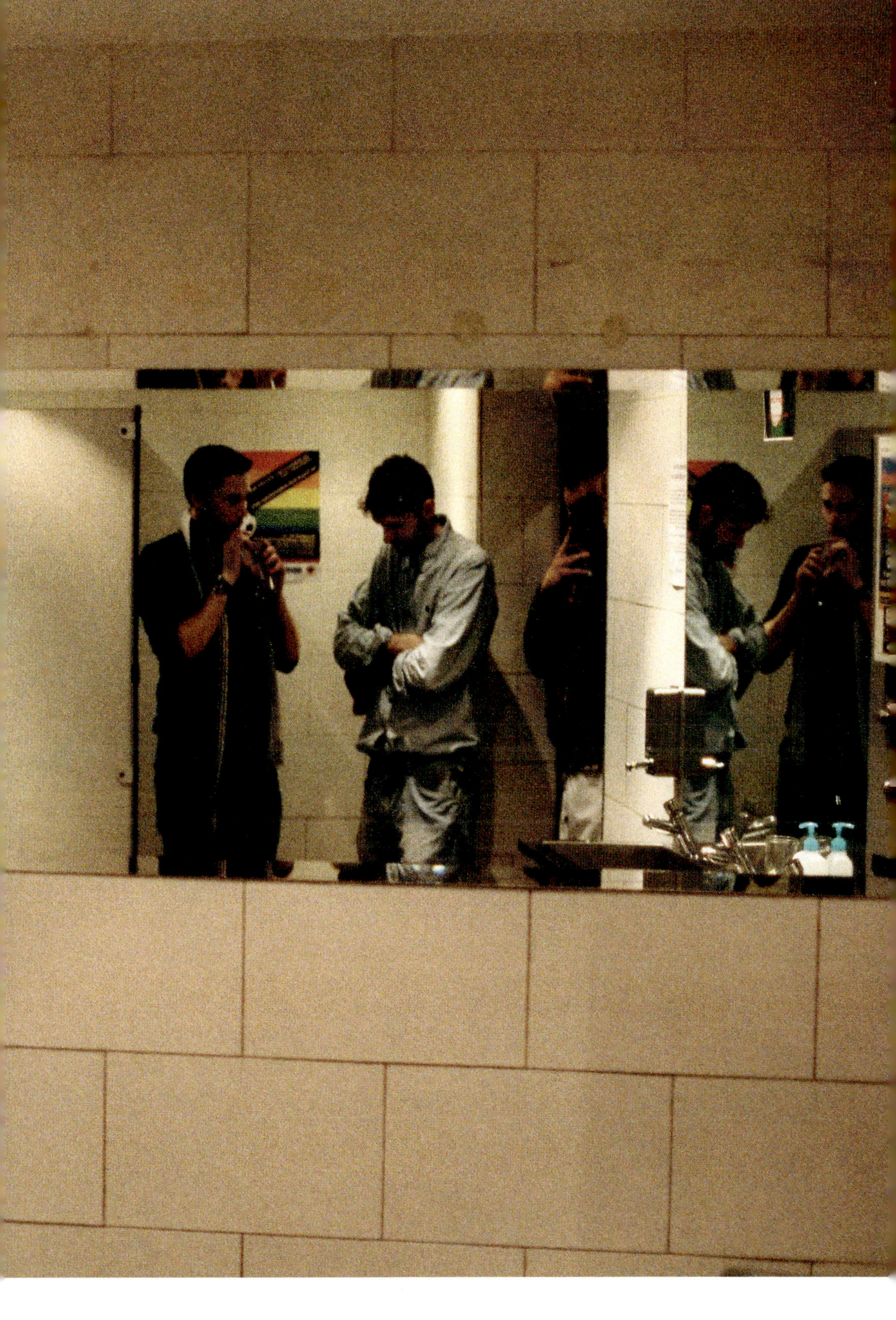

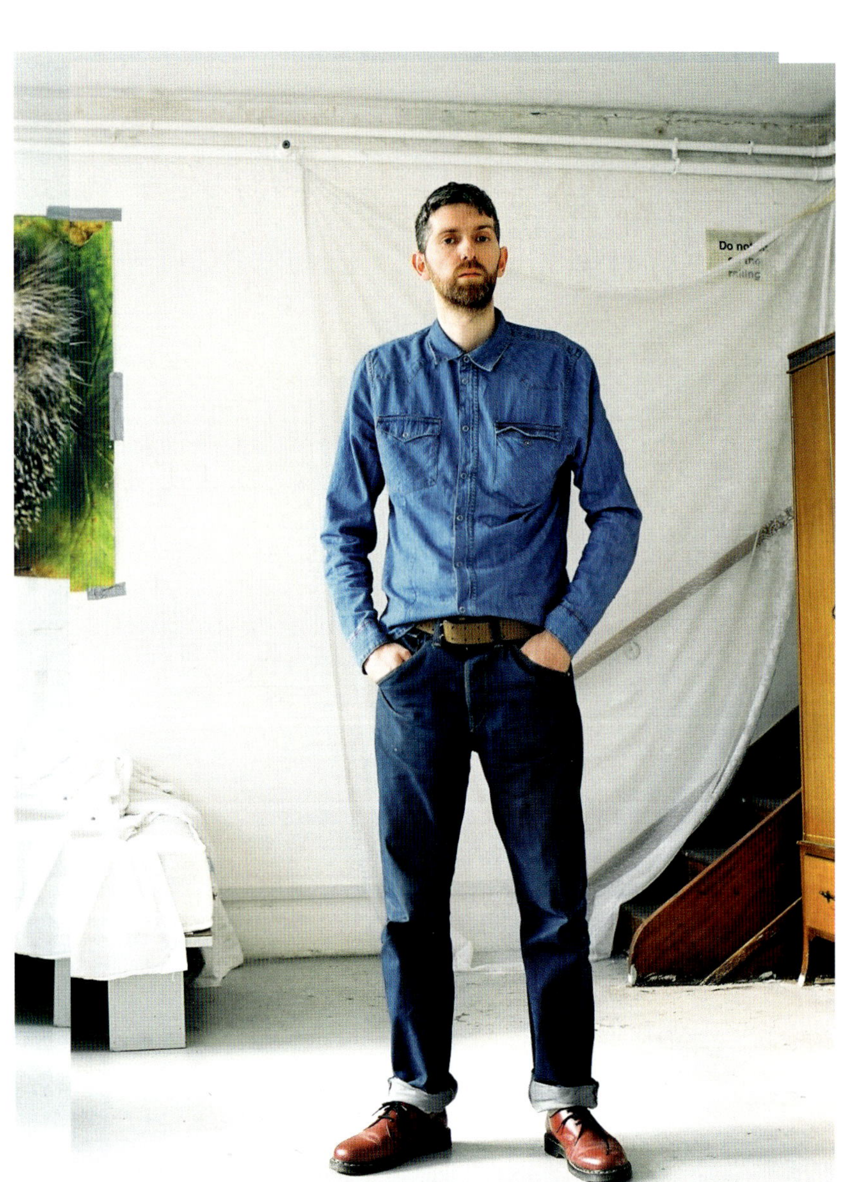

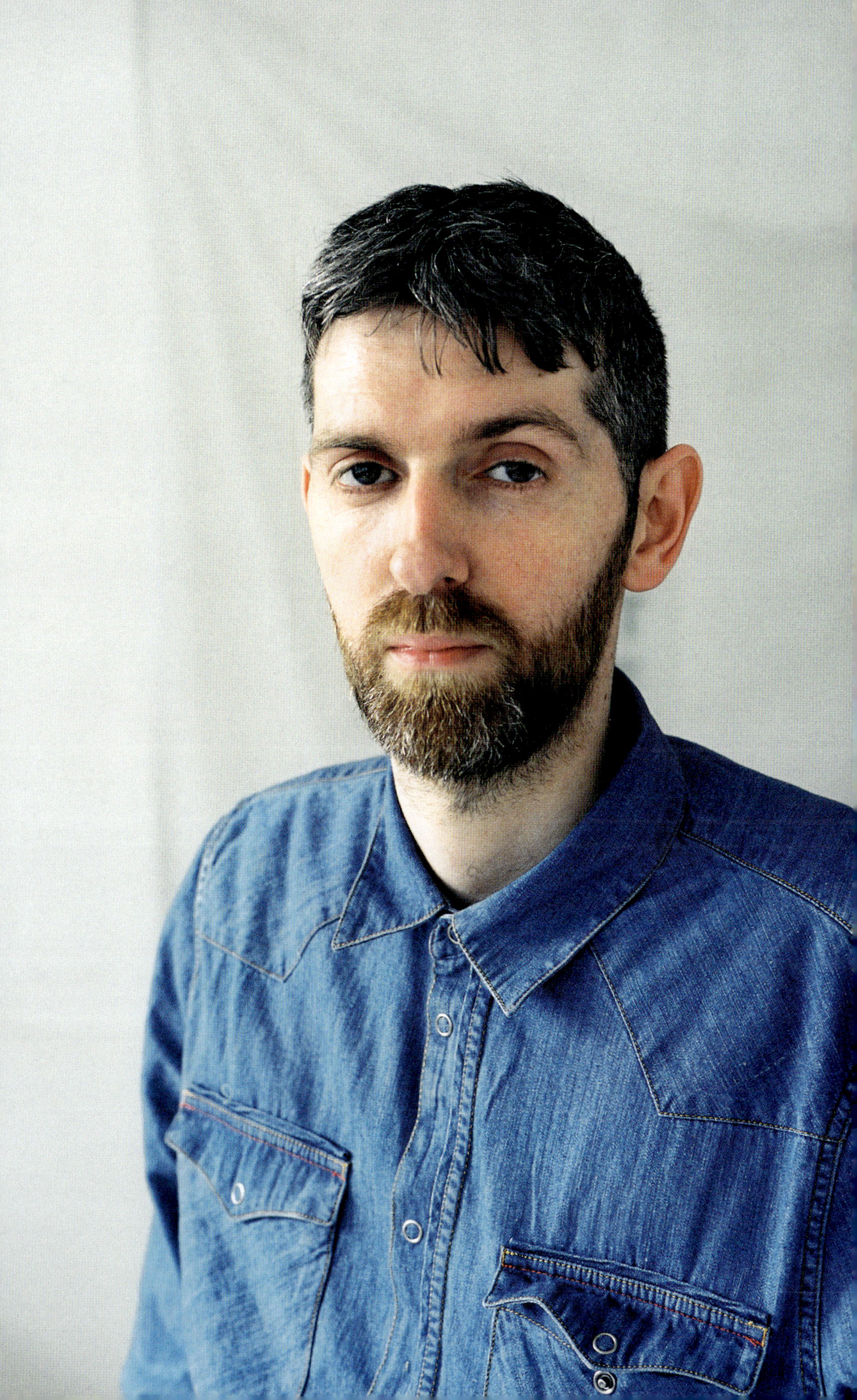

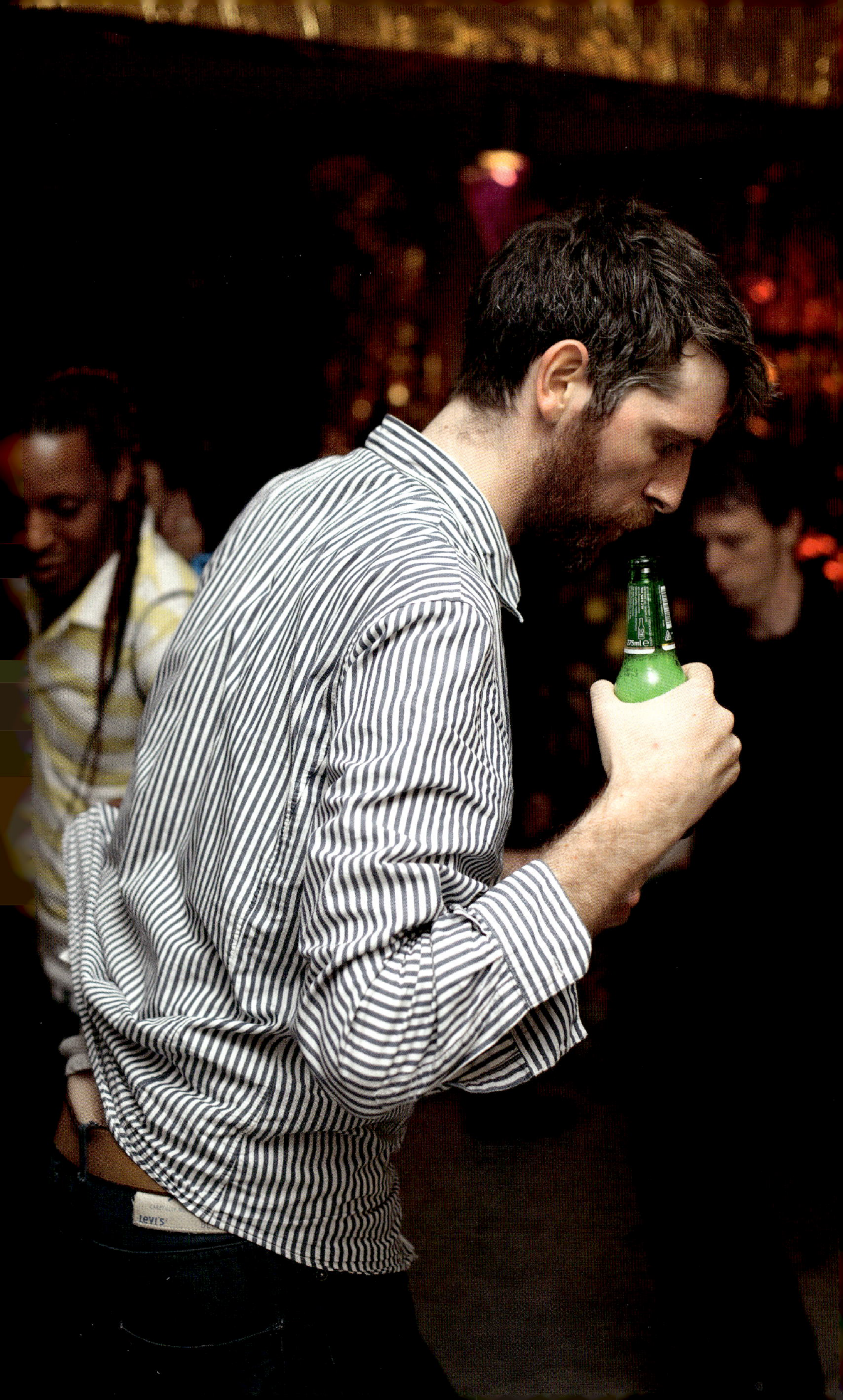
275ml
Levi's

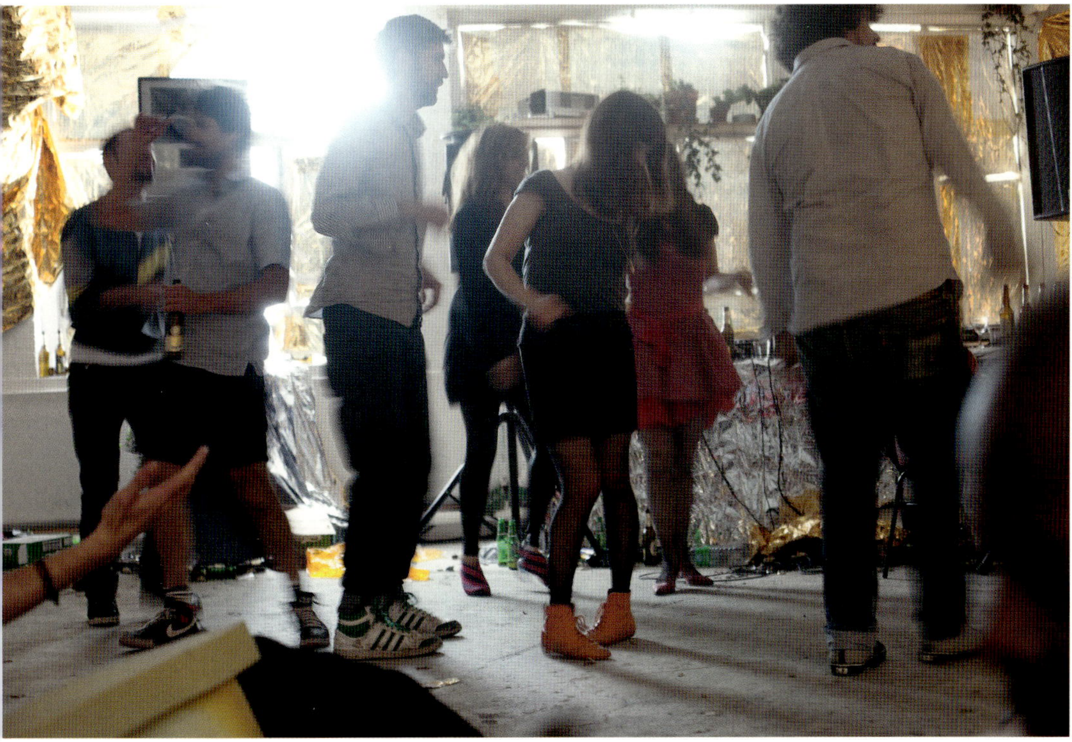

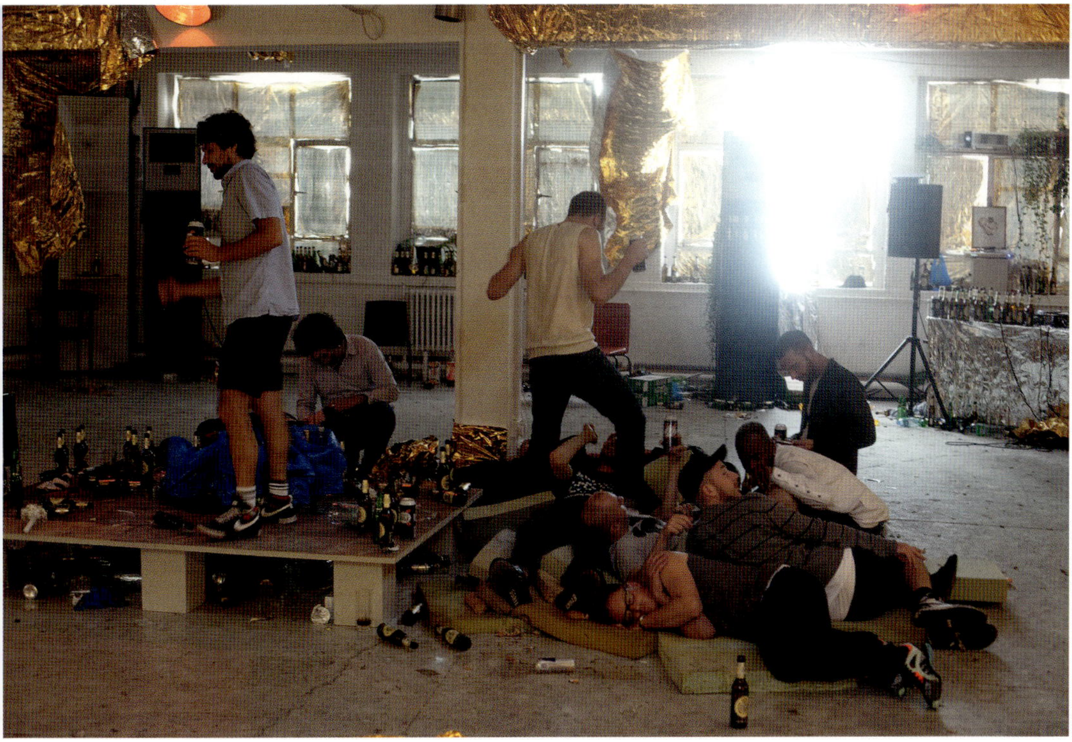

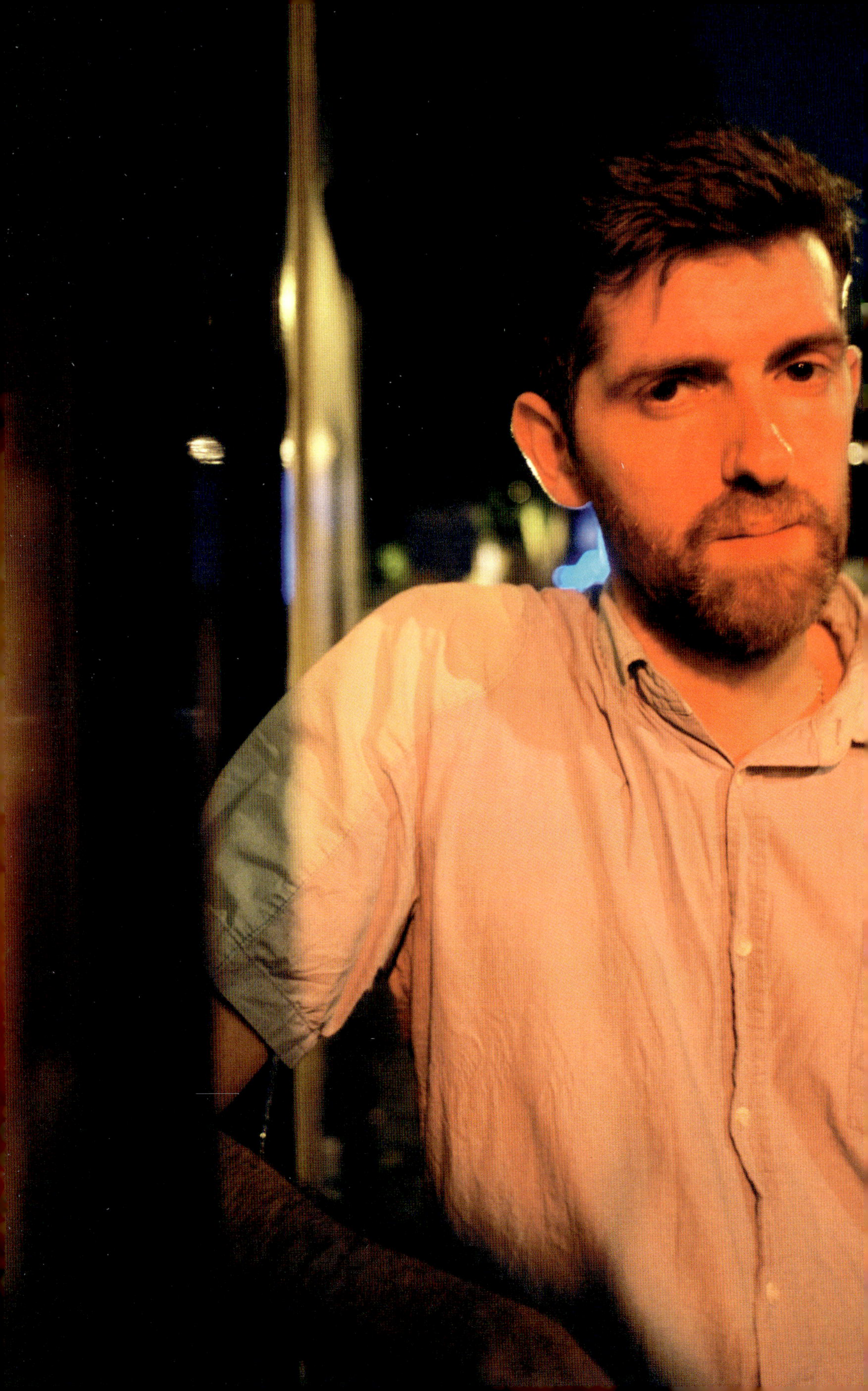

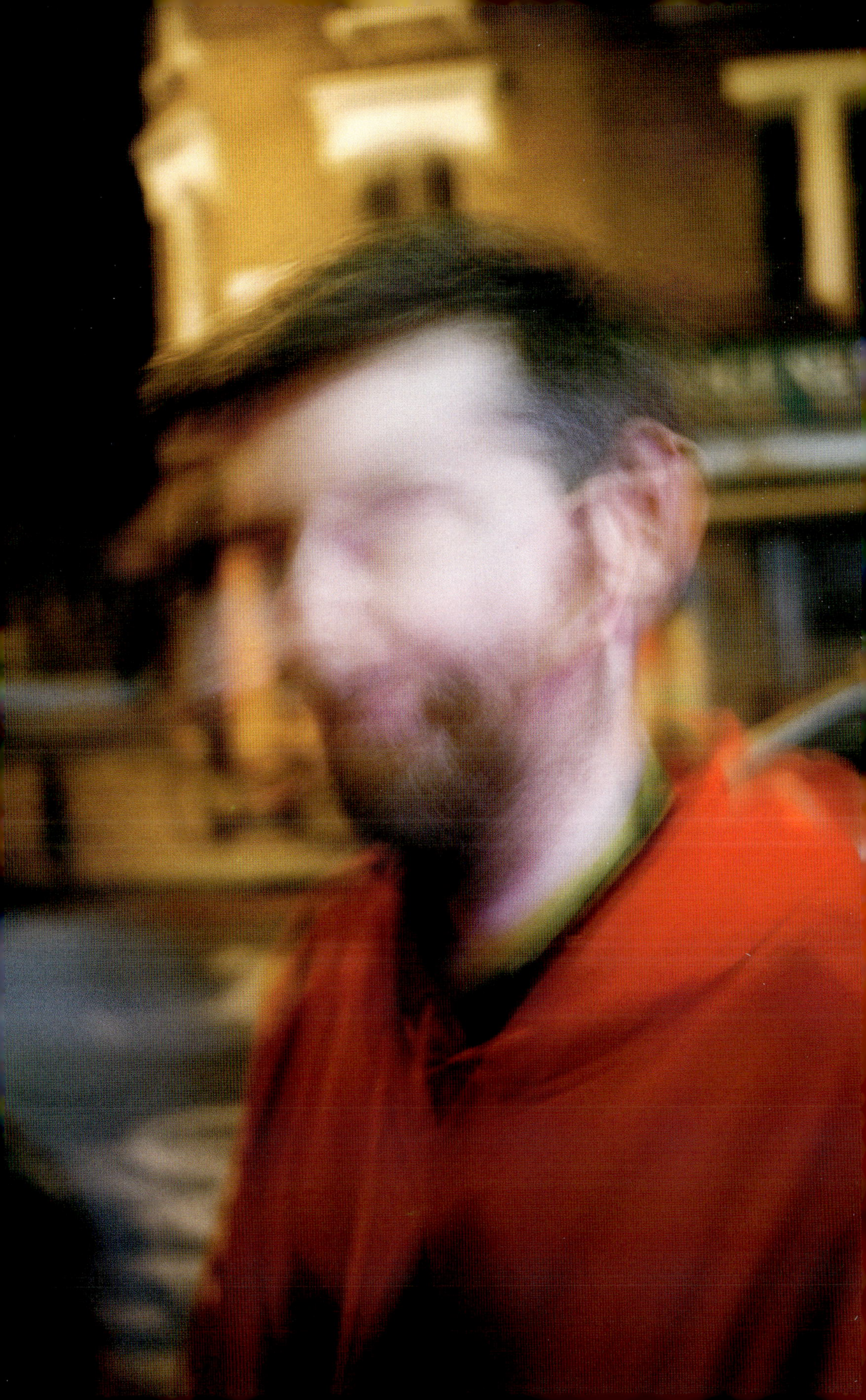

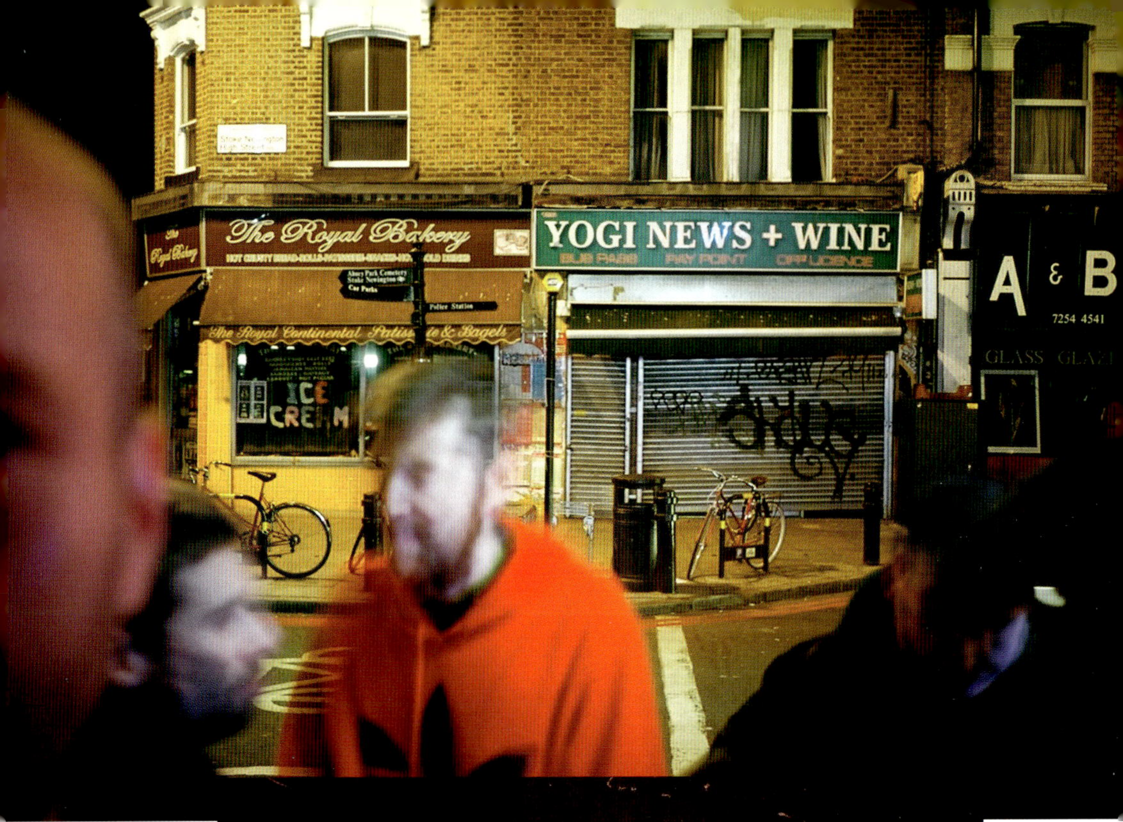
The Royal Bakery
YOGI NEWS + WINE
BUS PASS PAY POINT OFF LICENCE
ICE CREAM
A & B
7254 4541

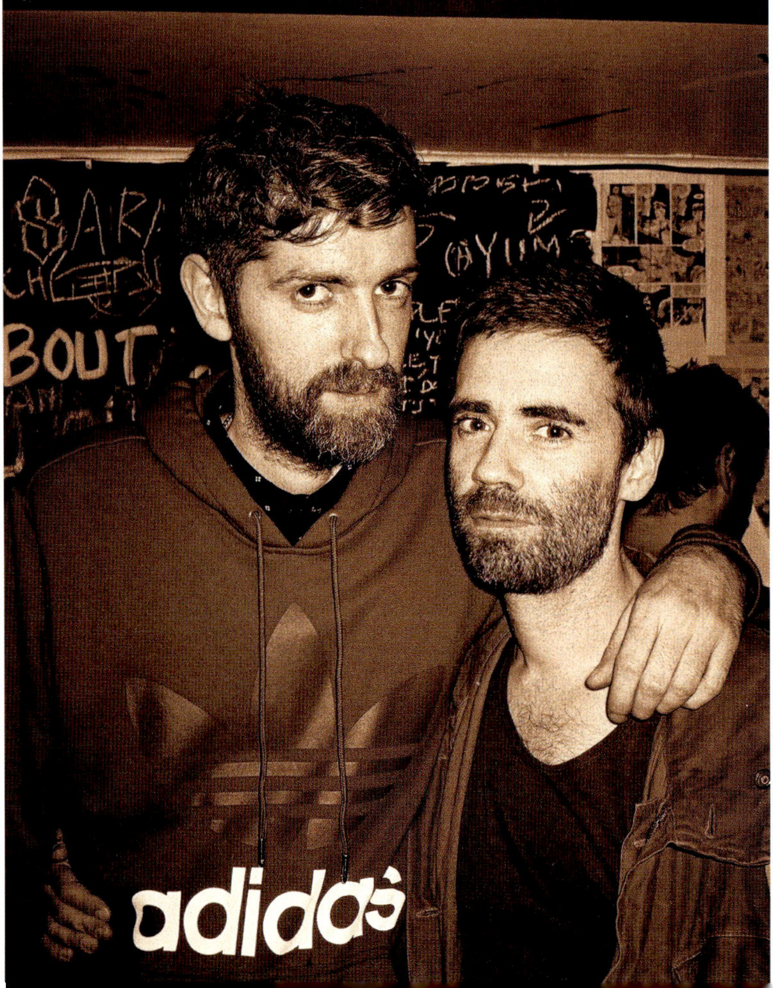
adidas

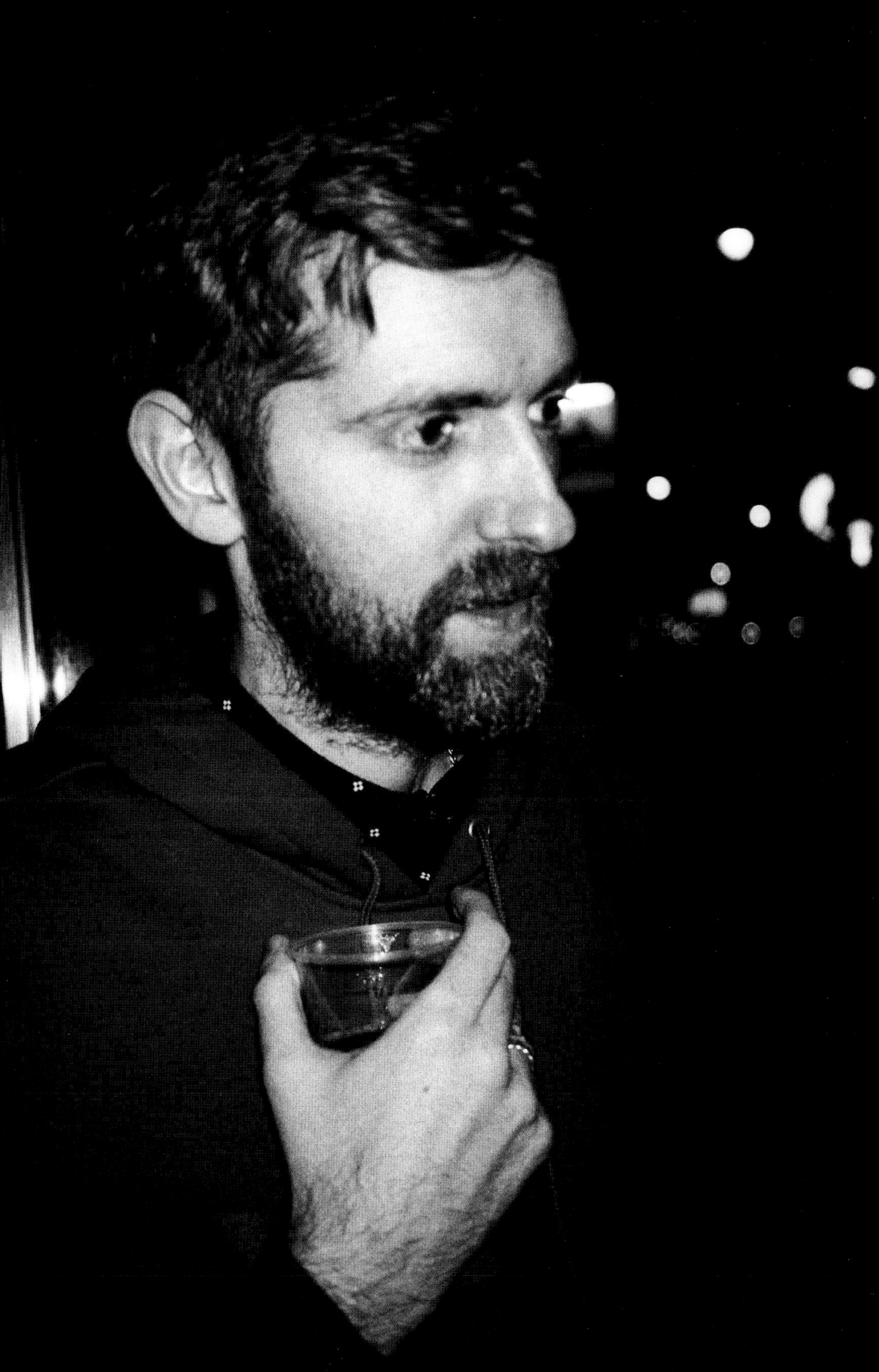

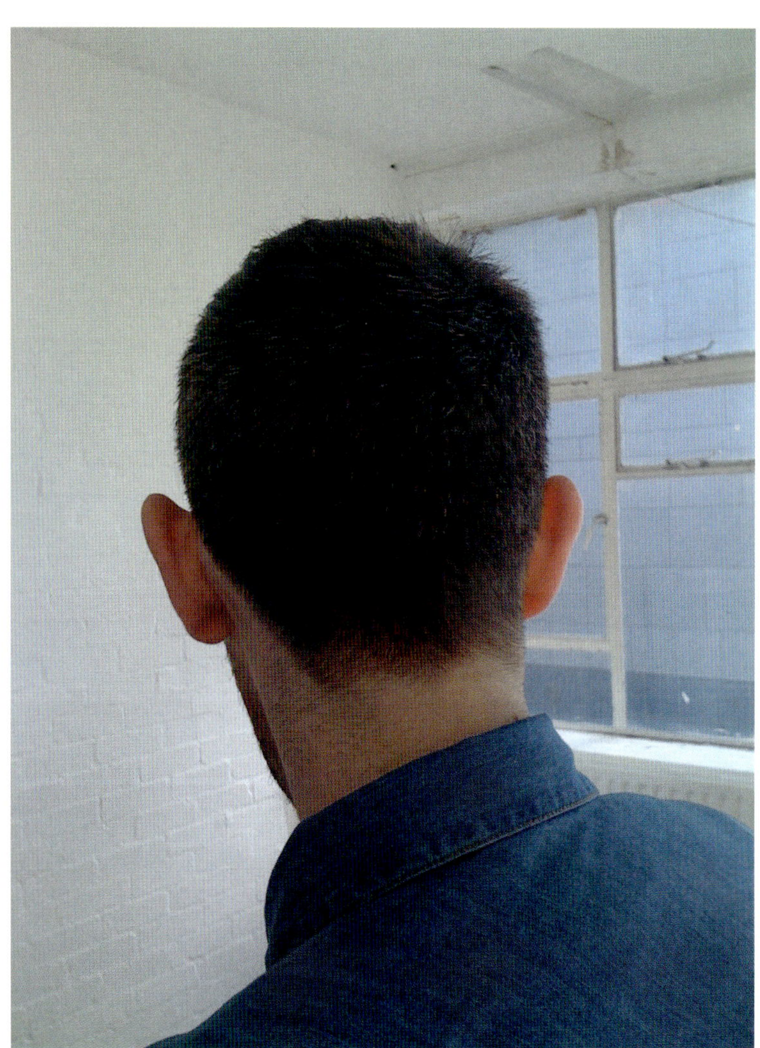

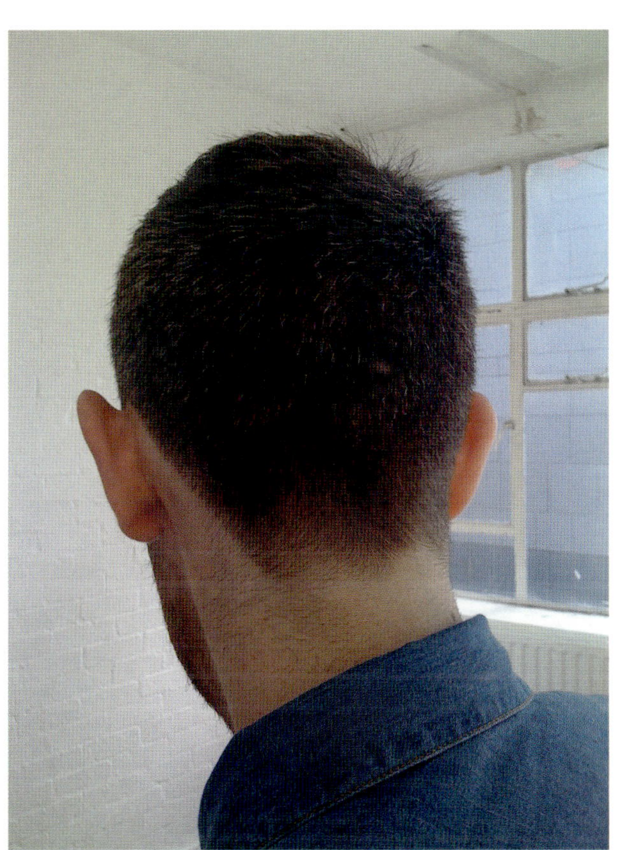

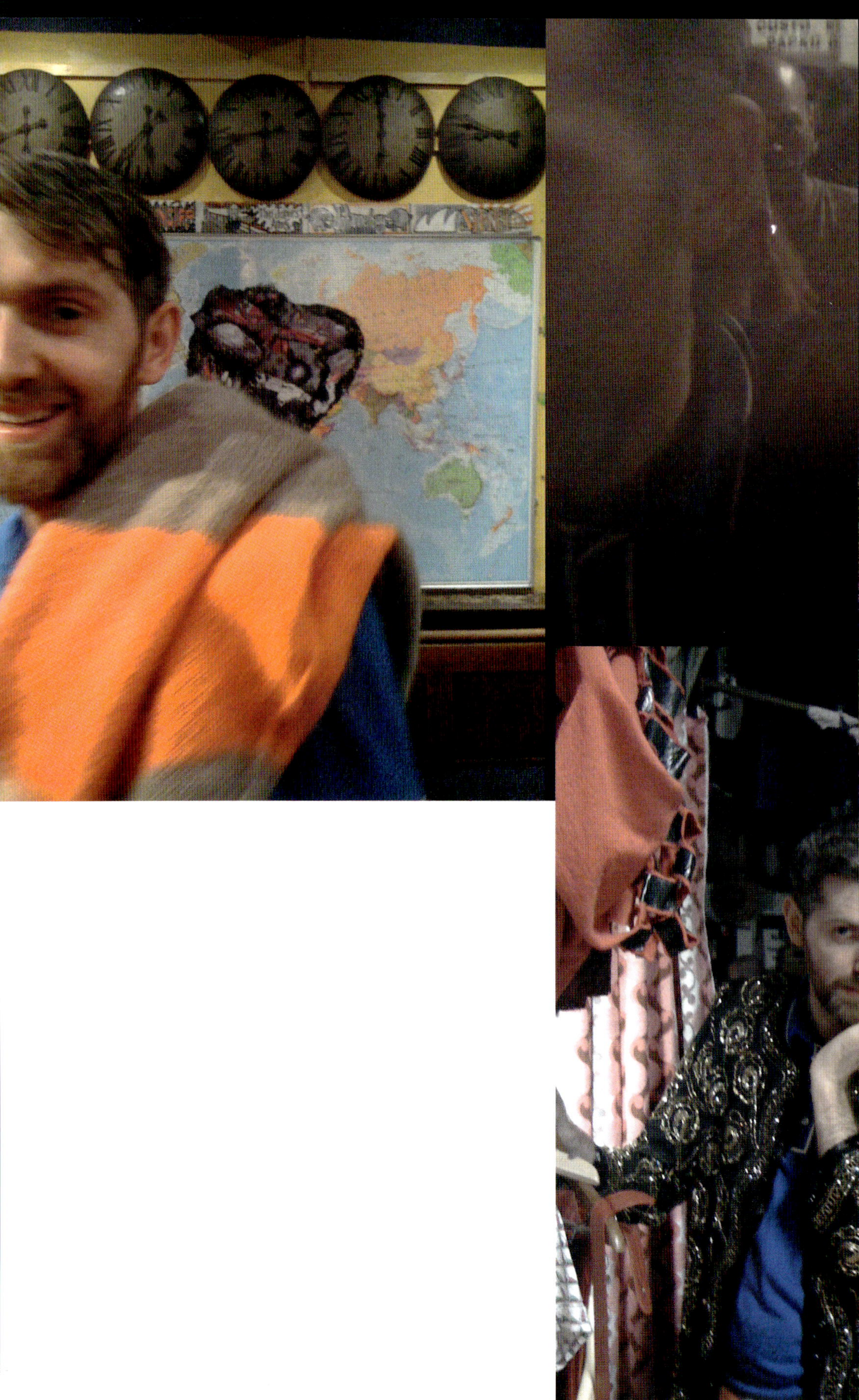

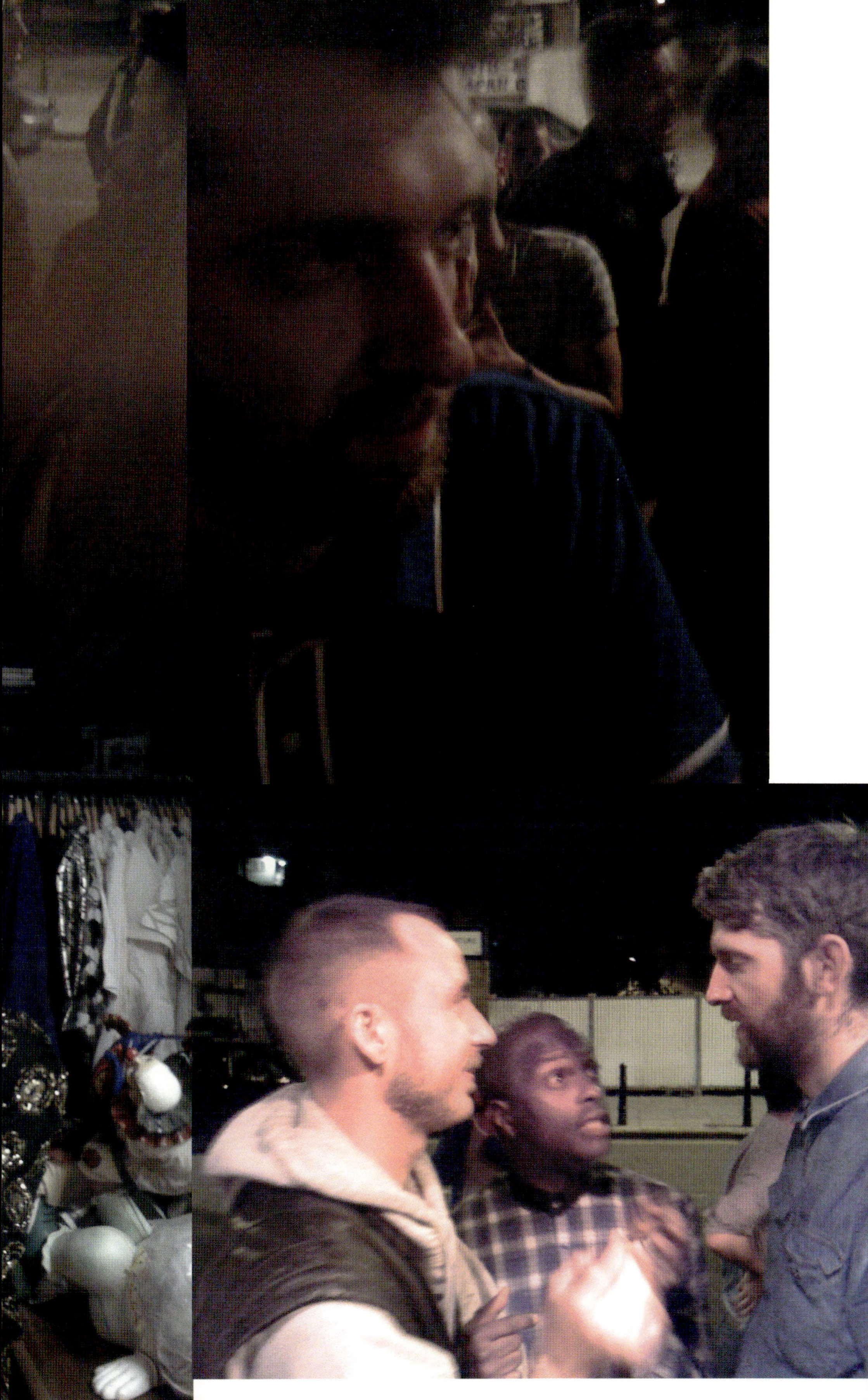

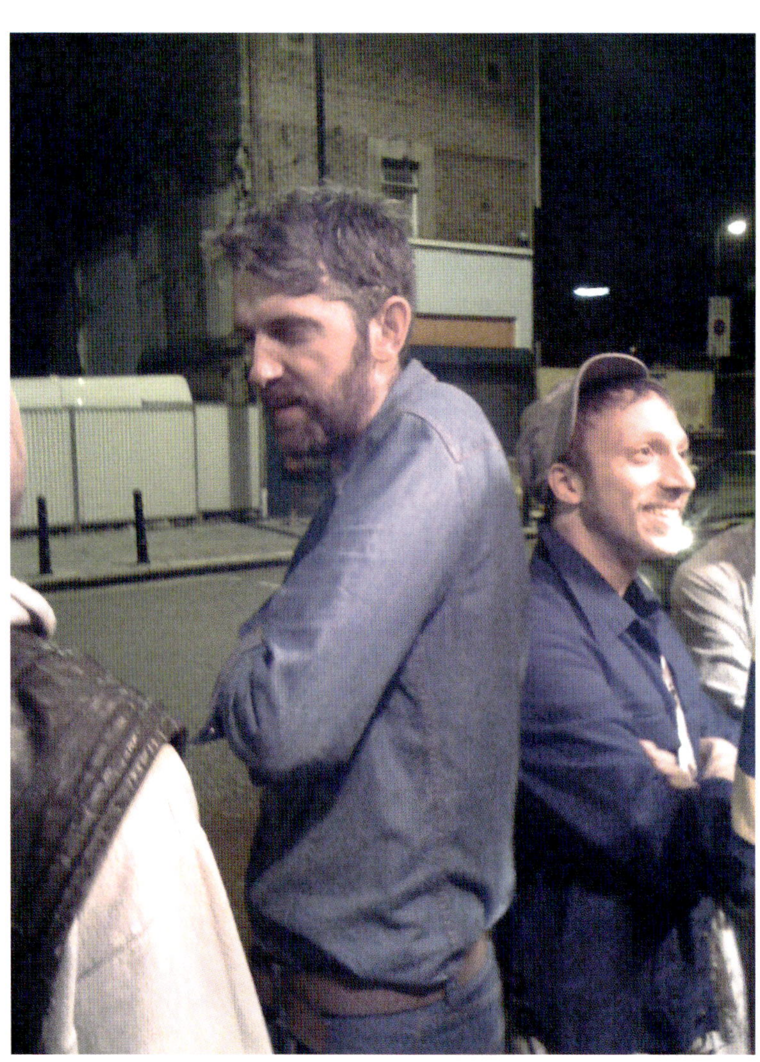

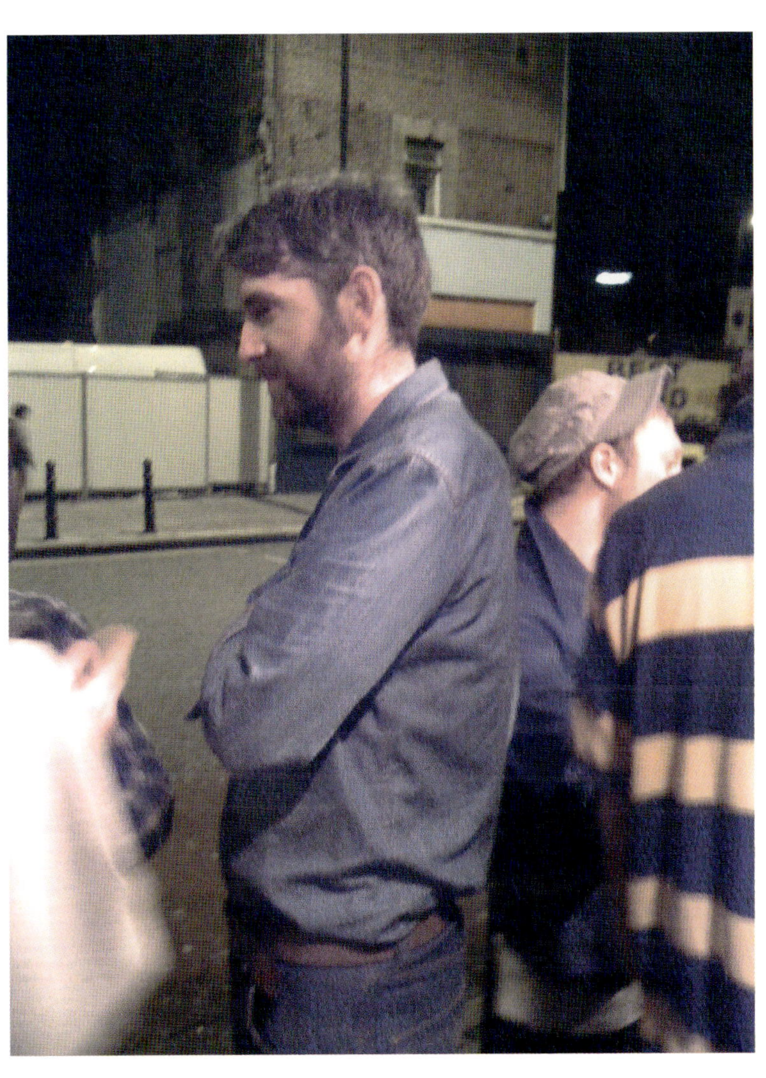

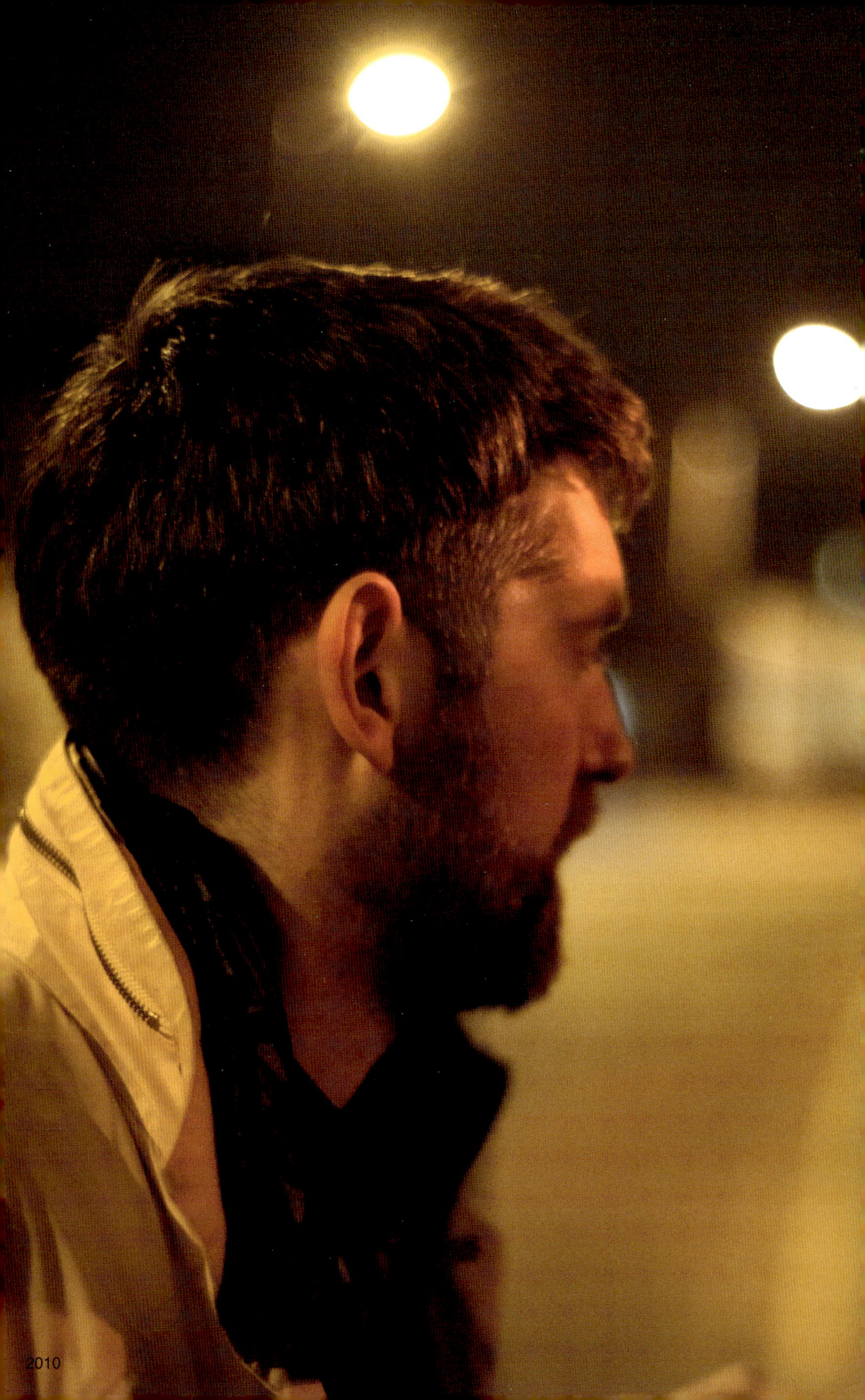

2010

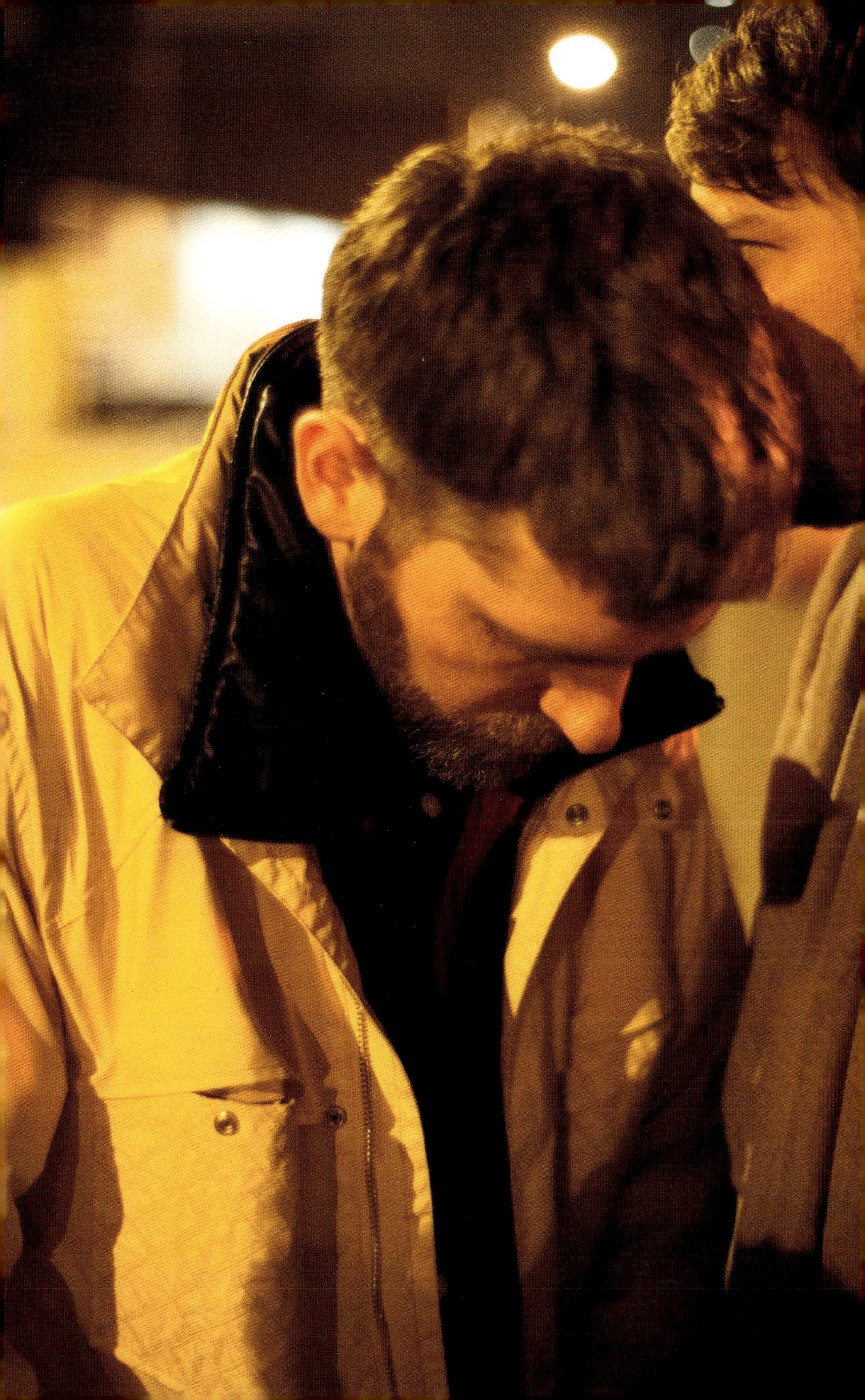

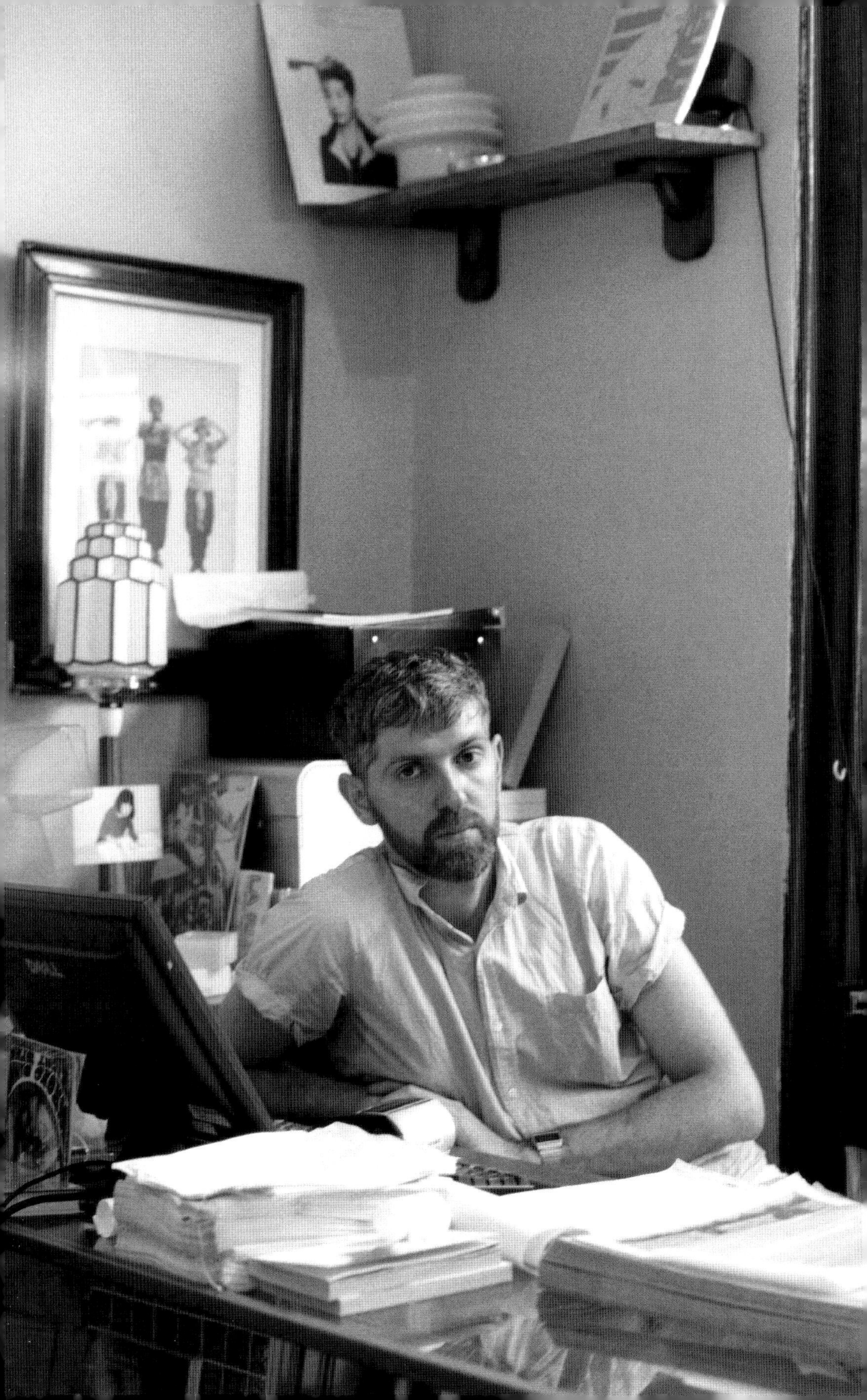

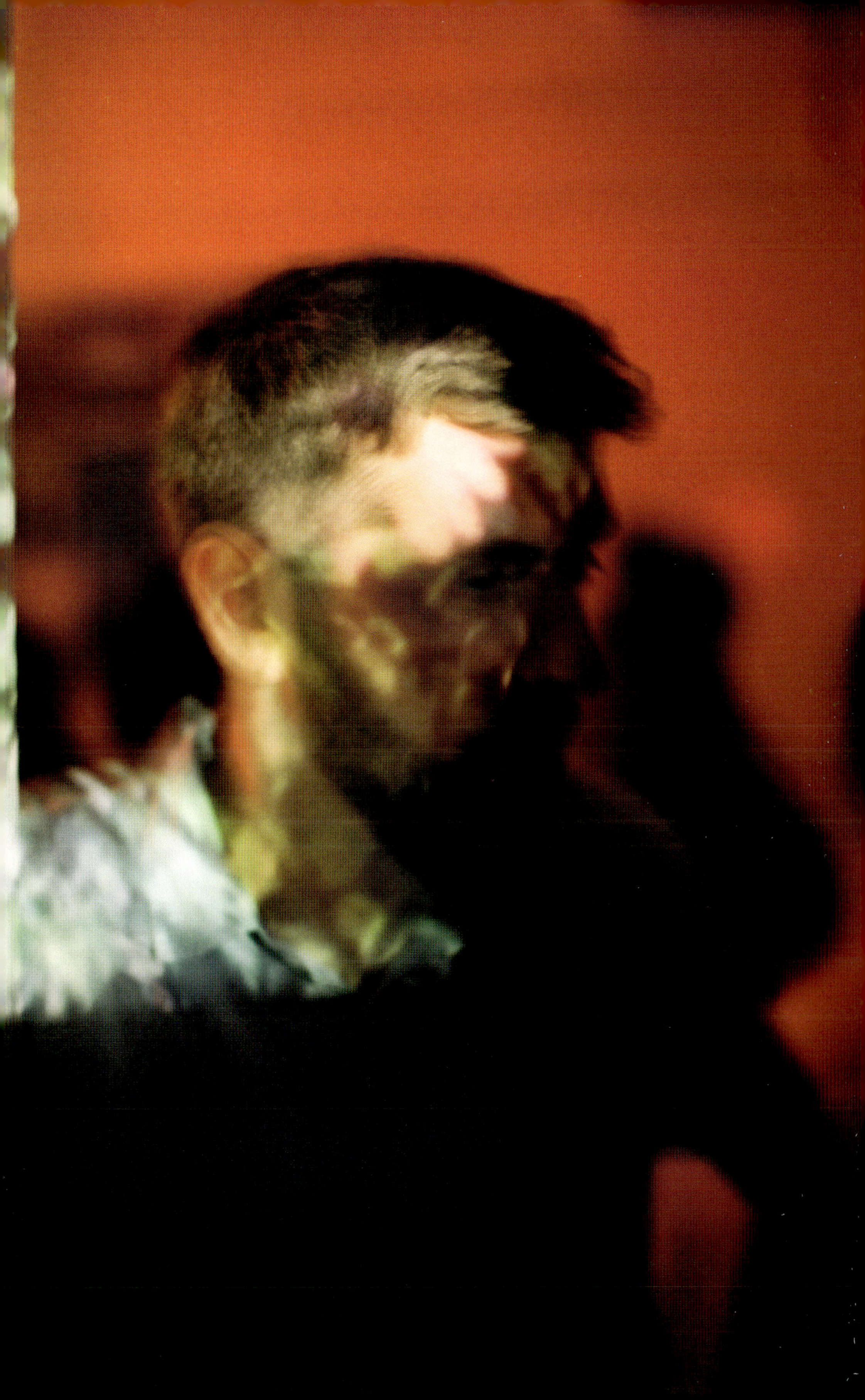

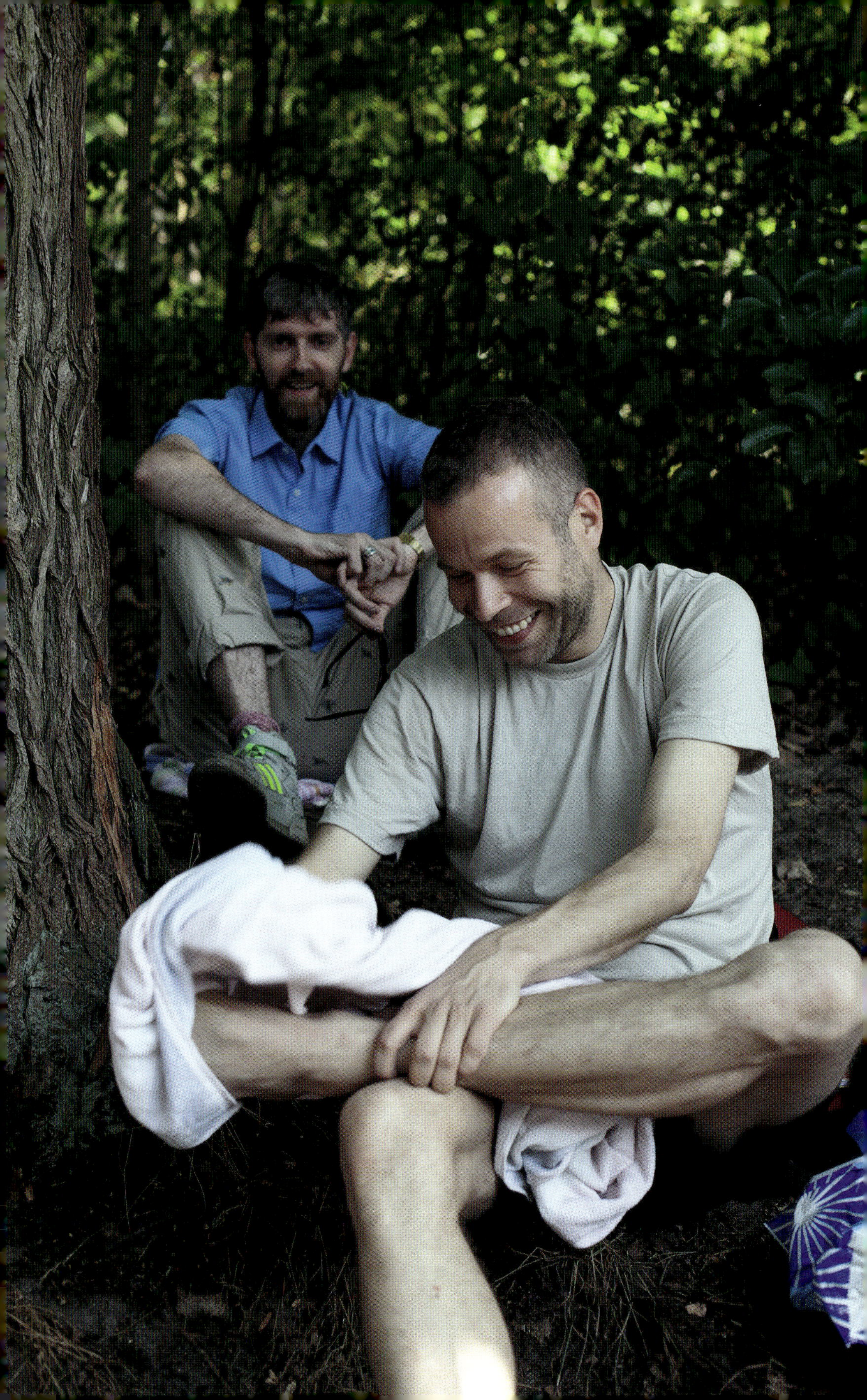

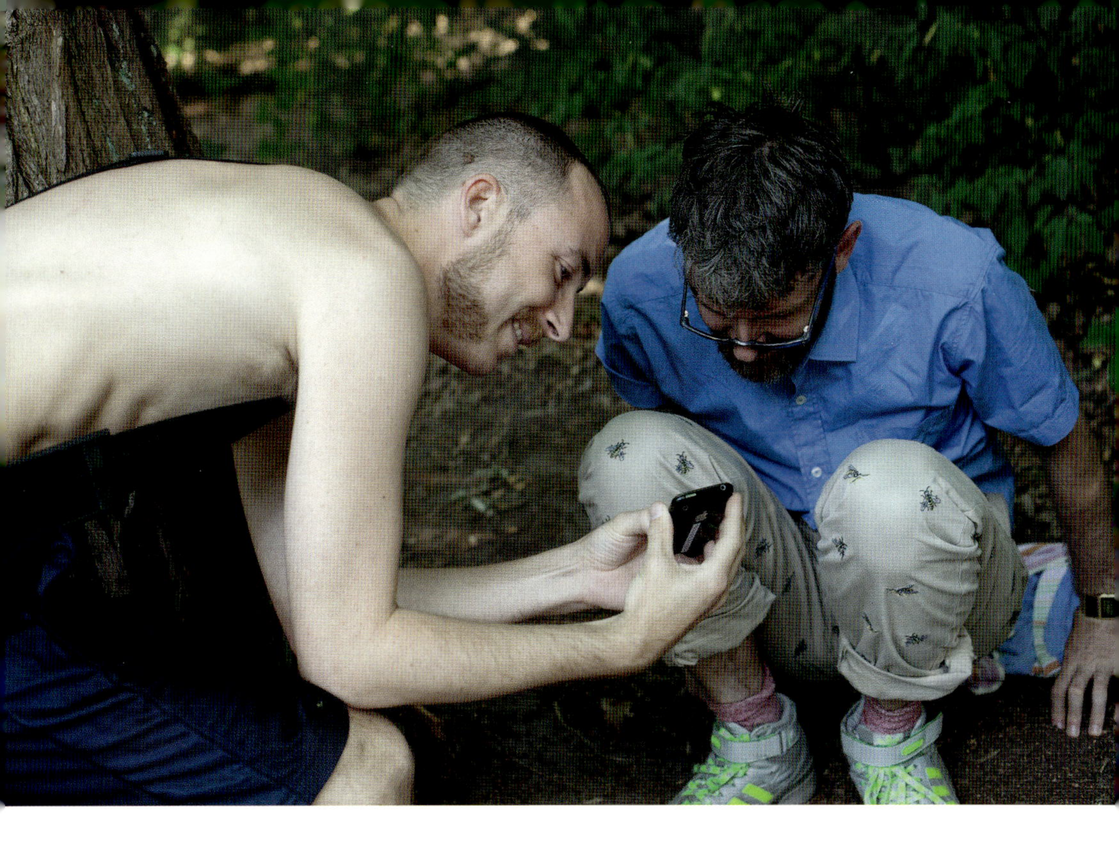

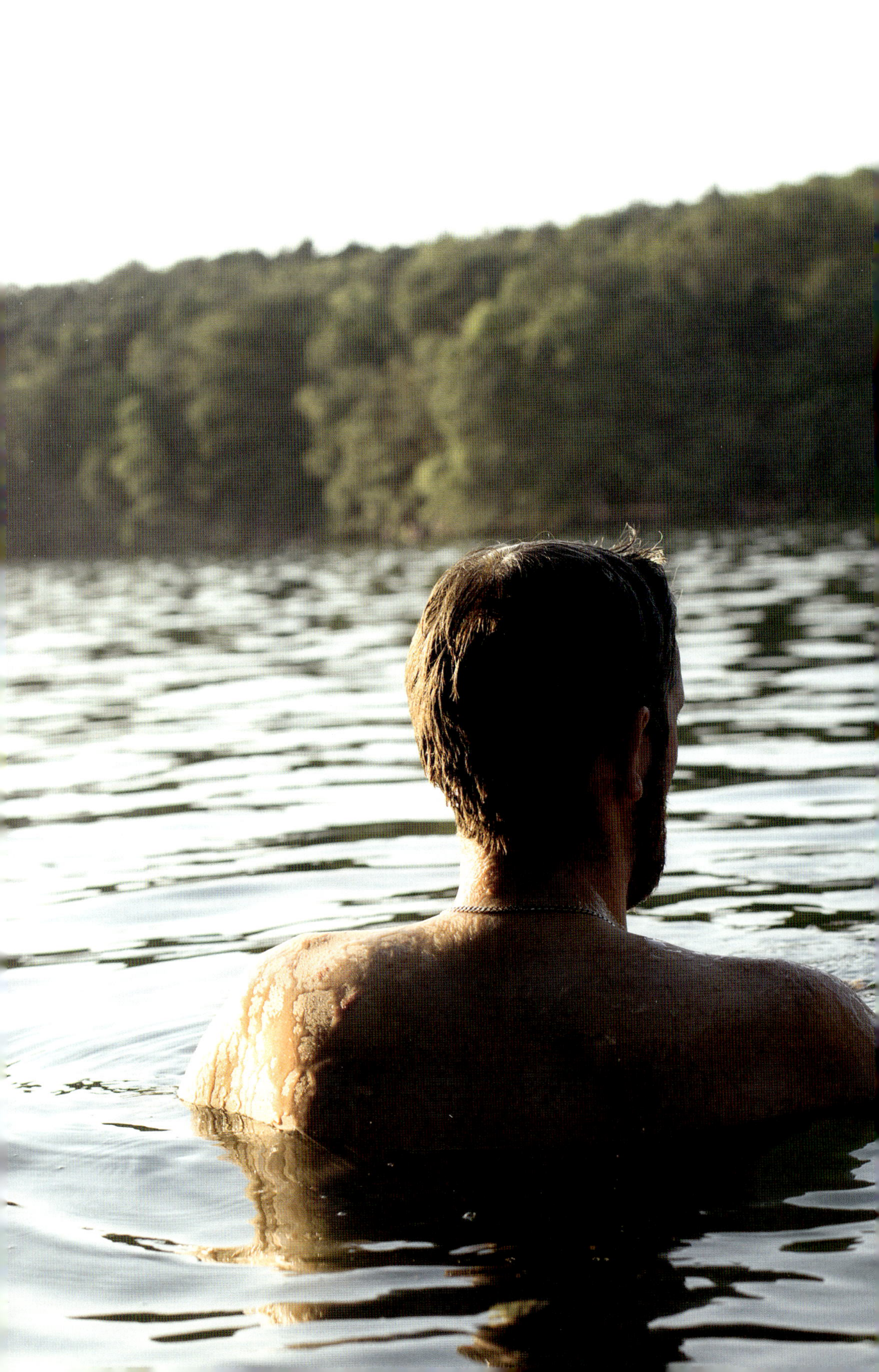

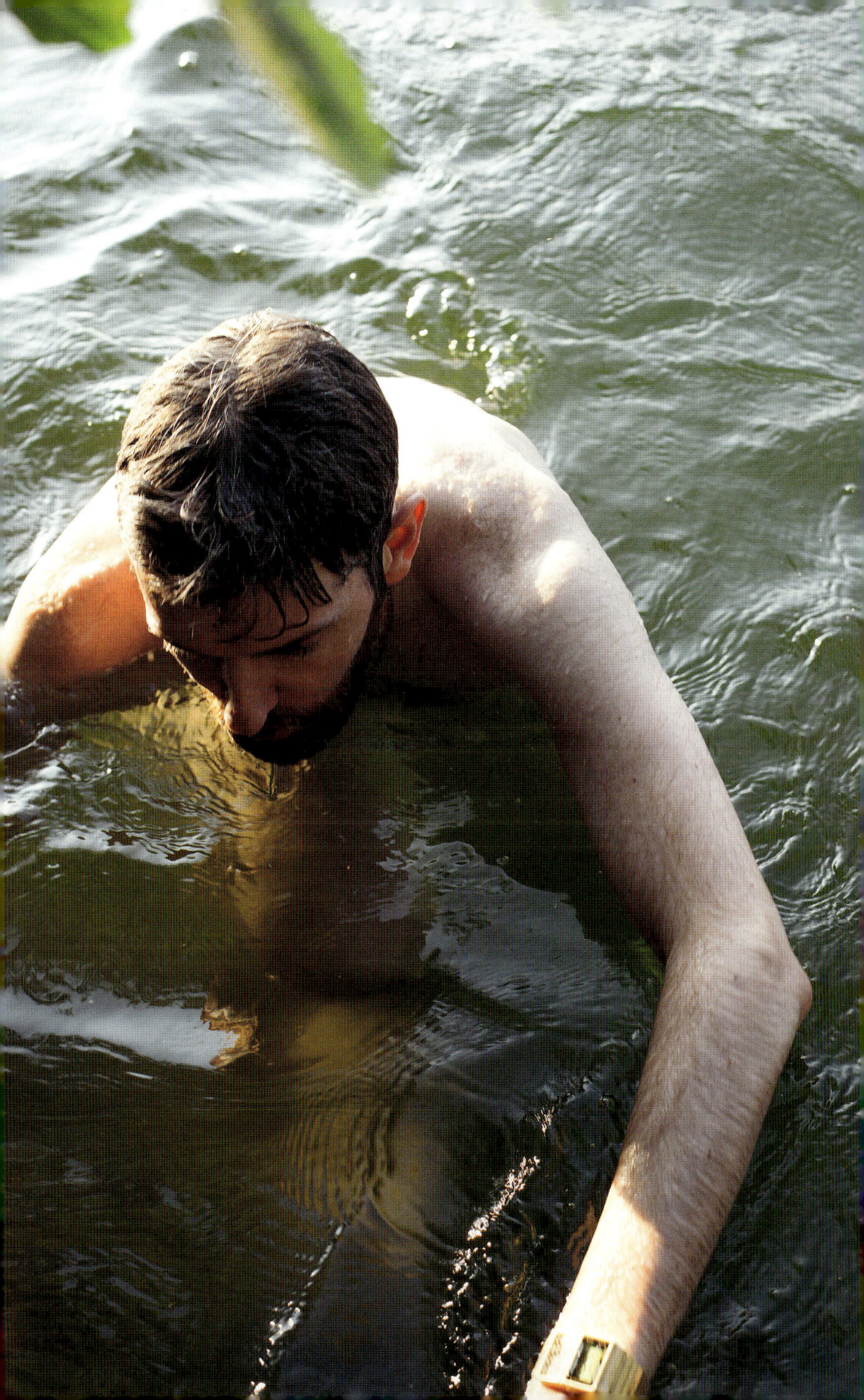

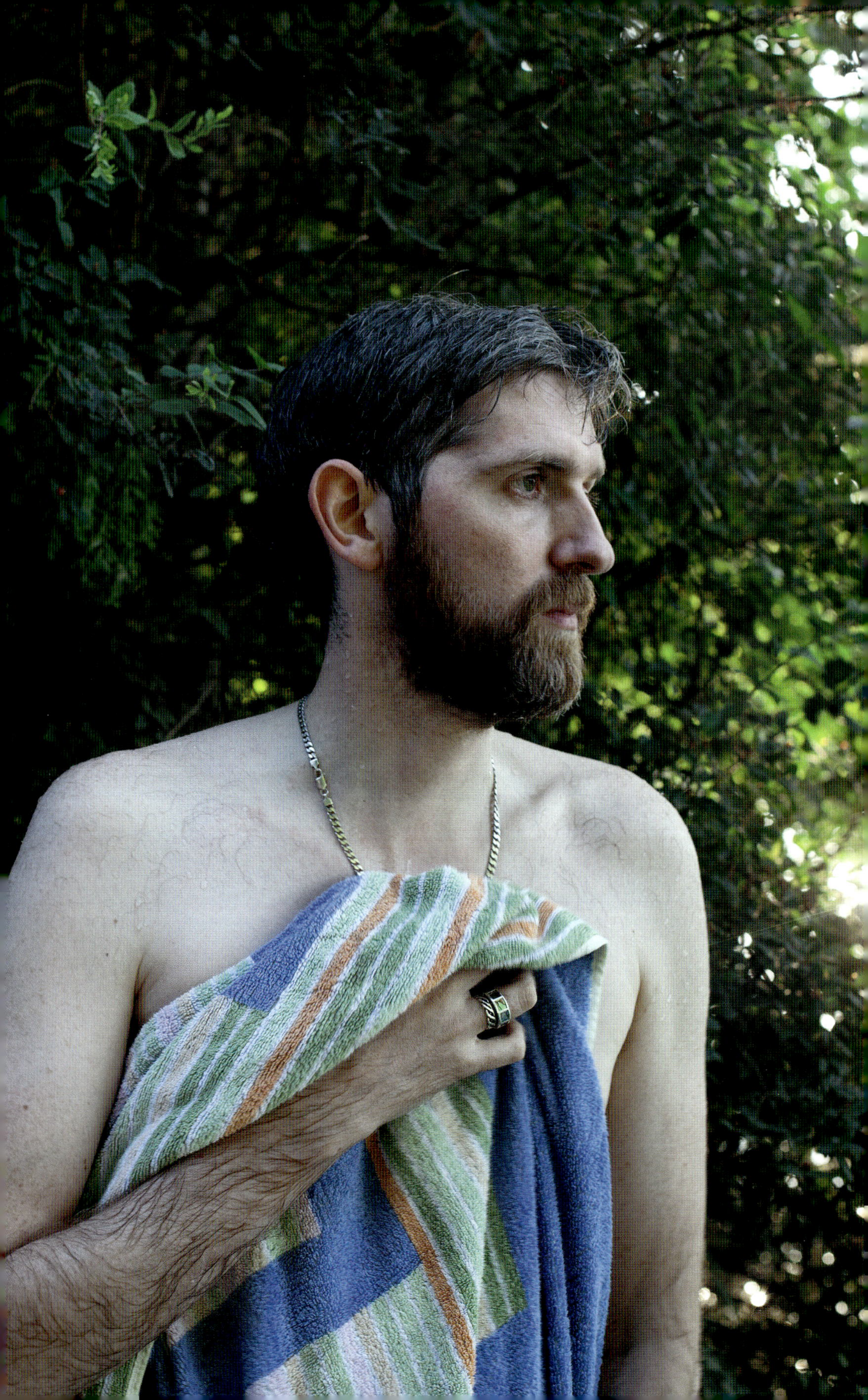

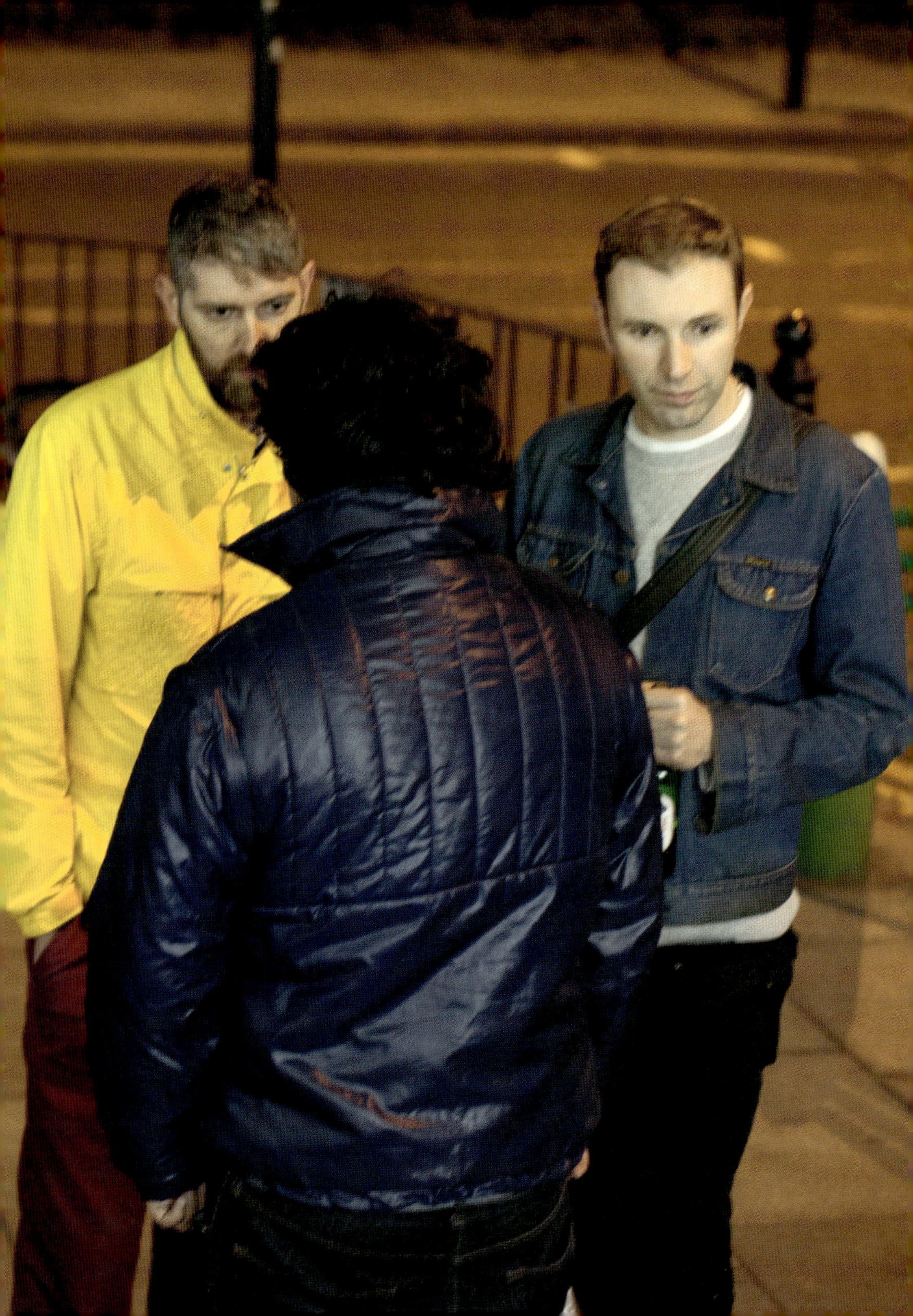

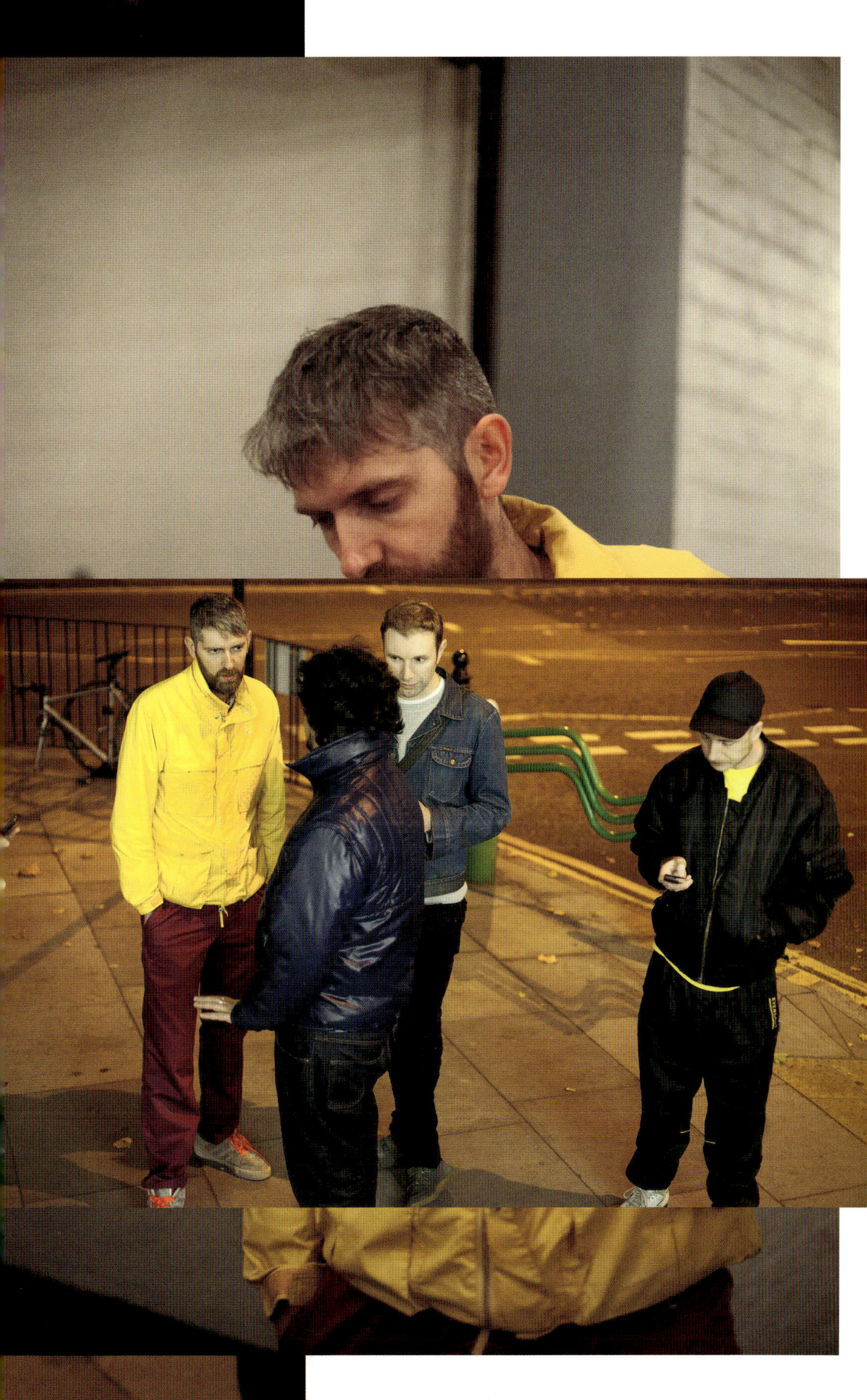

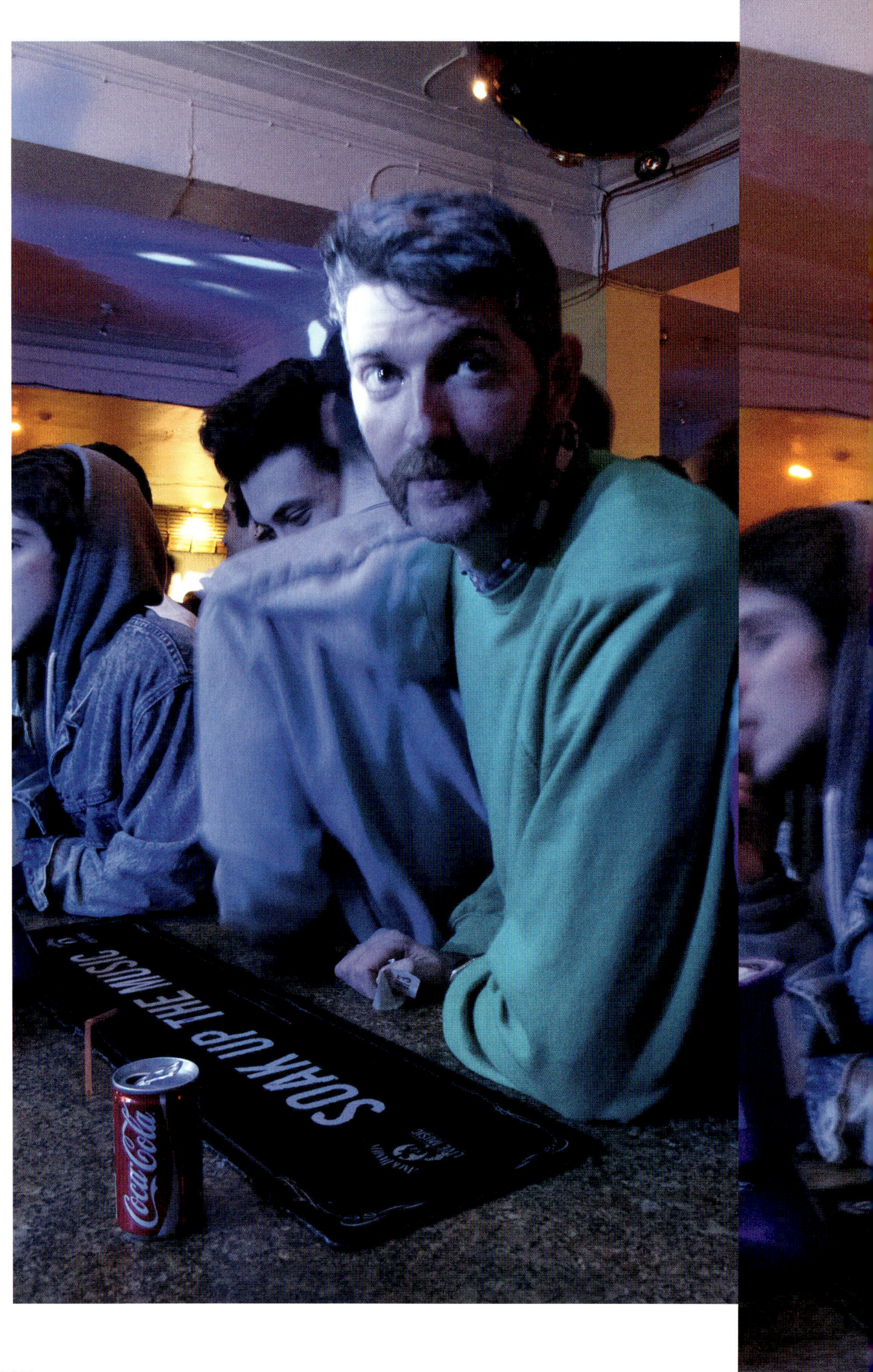

2011

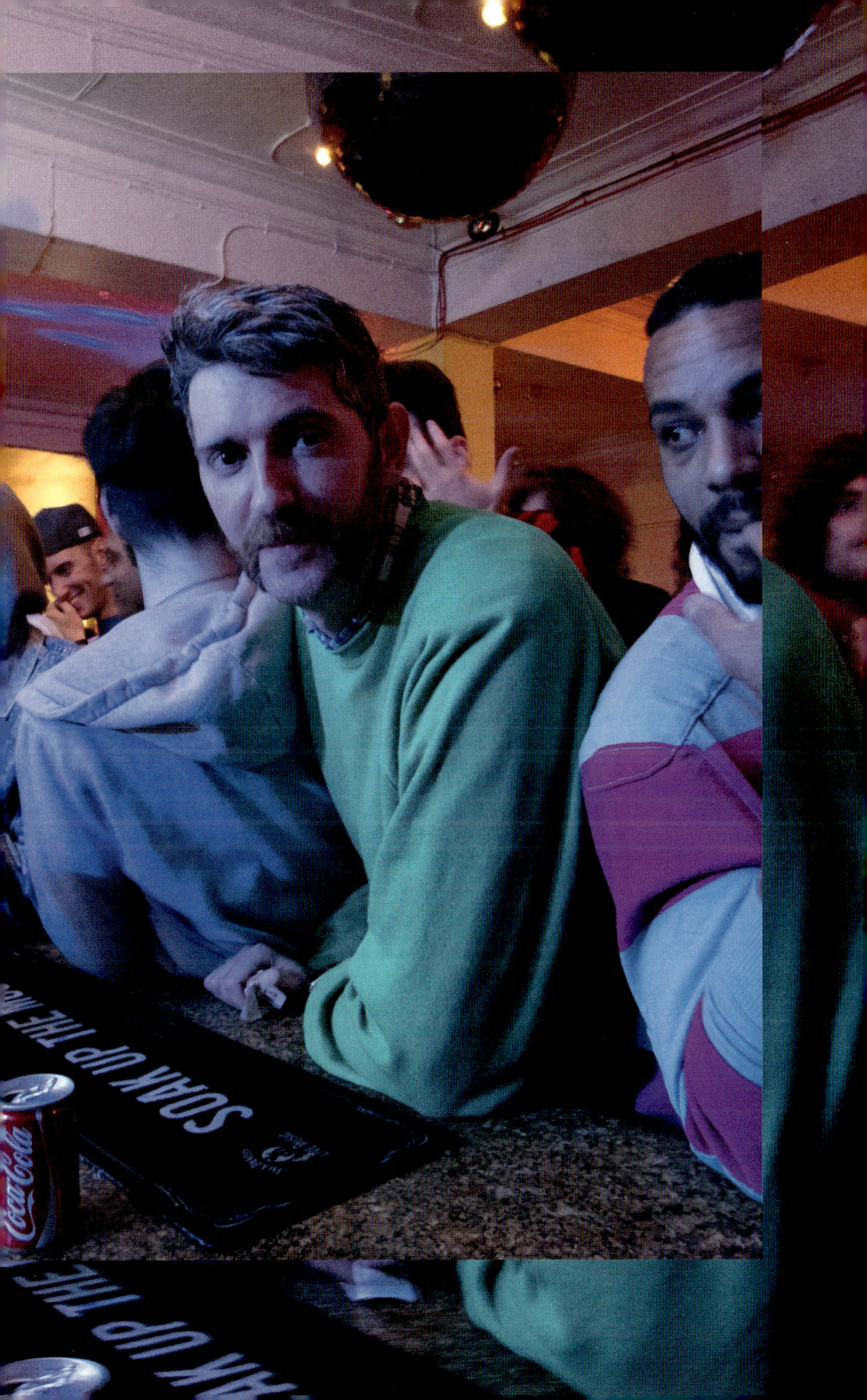
SOAK UP THE
Coca-Cola

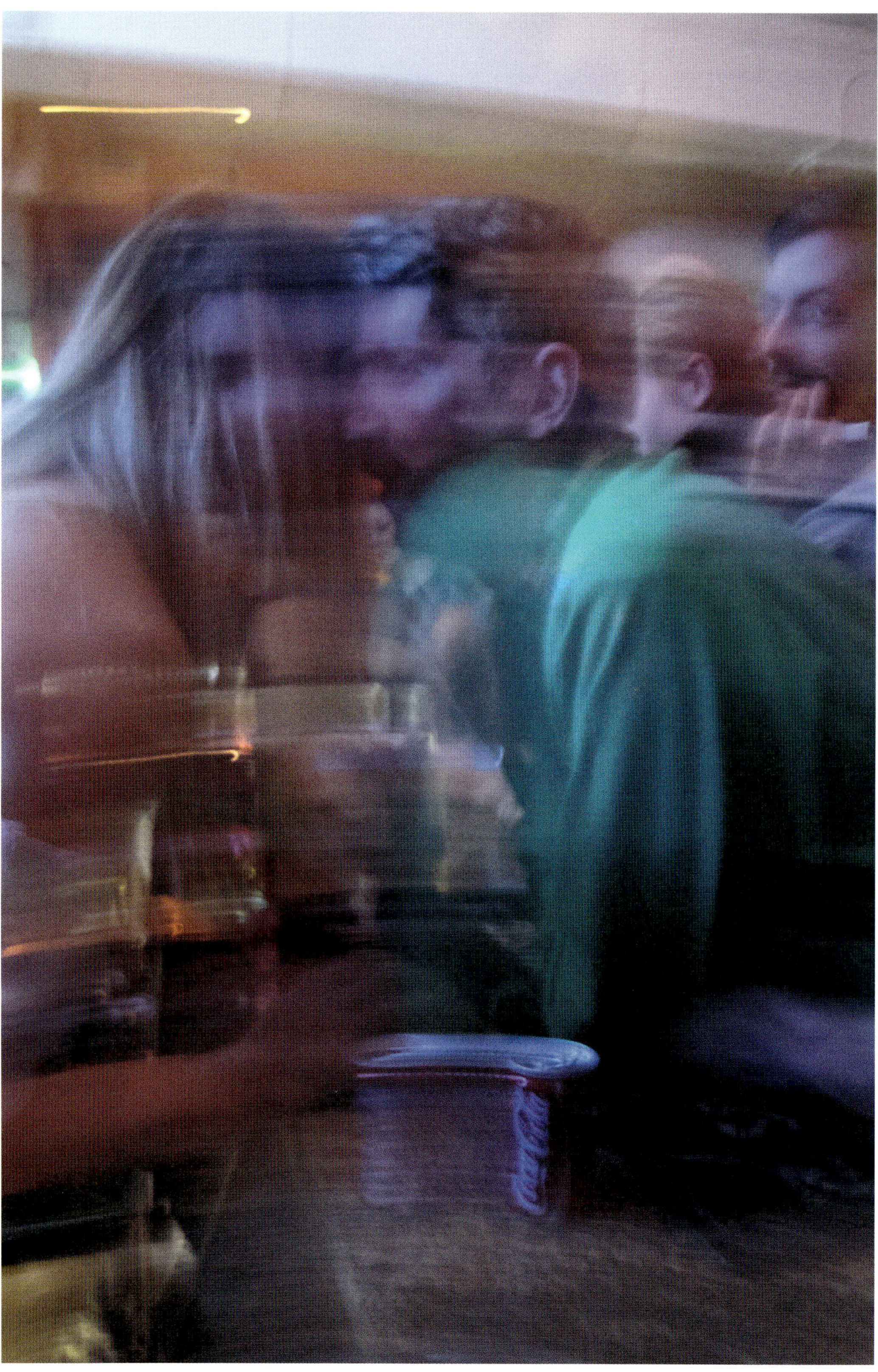

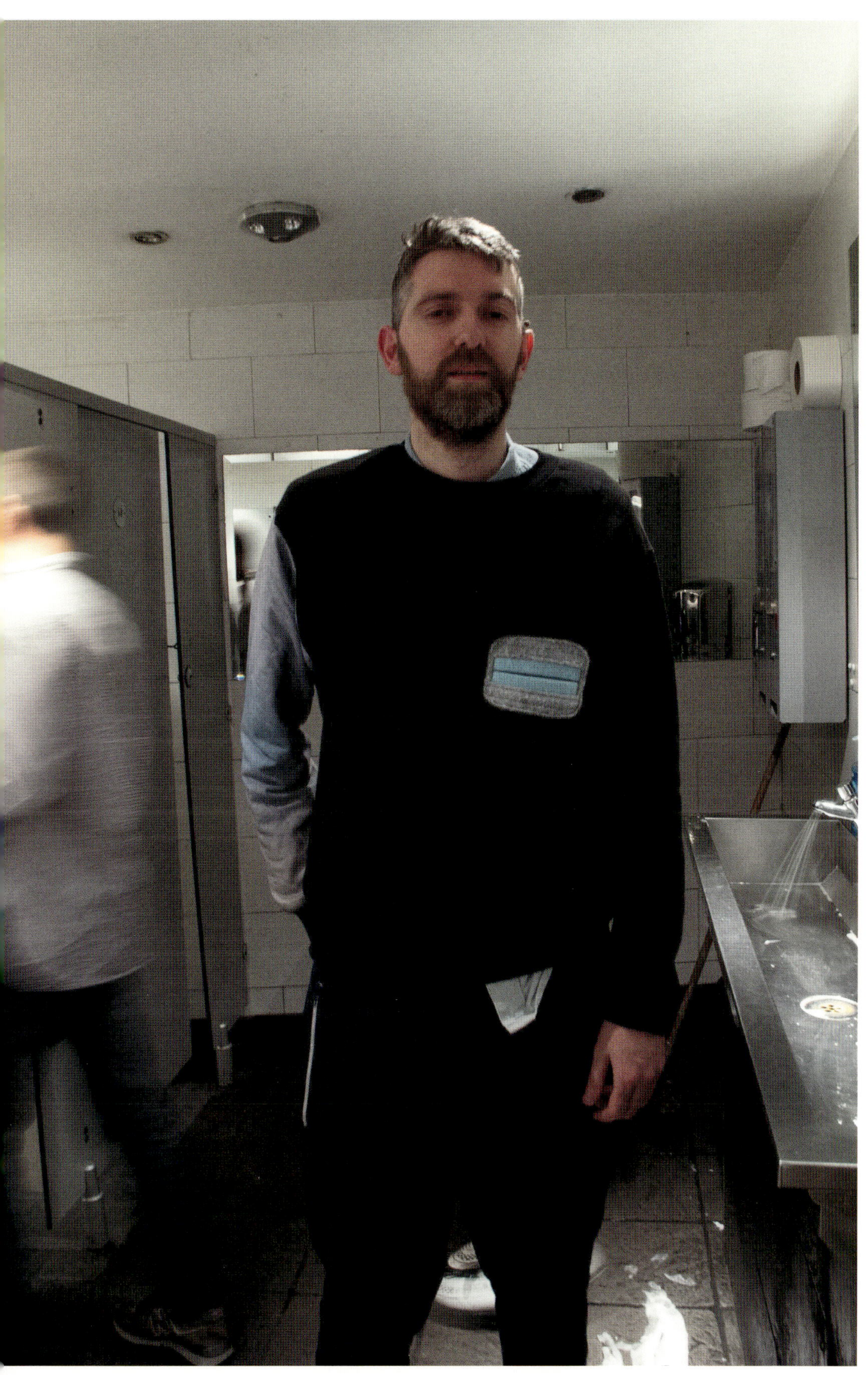

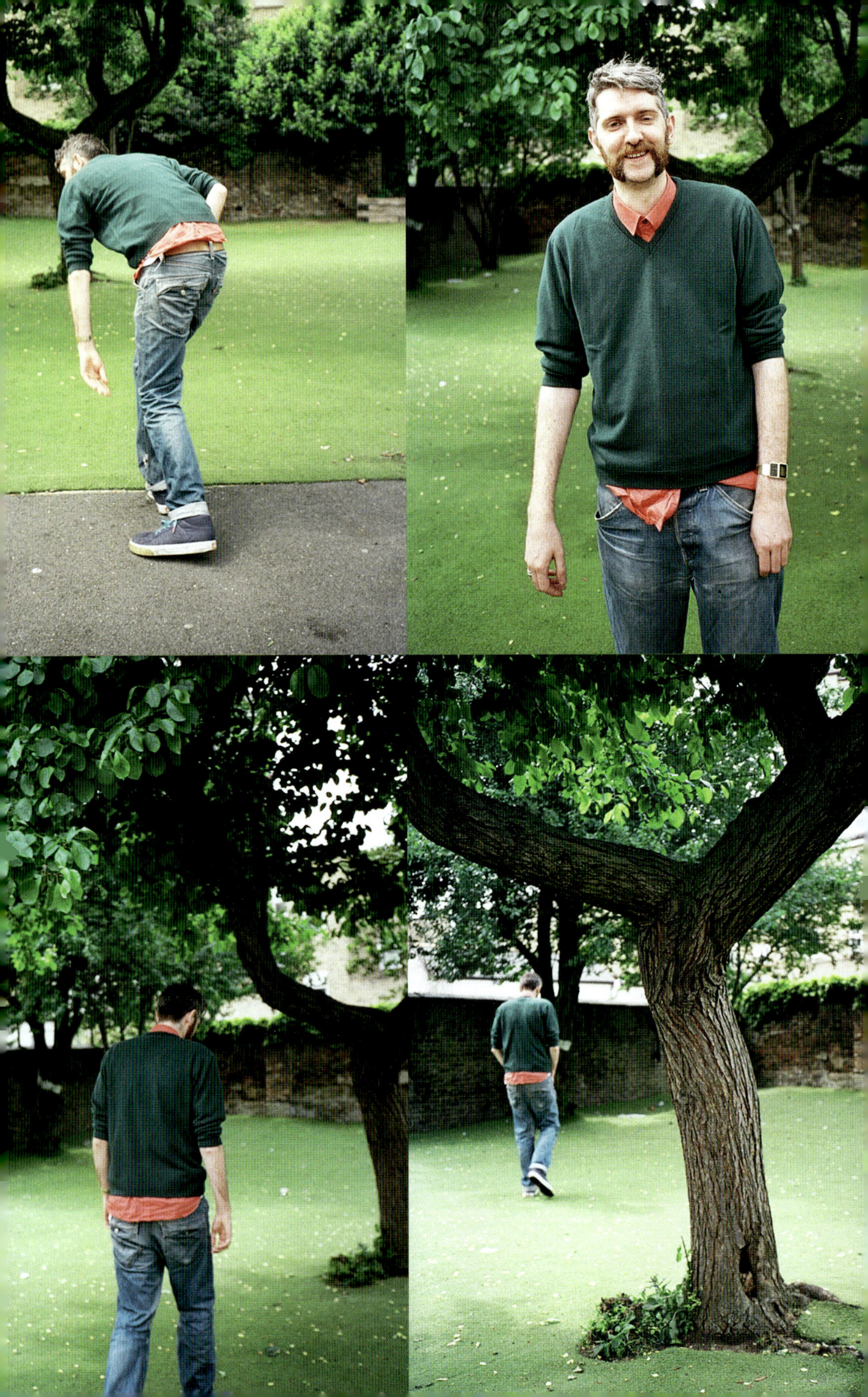

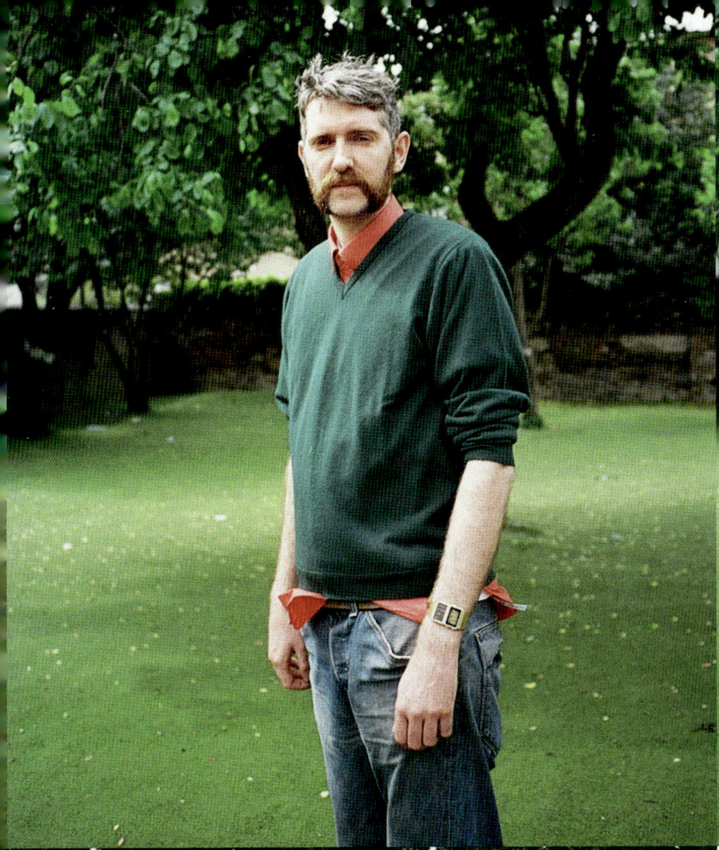

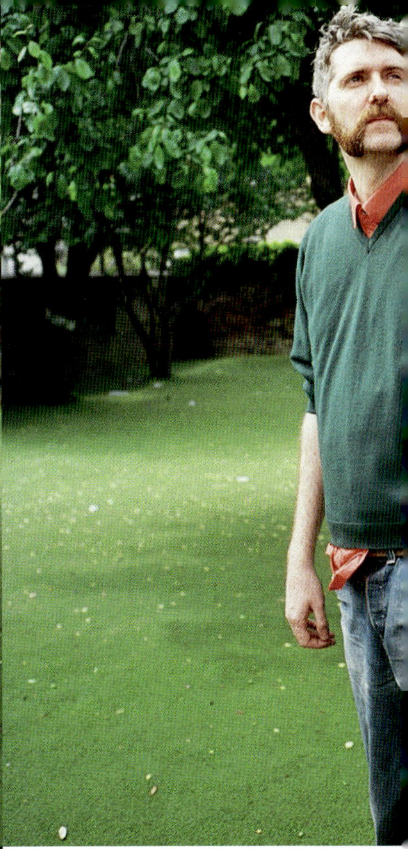

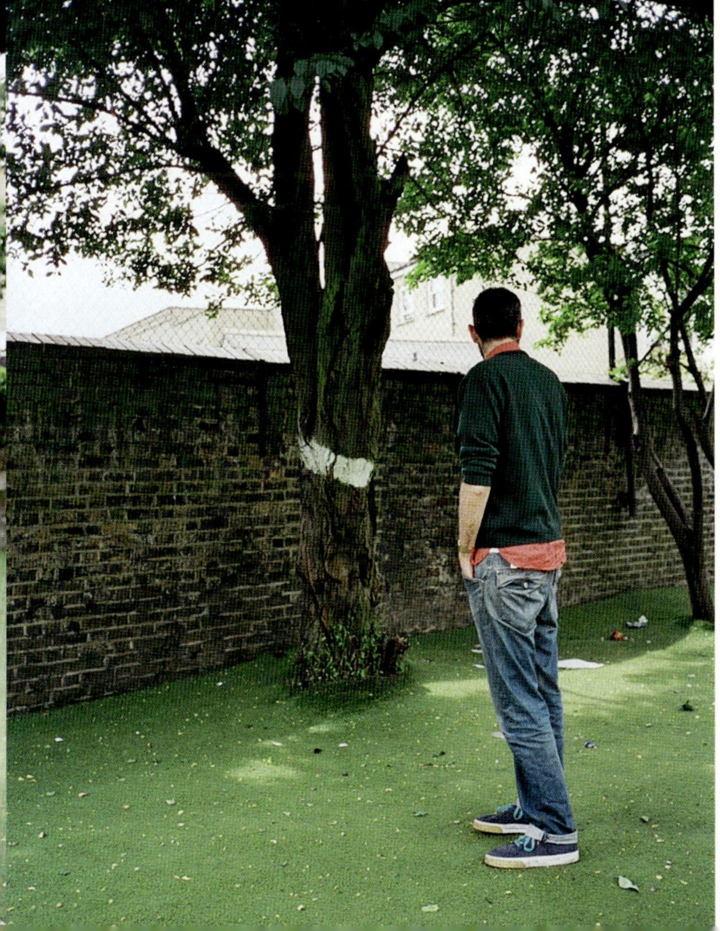

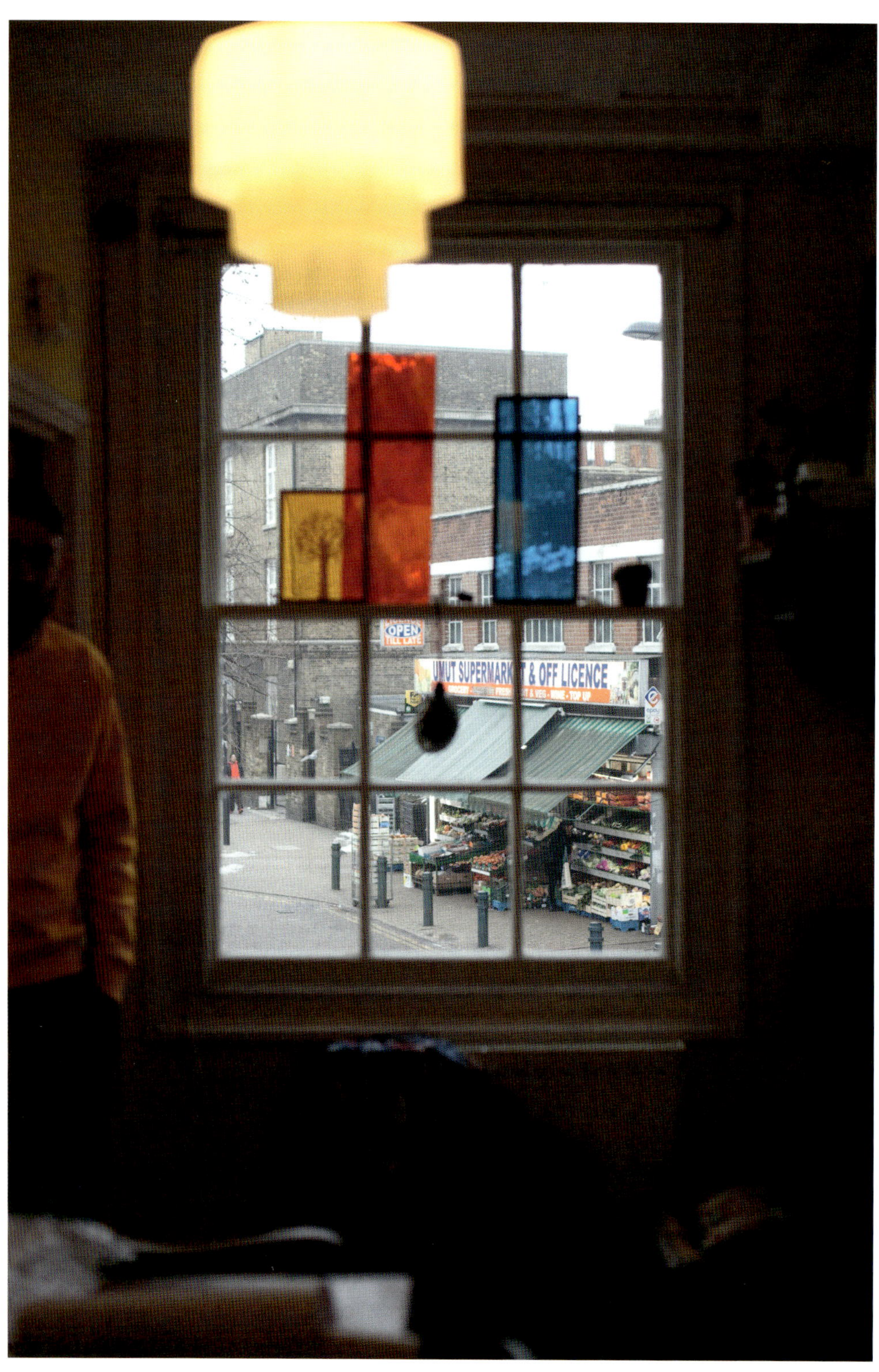

2012

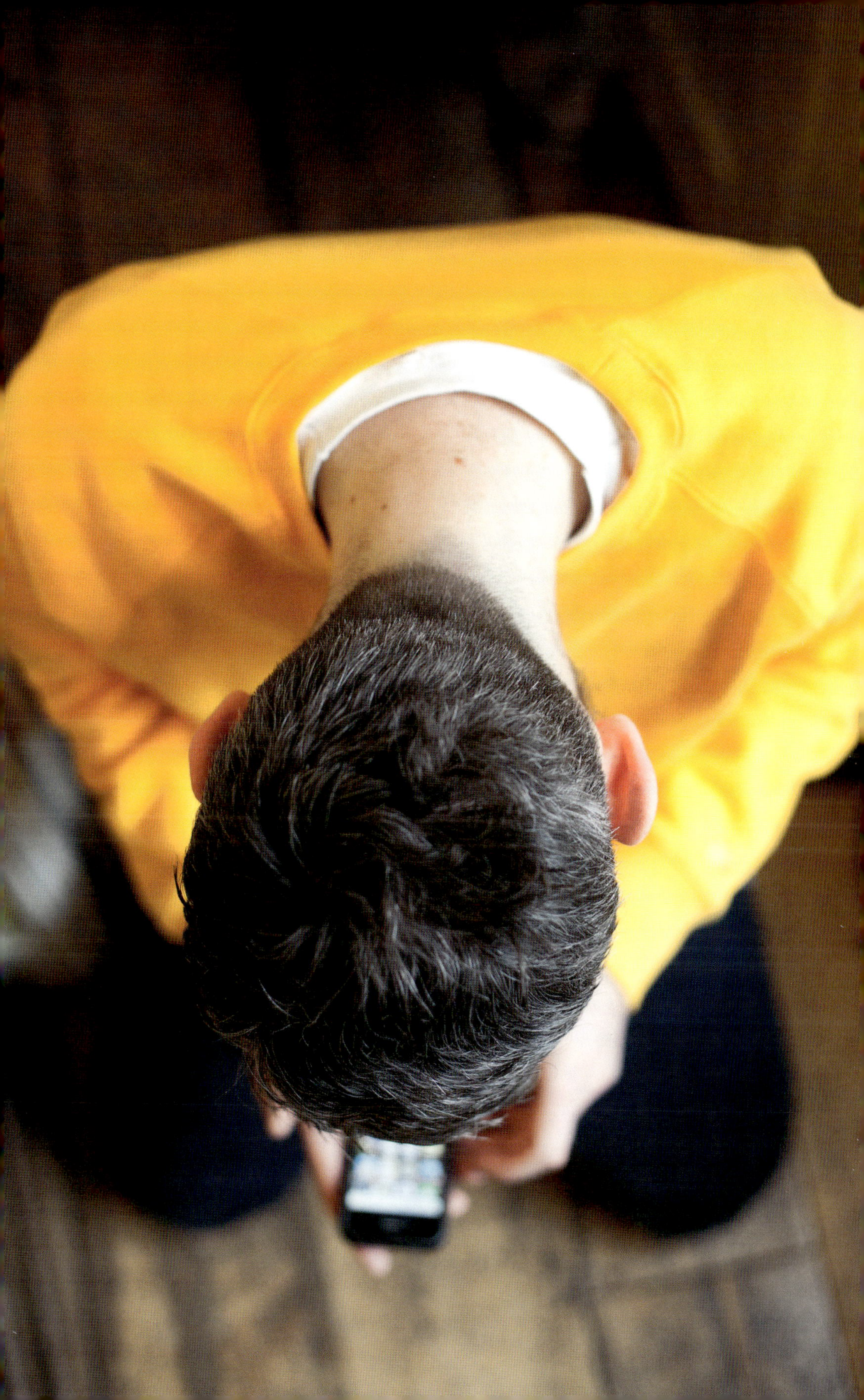

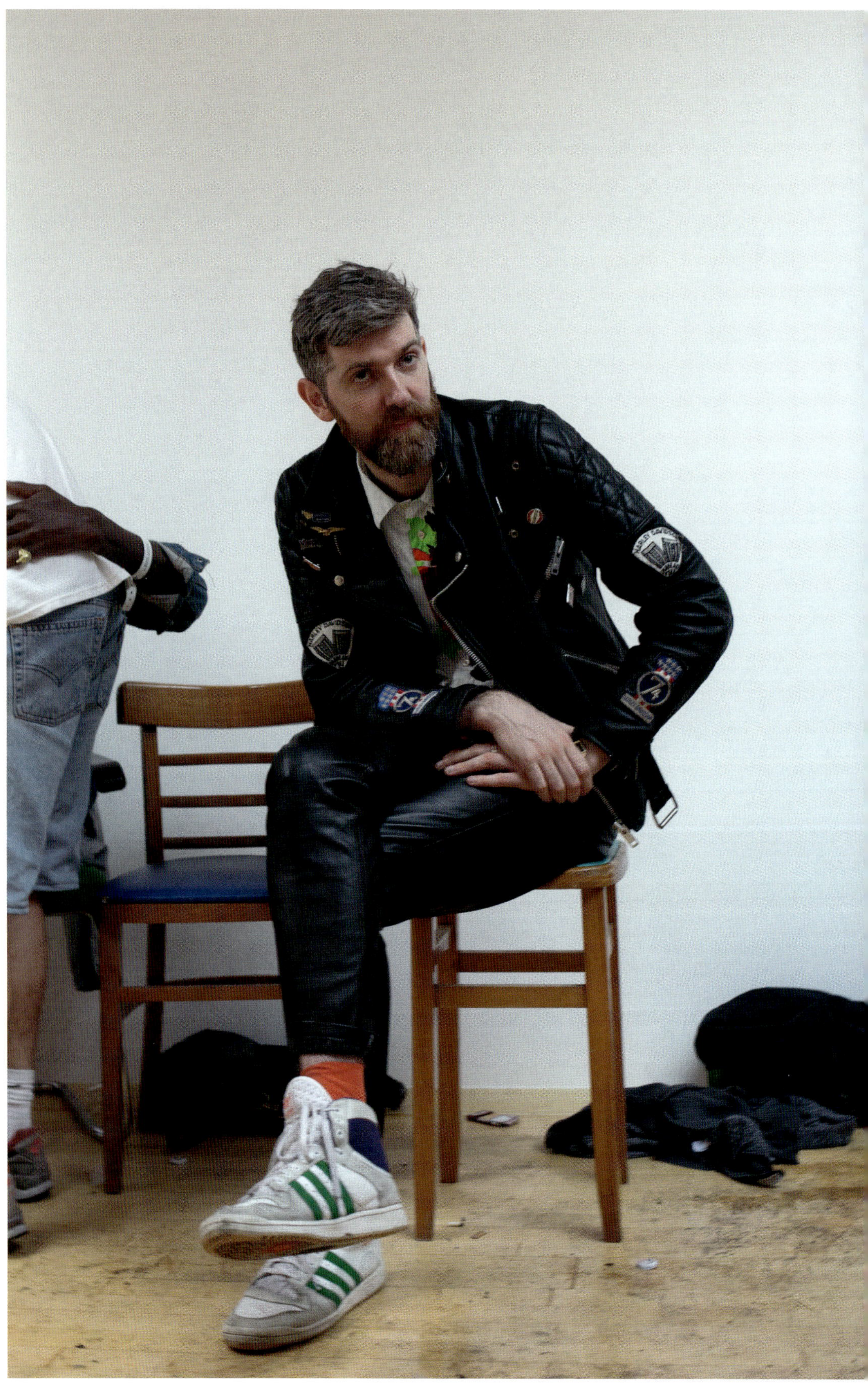

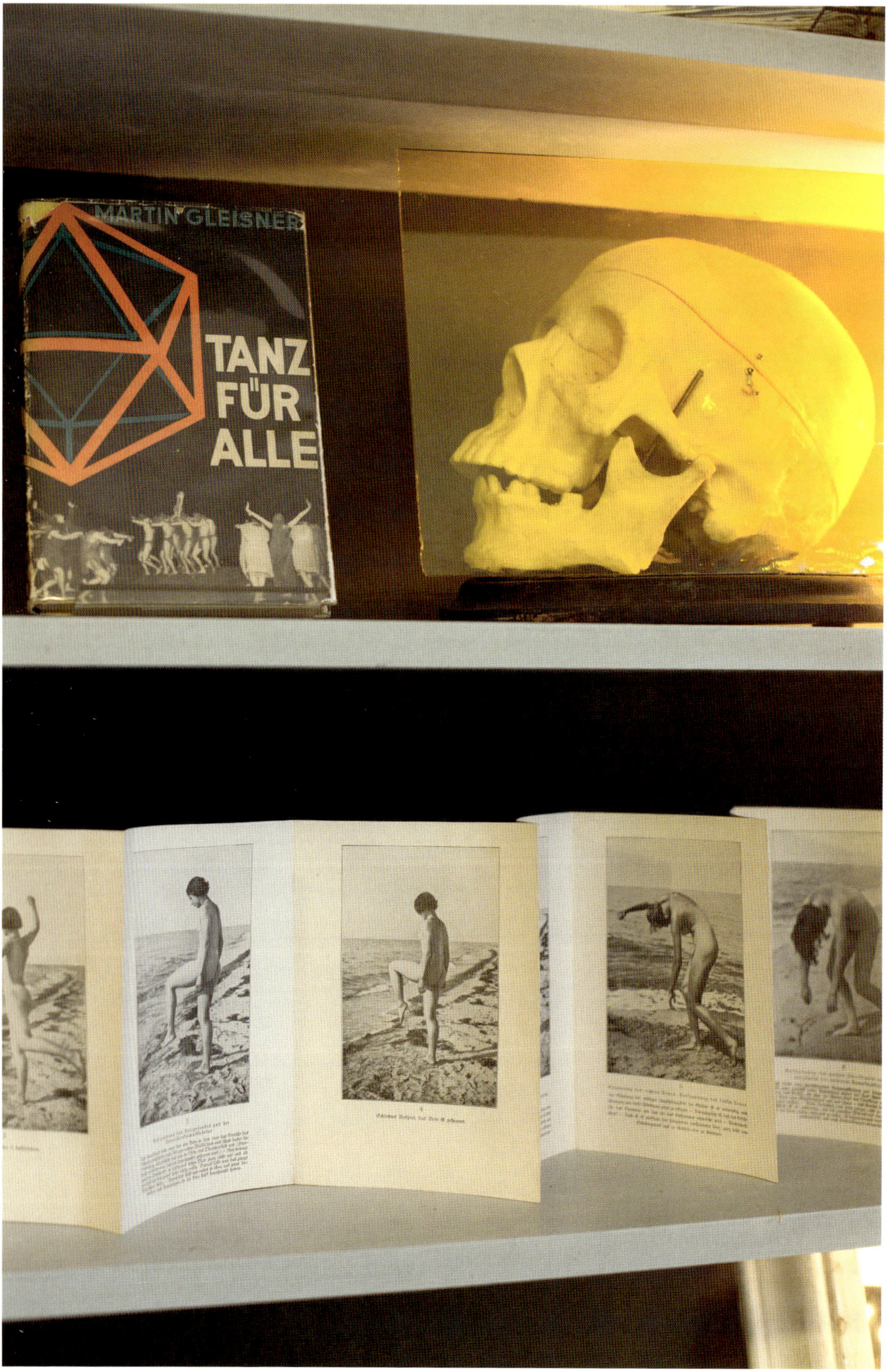

MARTIN GLEISNER
TANZ
FÜR
ALLE

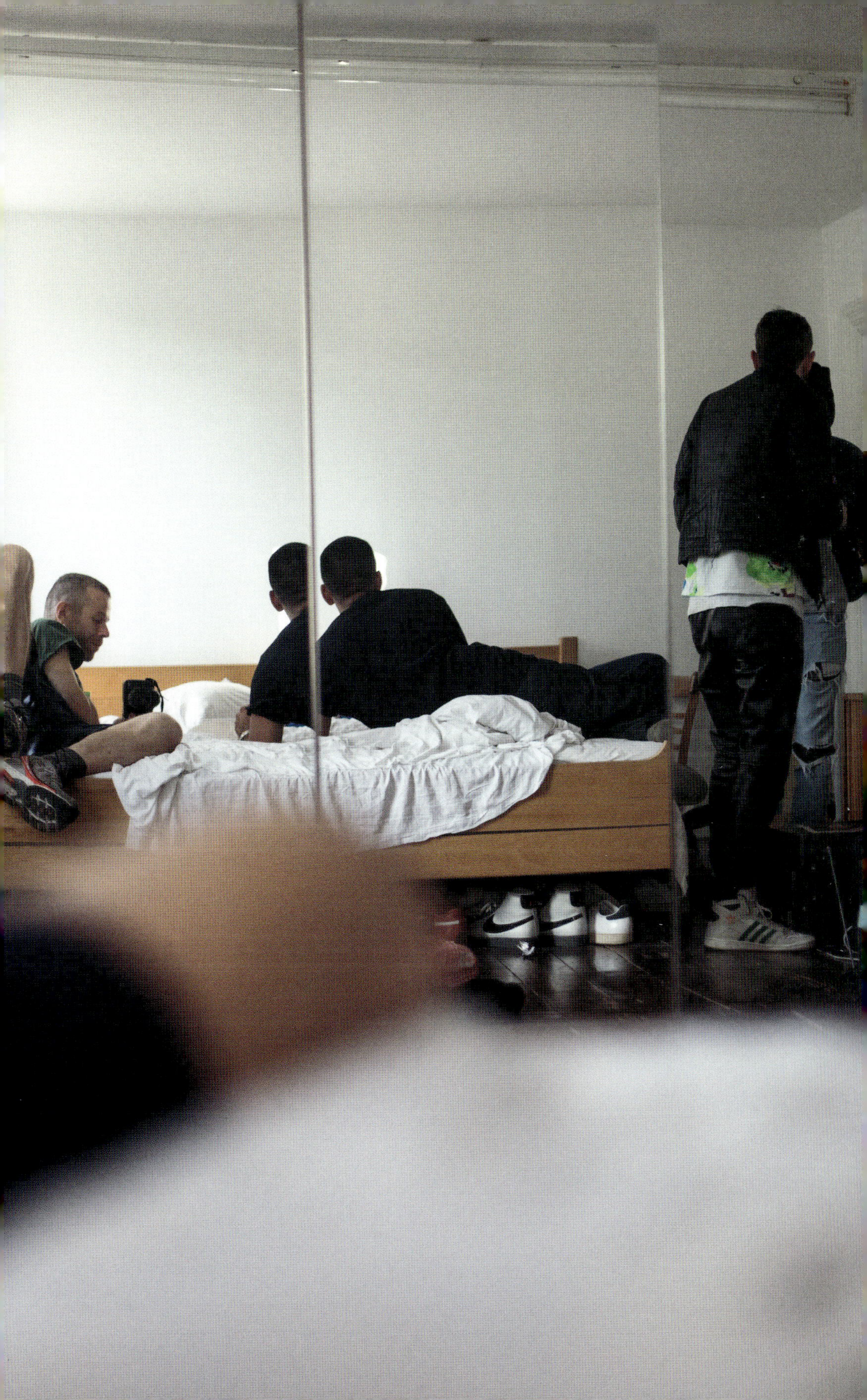

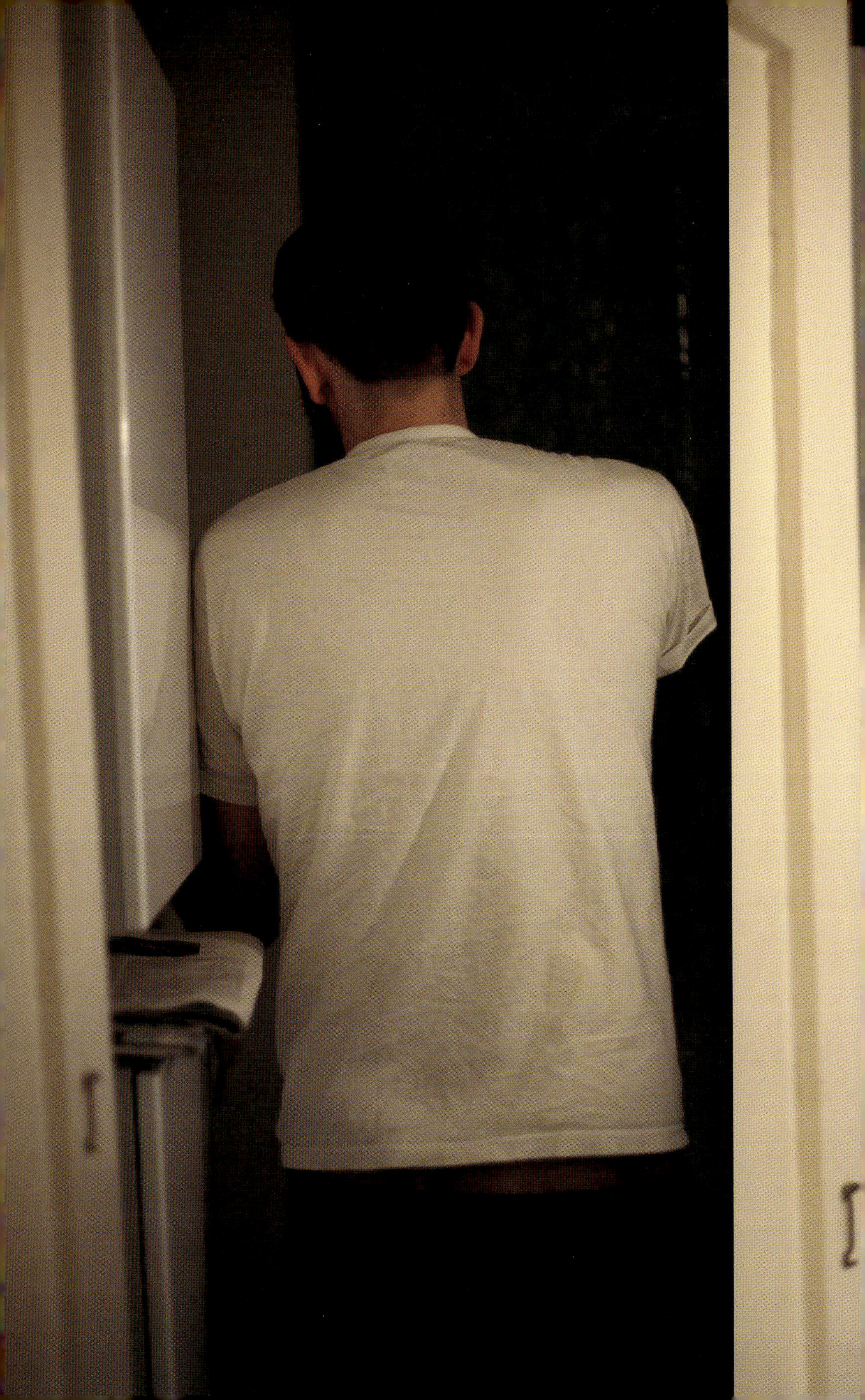

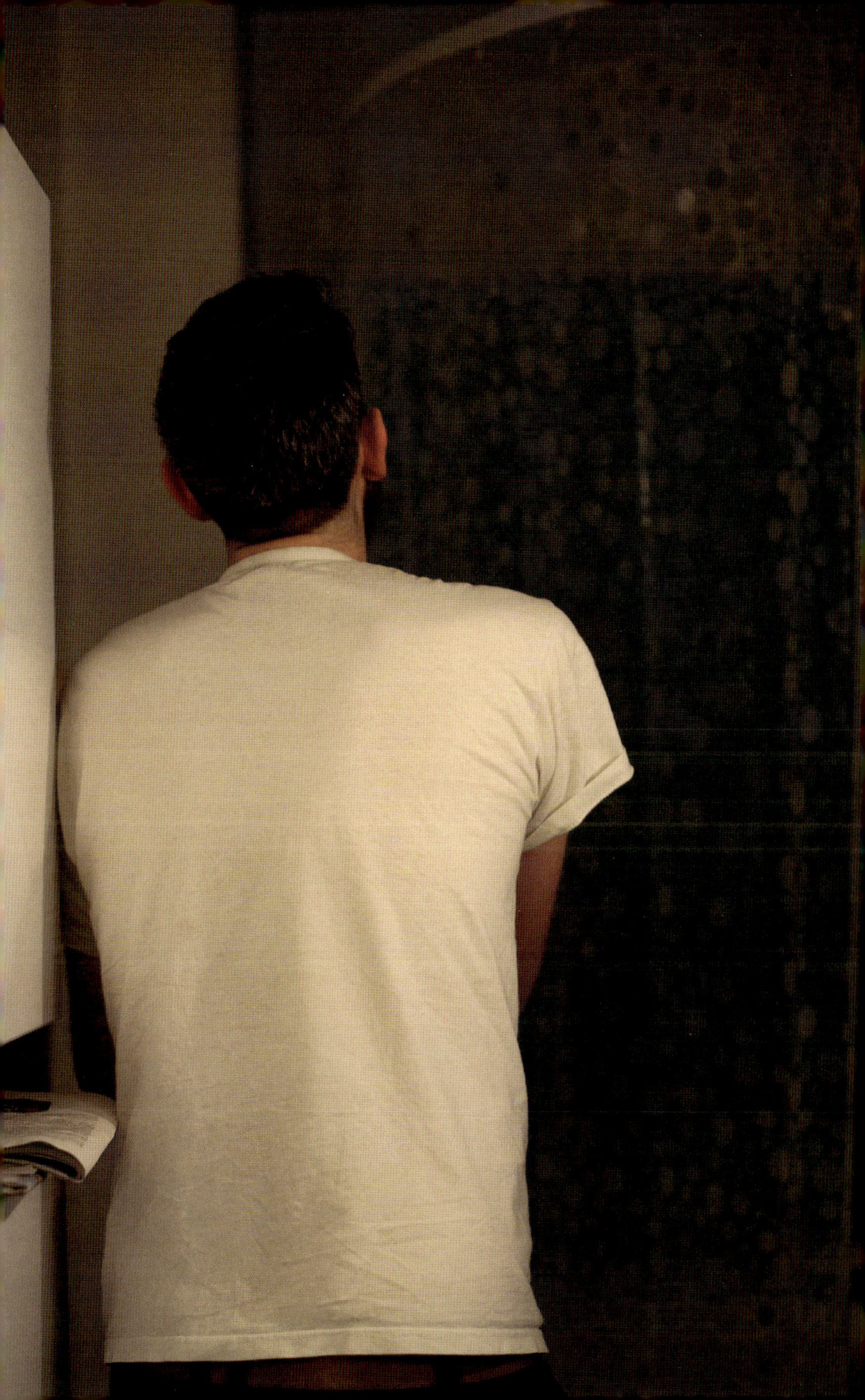

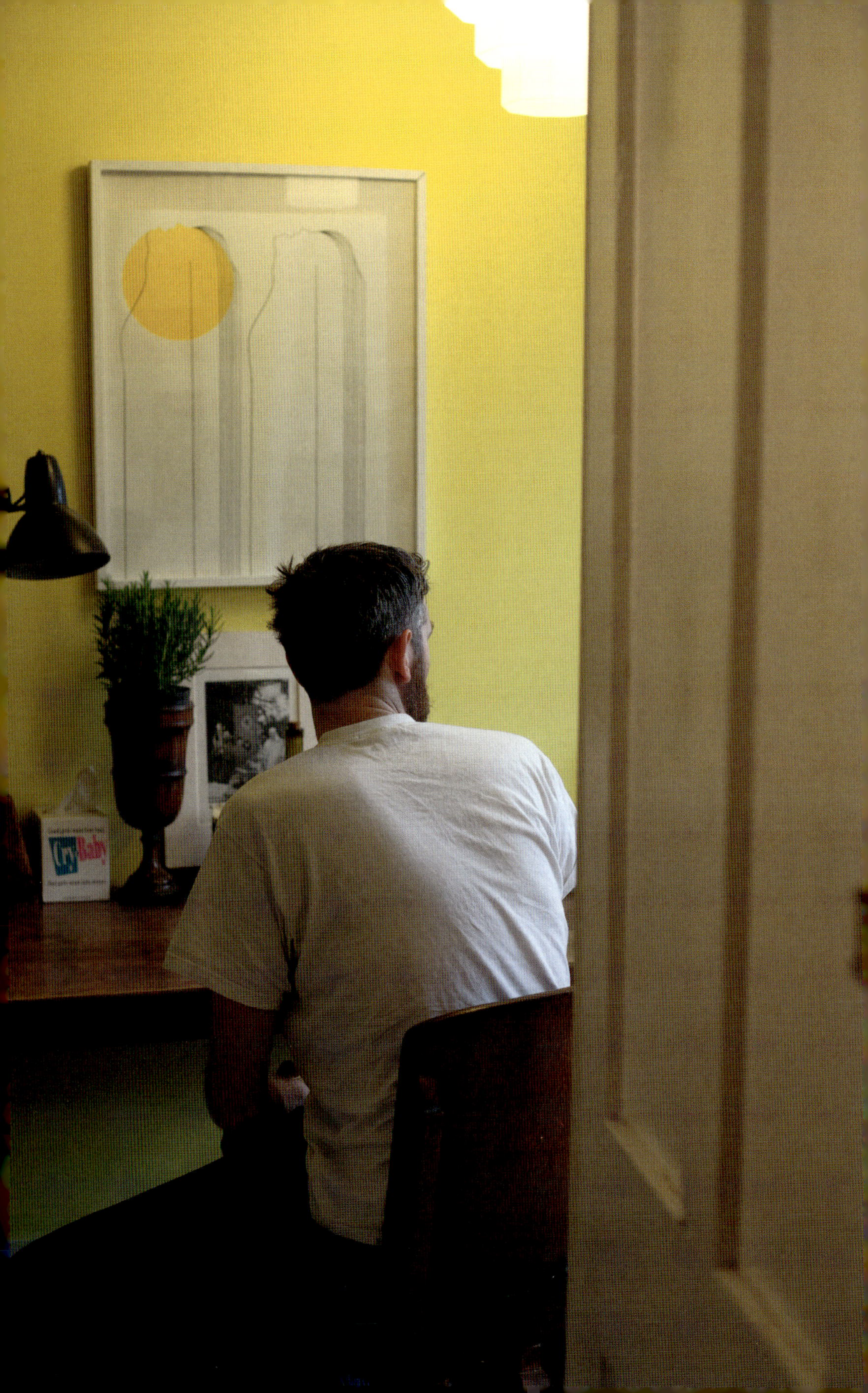
CryBaby

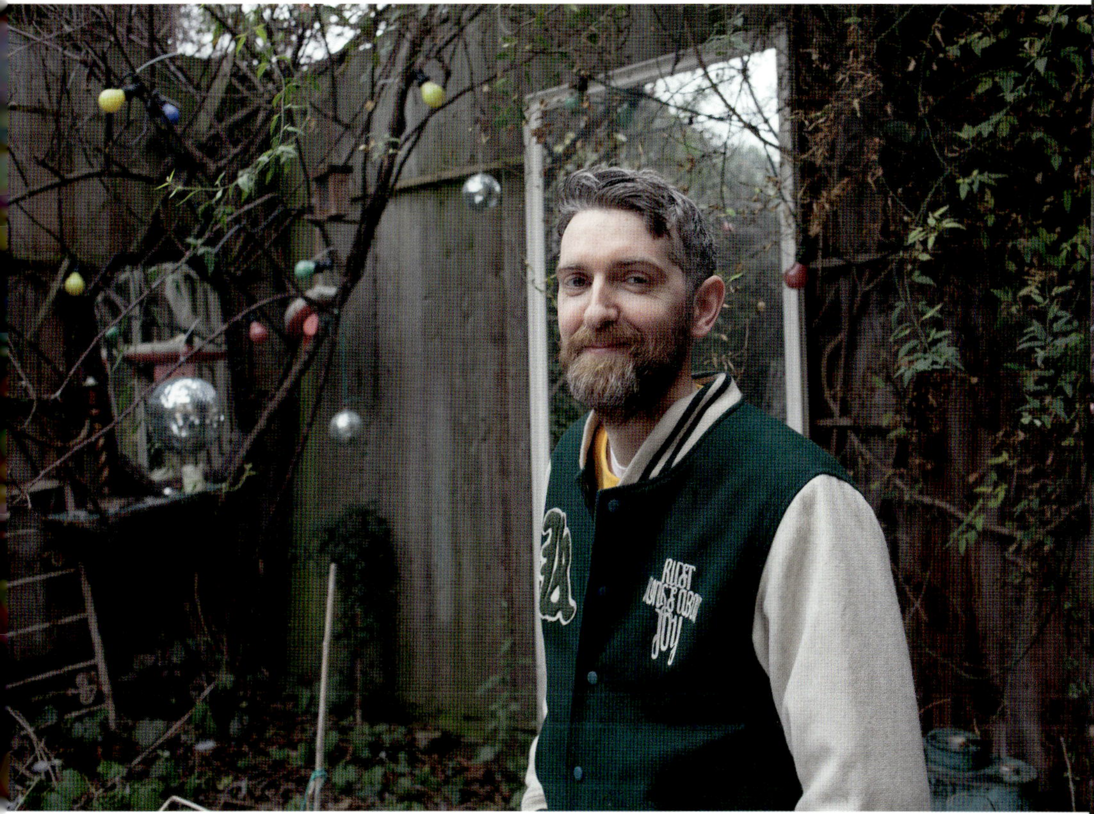

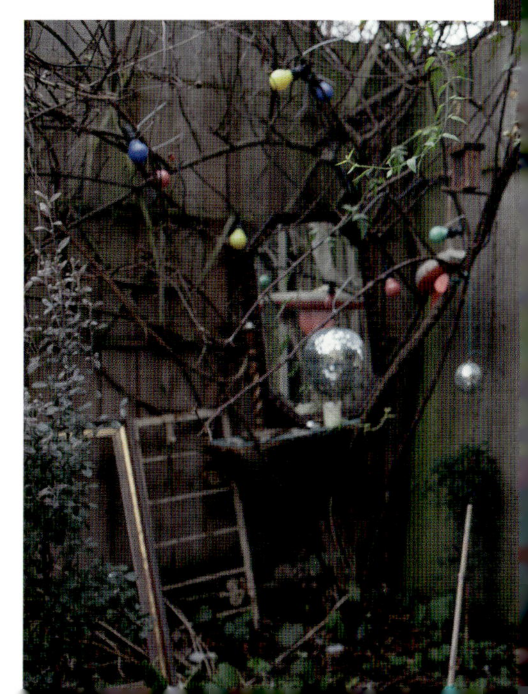

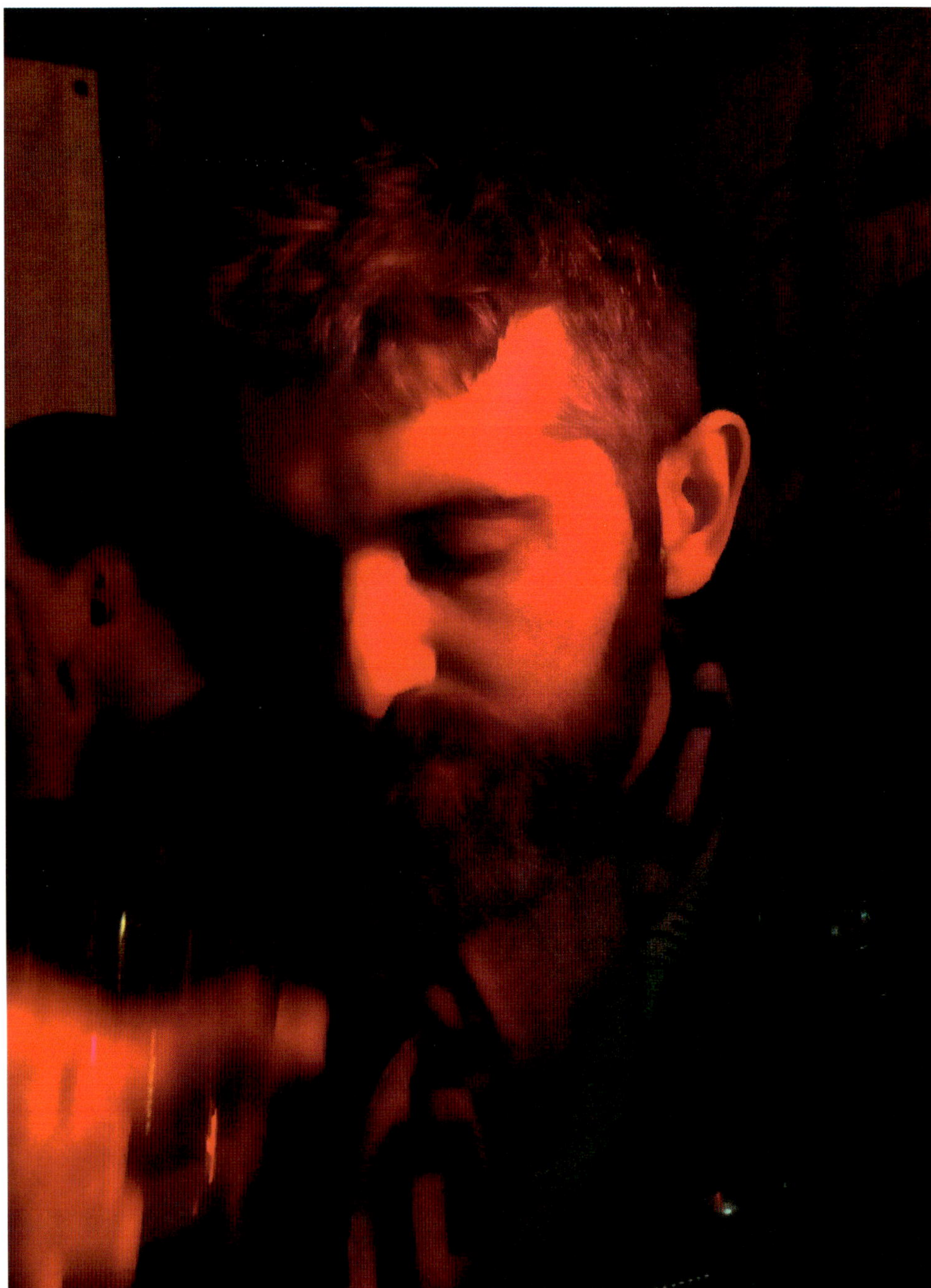

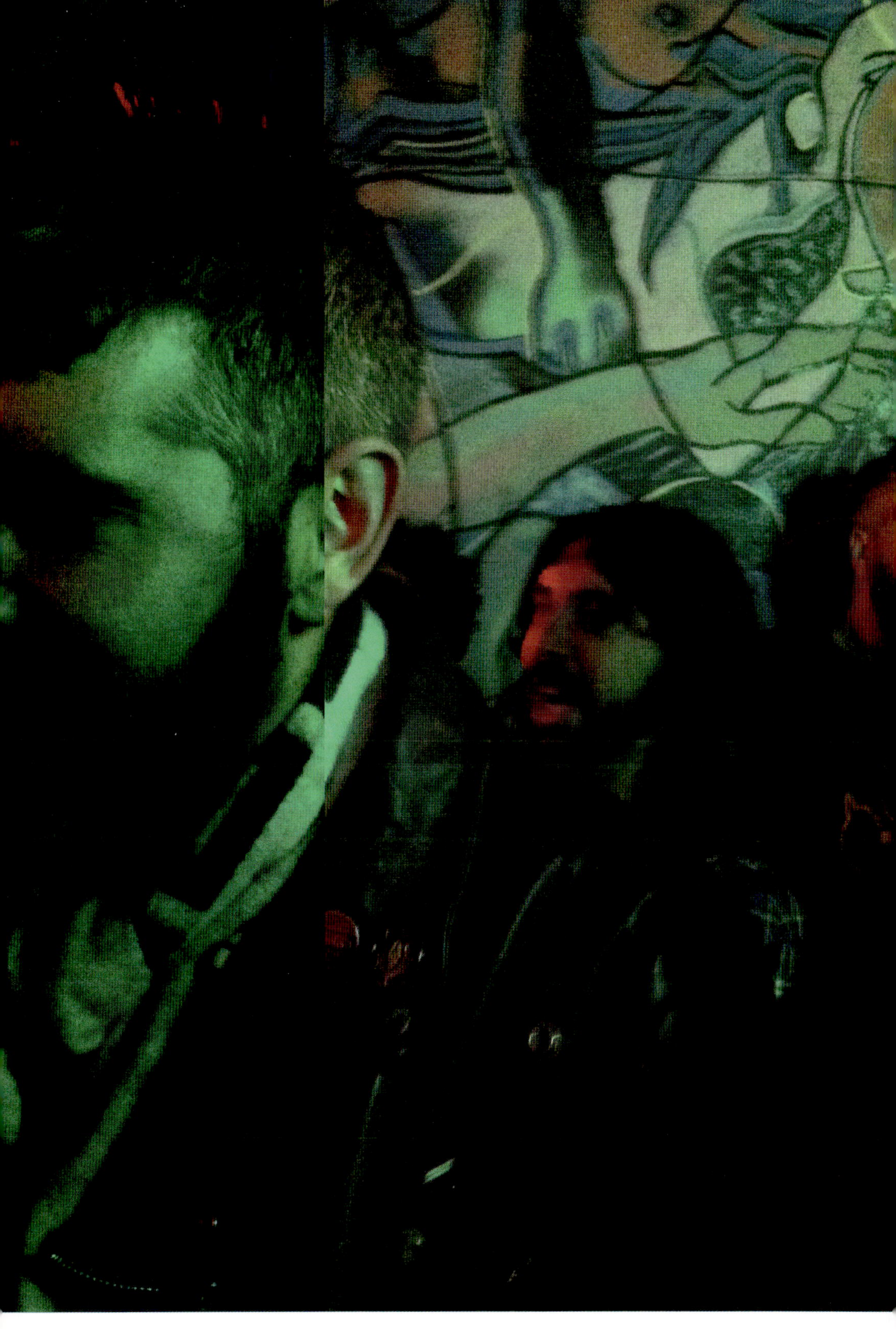

2013

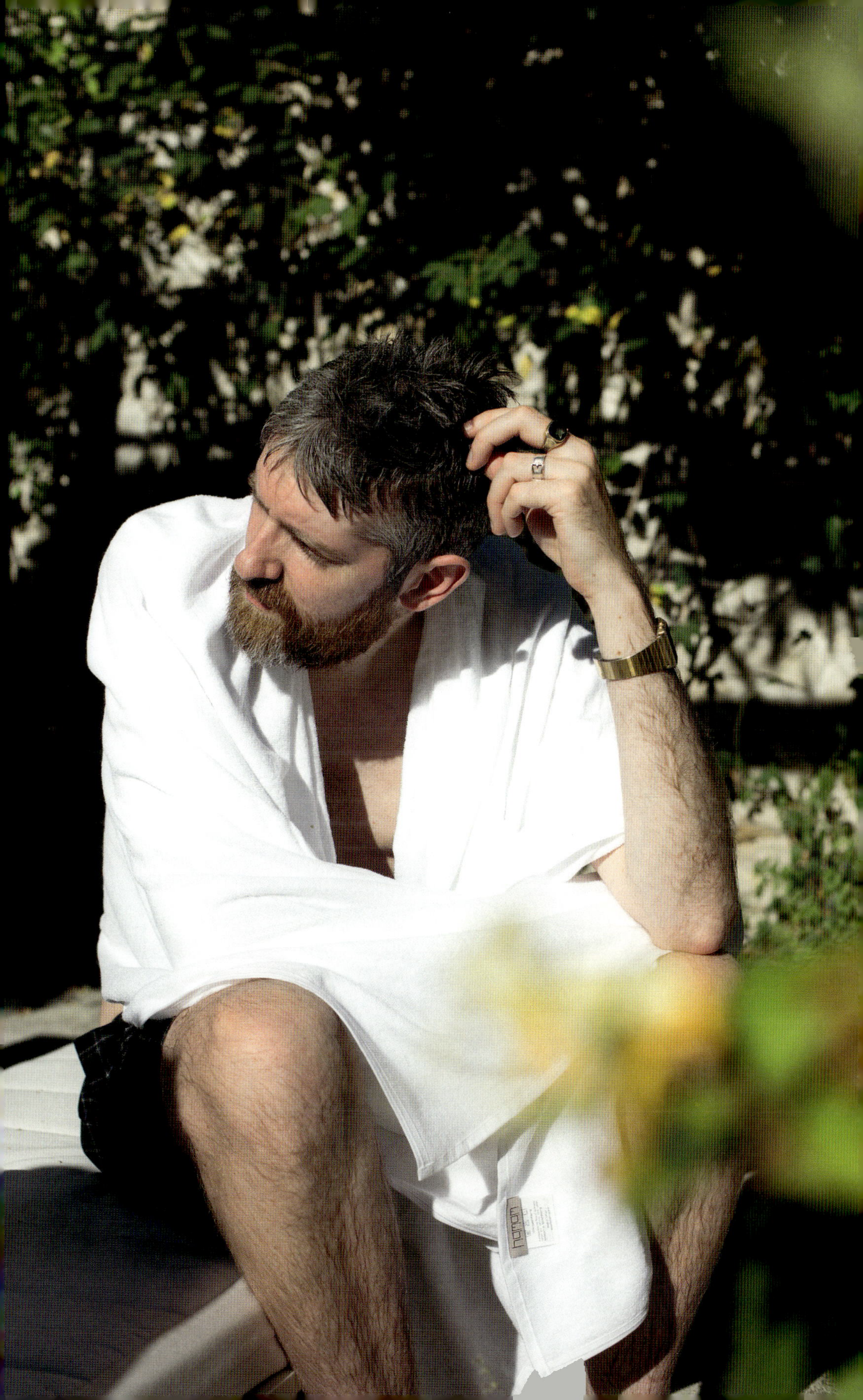

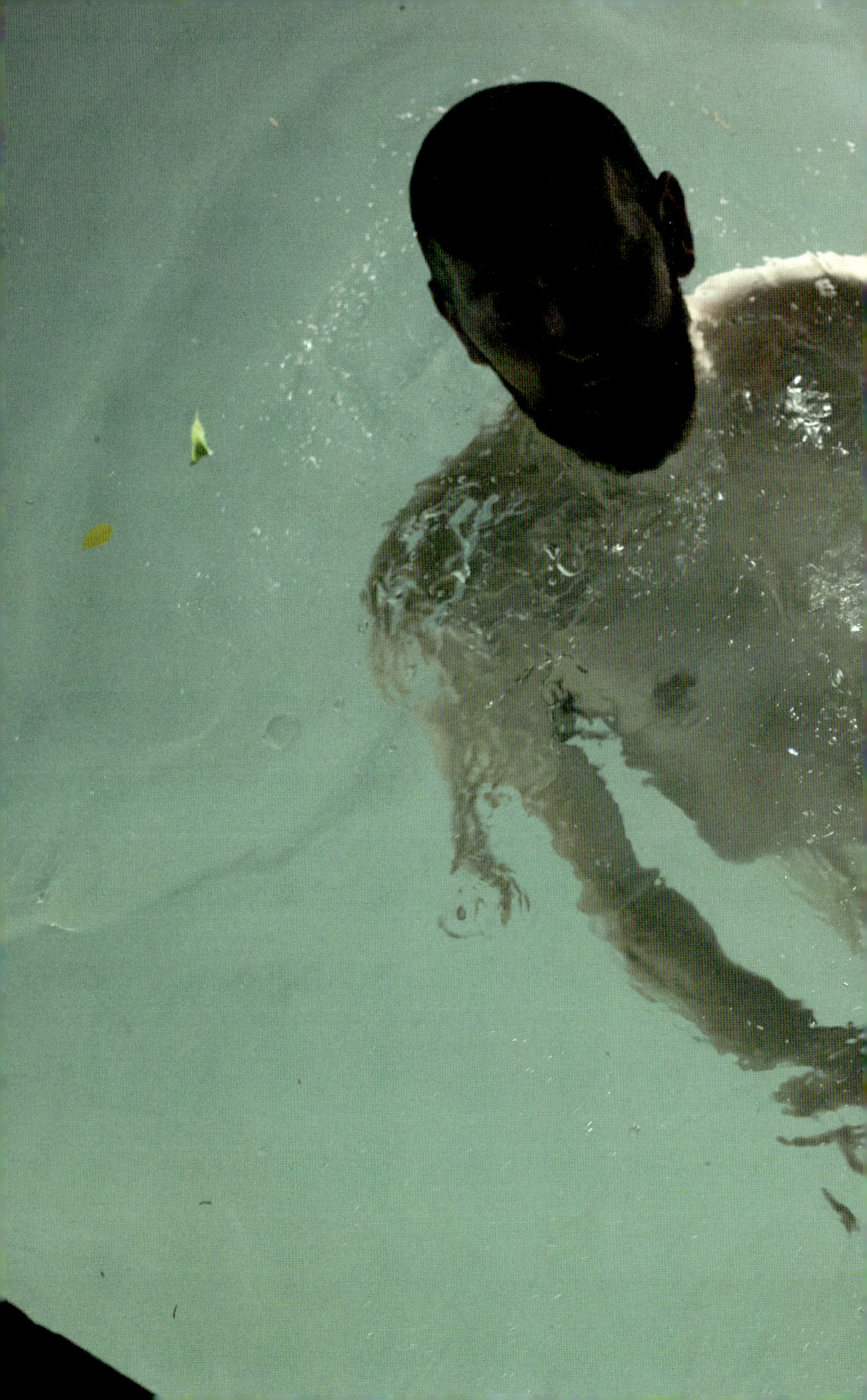

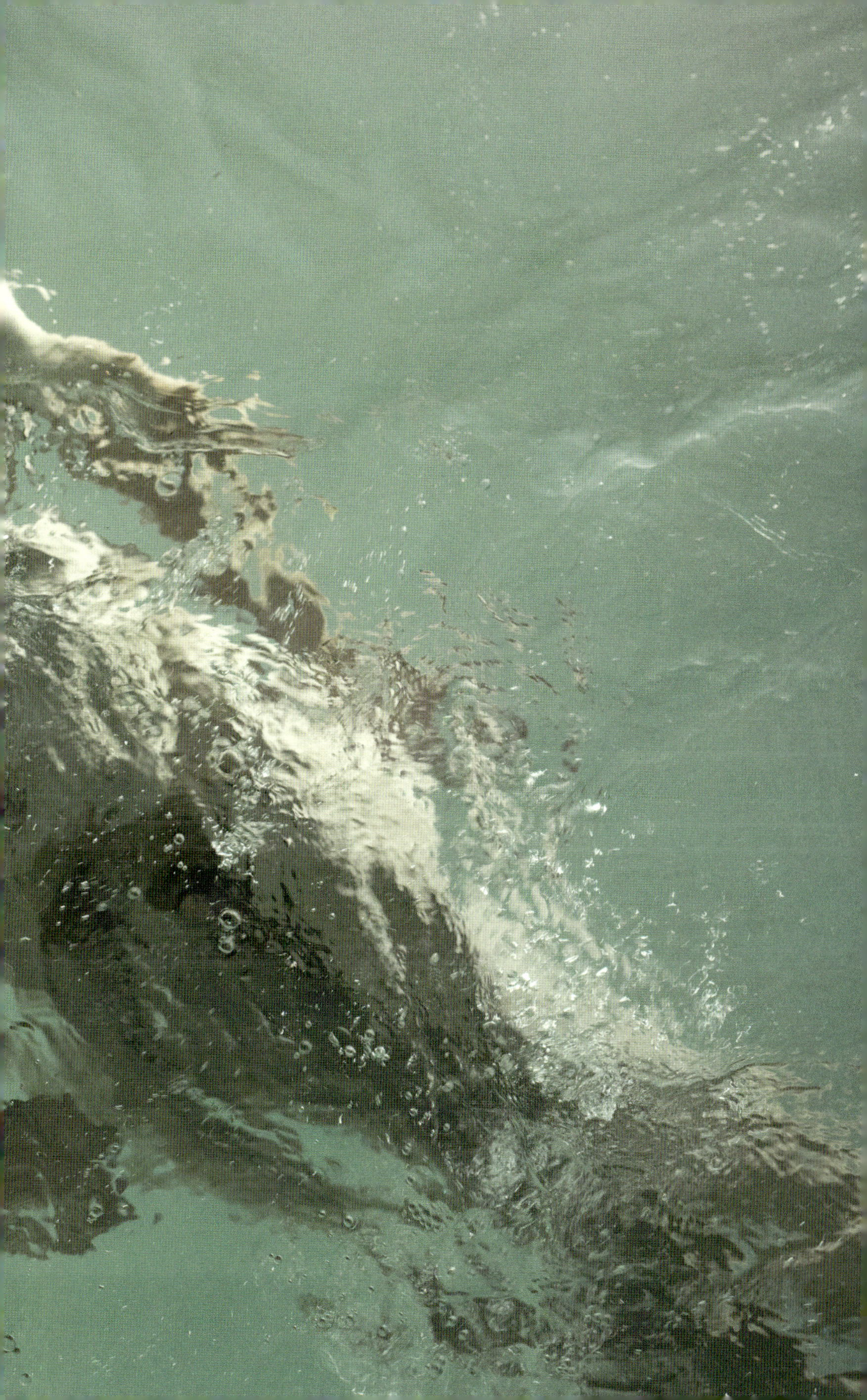

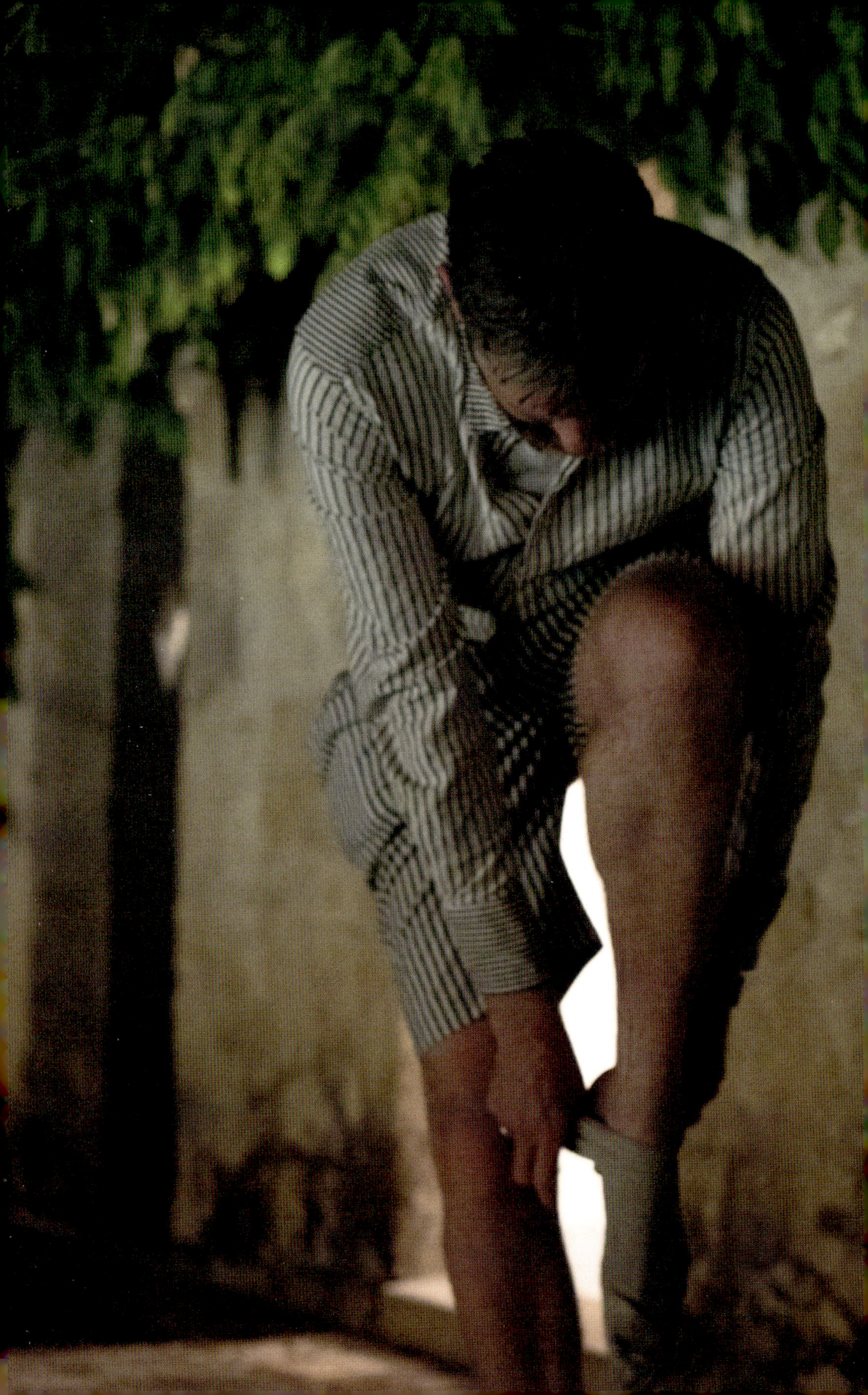

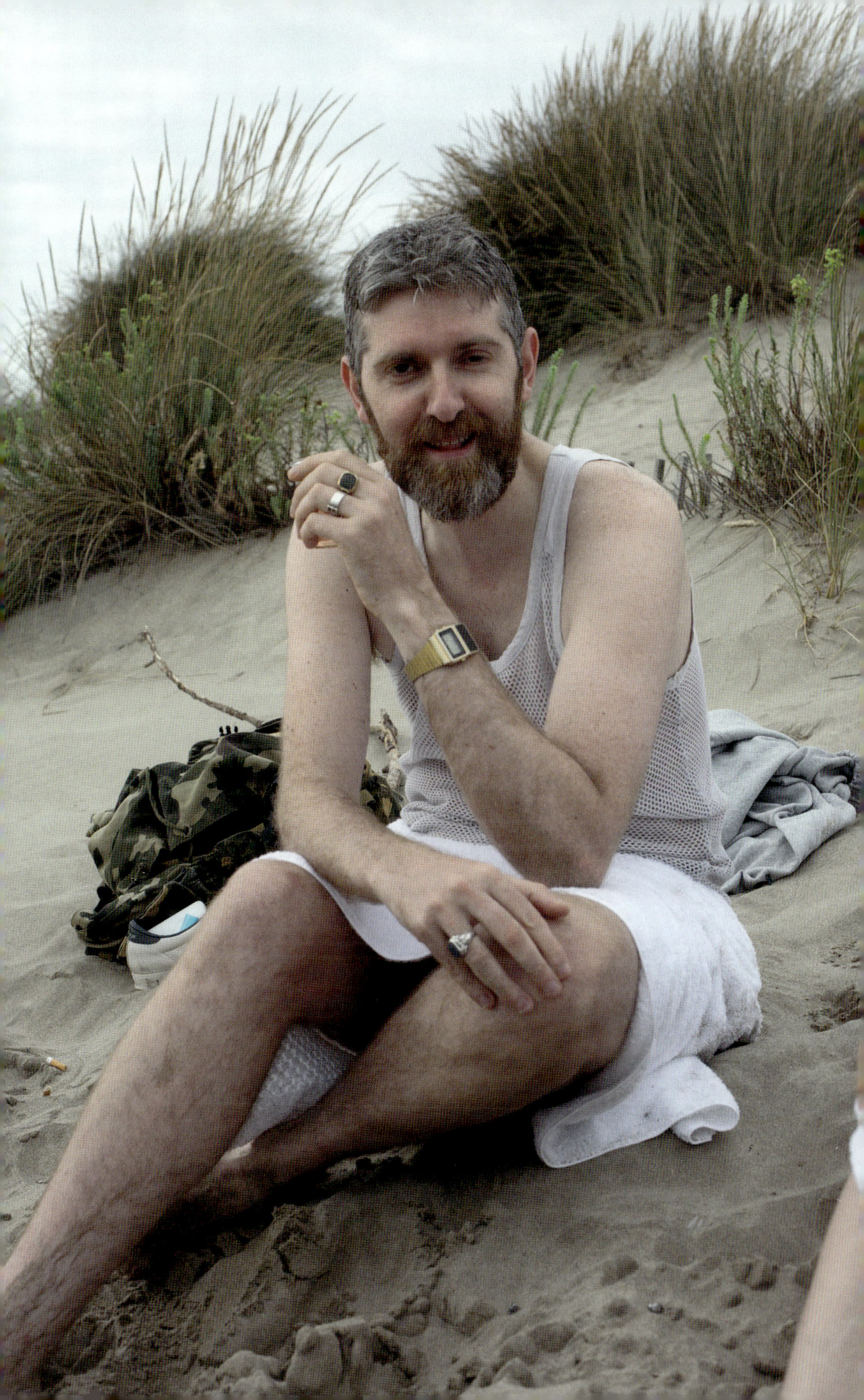

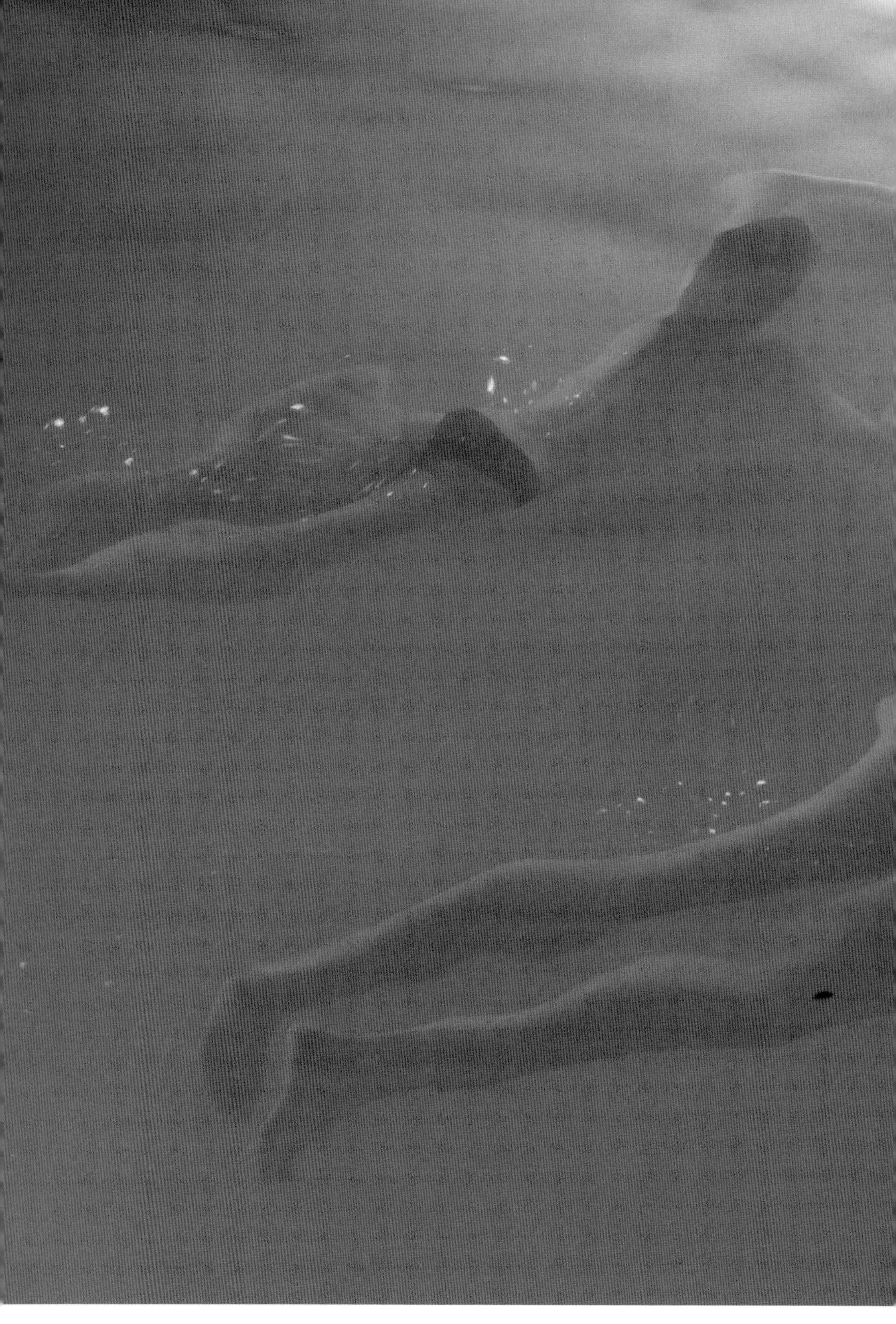

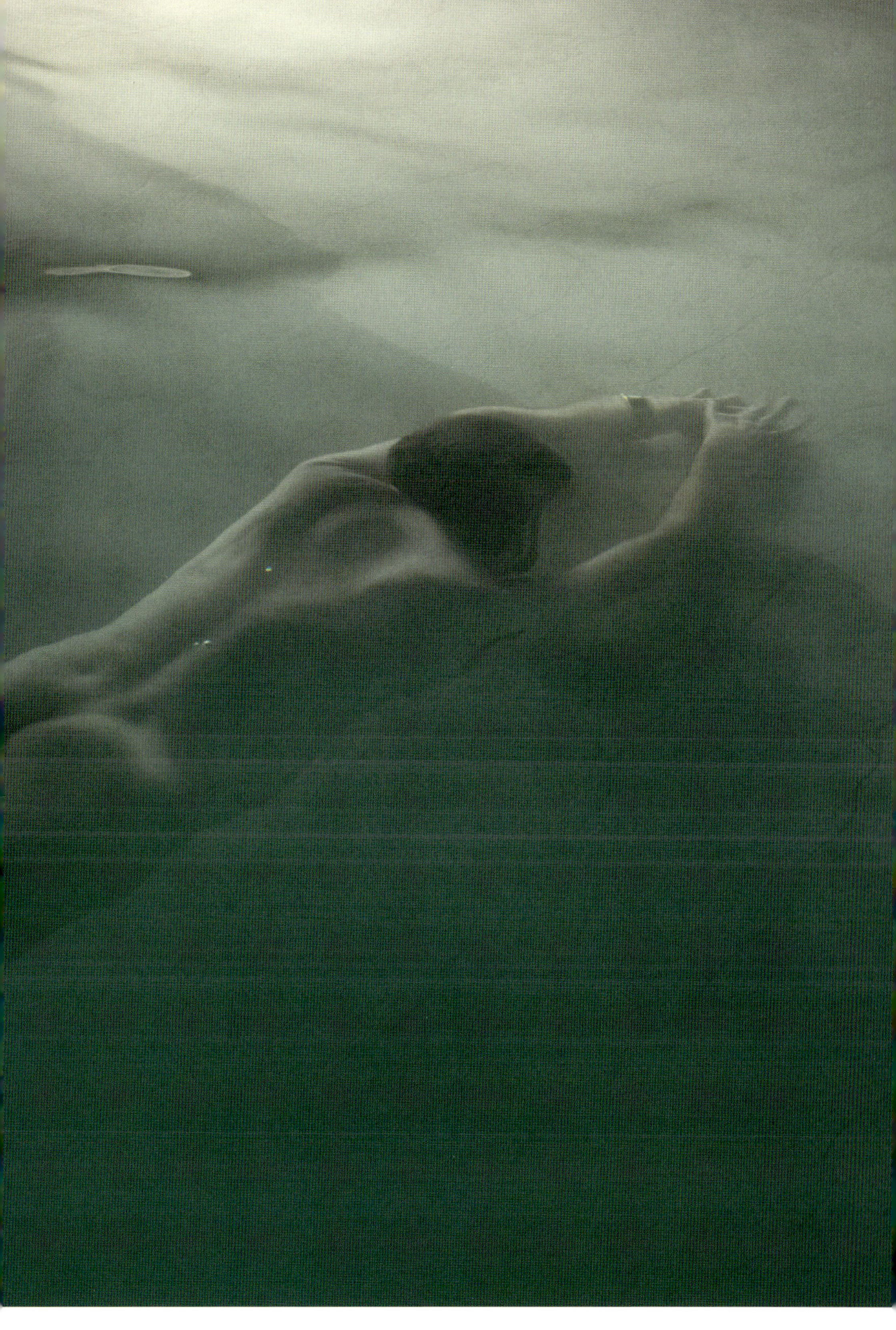

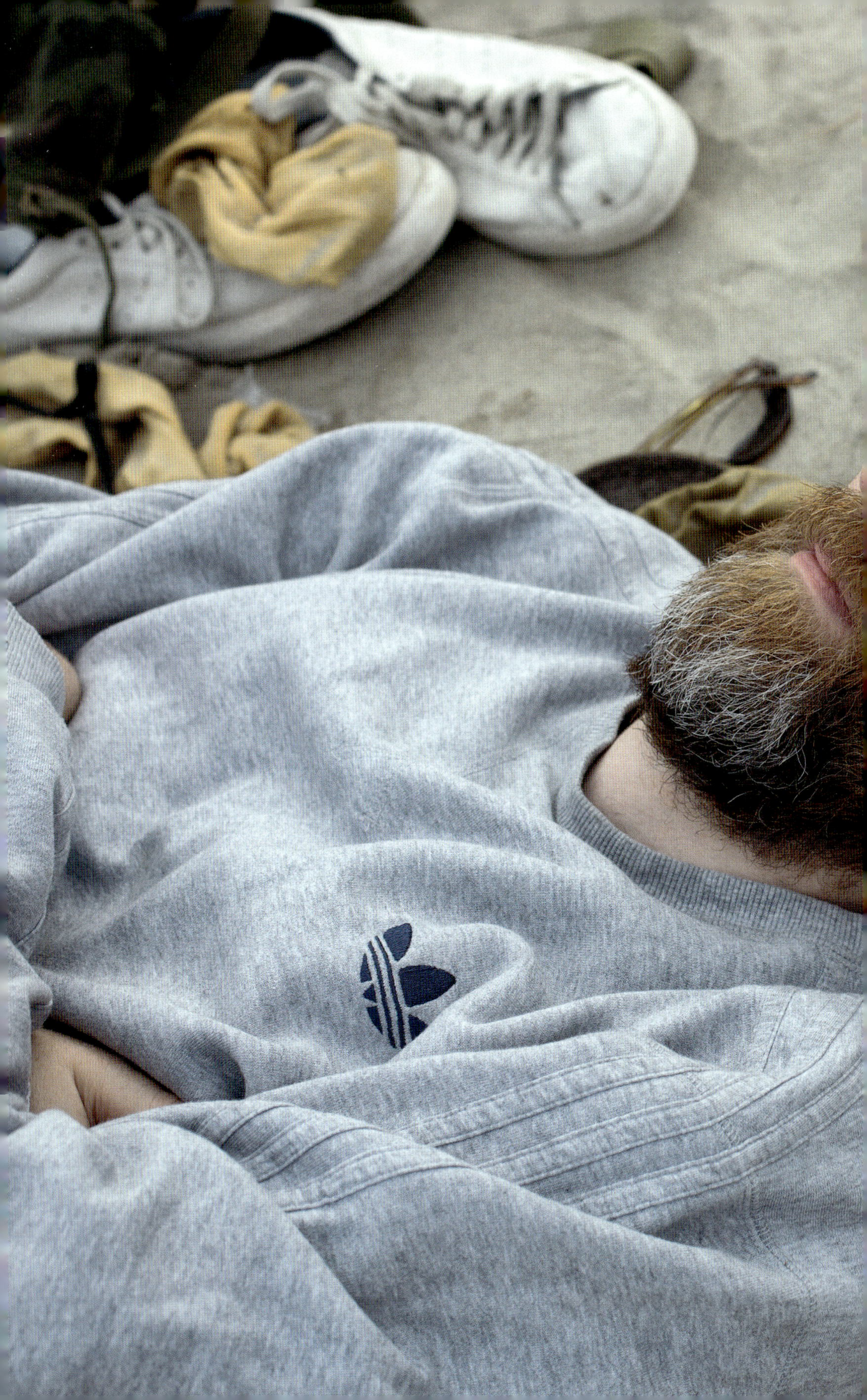

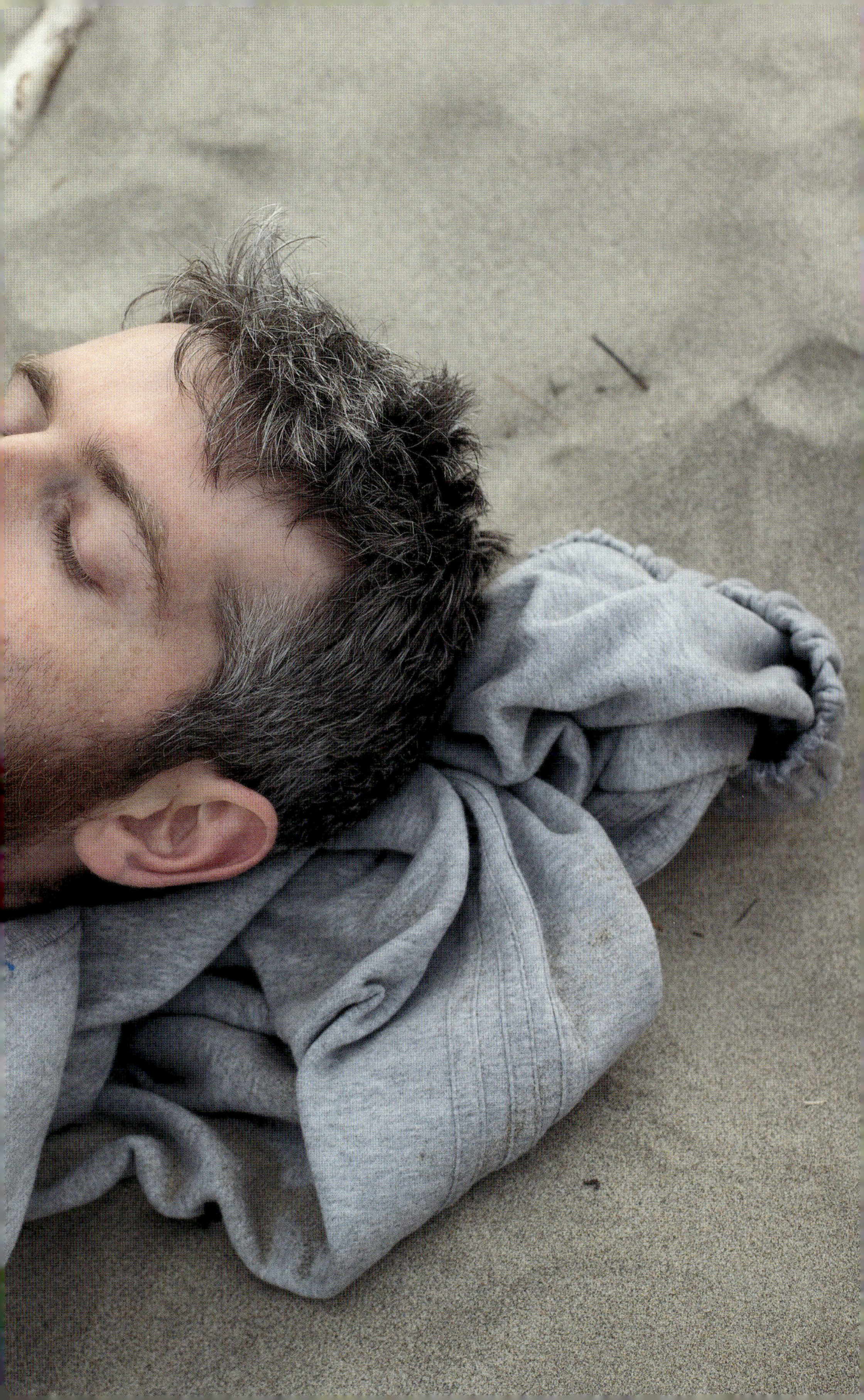

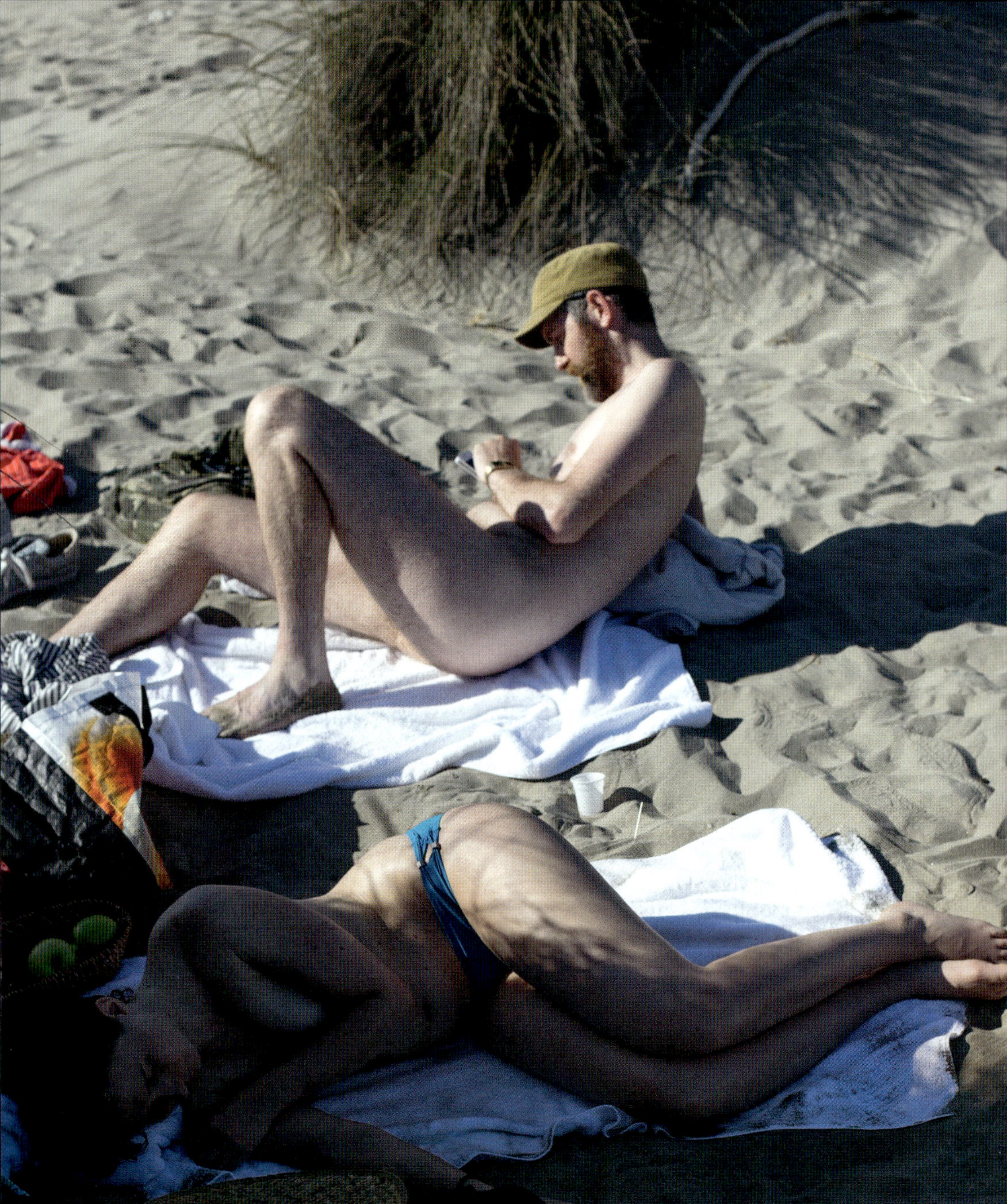

2014

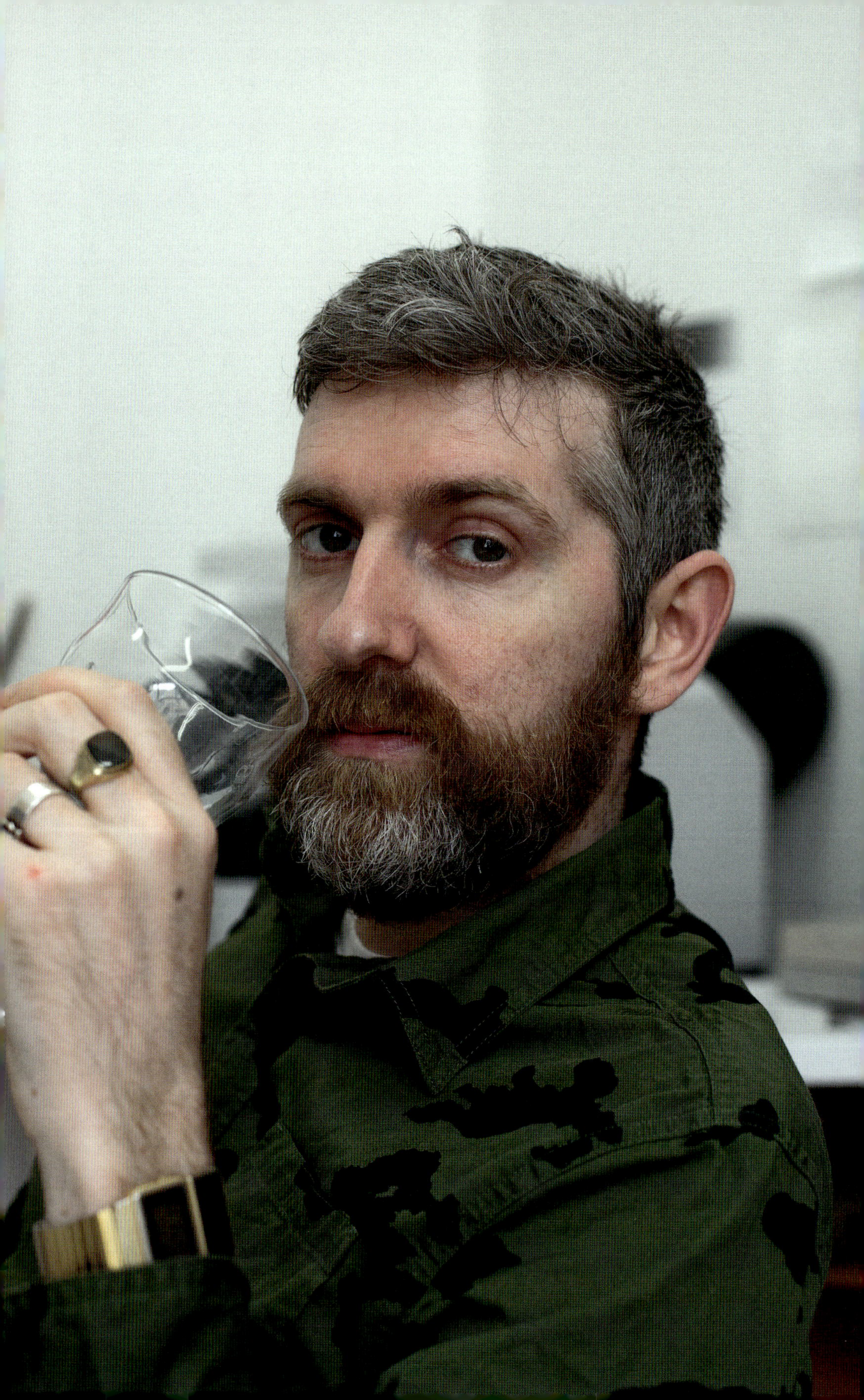

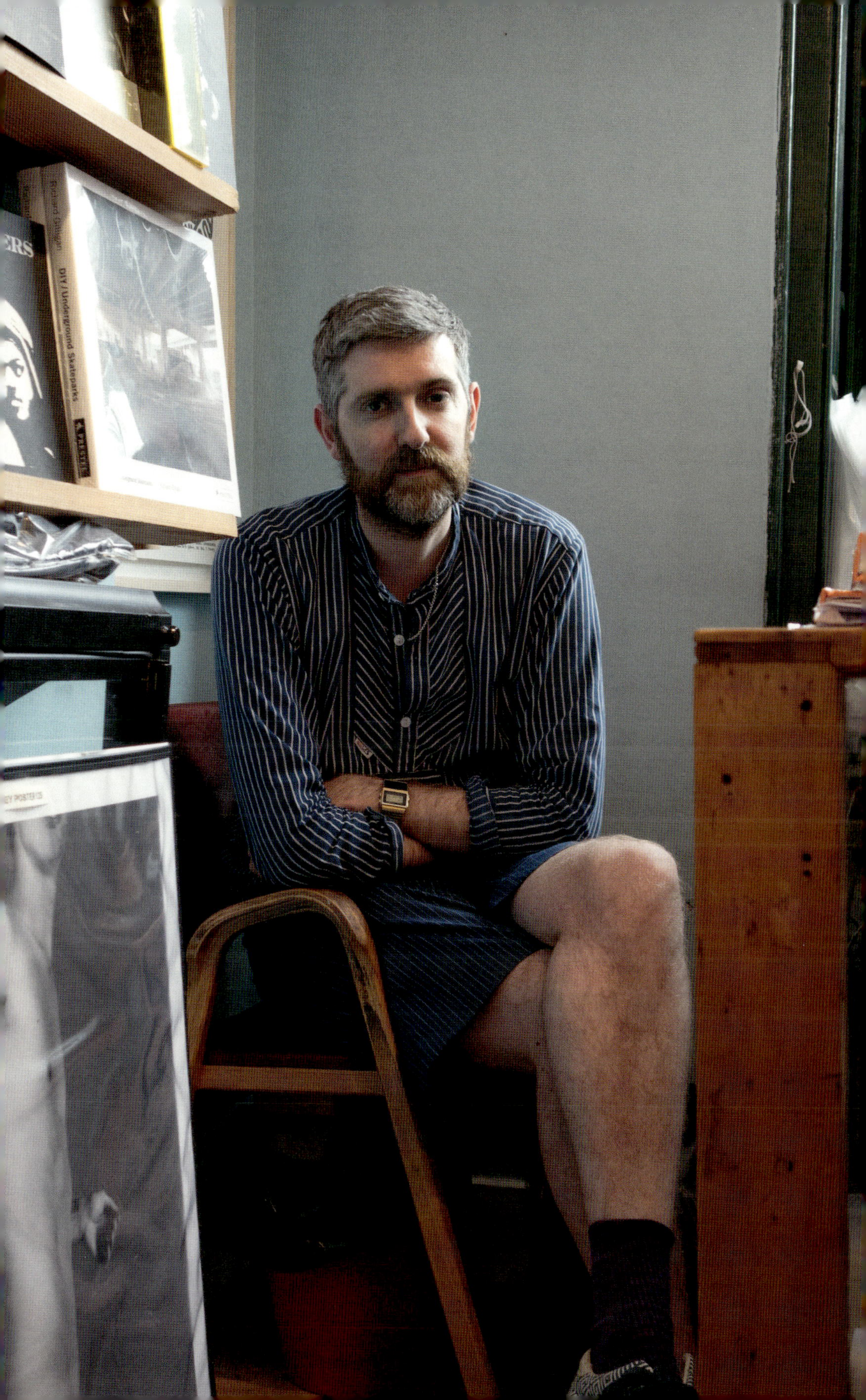
Richard Gilligan
DIY / Underground Skateparks
ERS

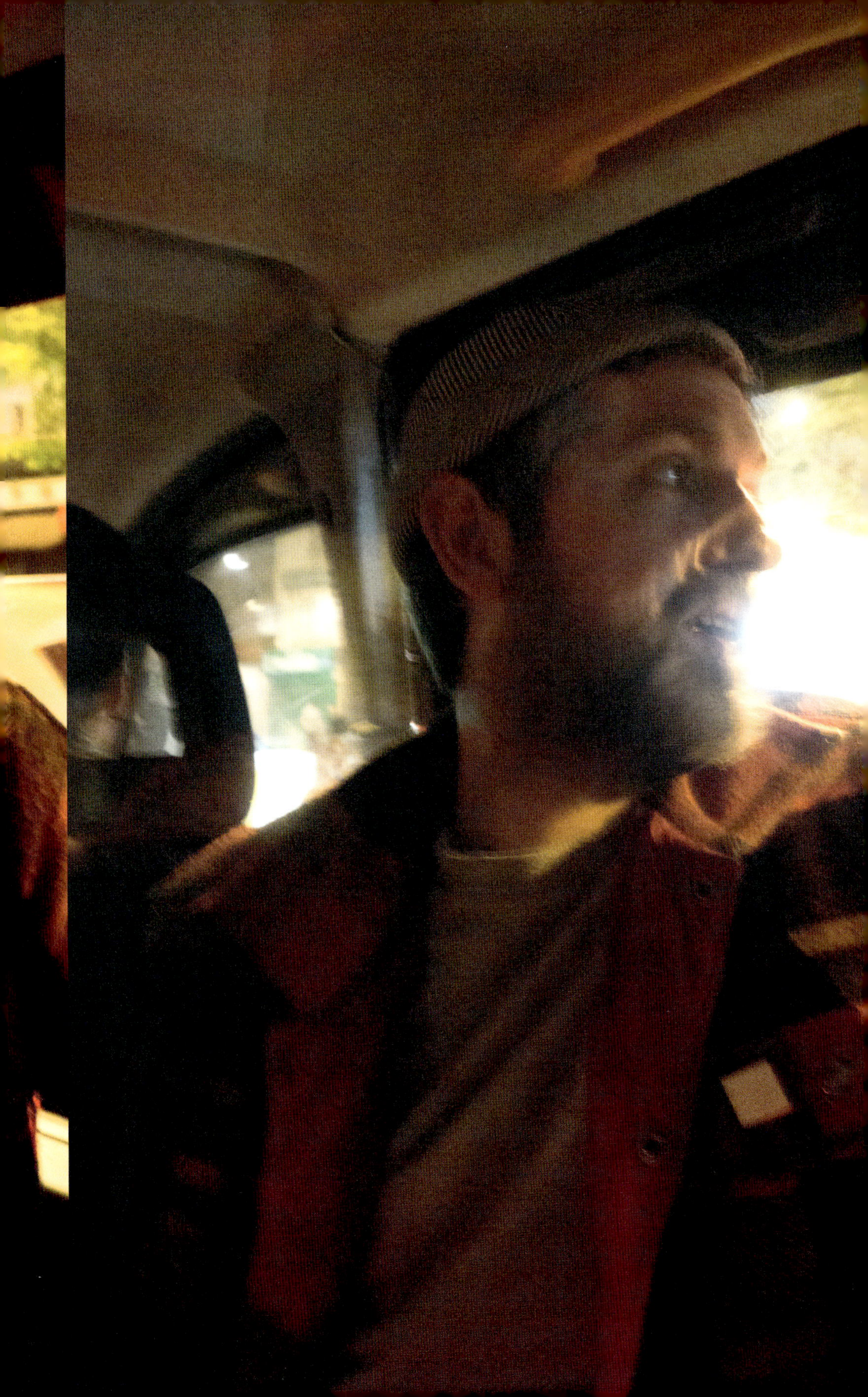

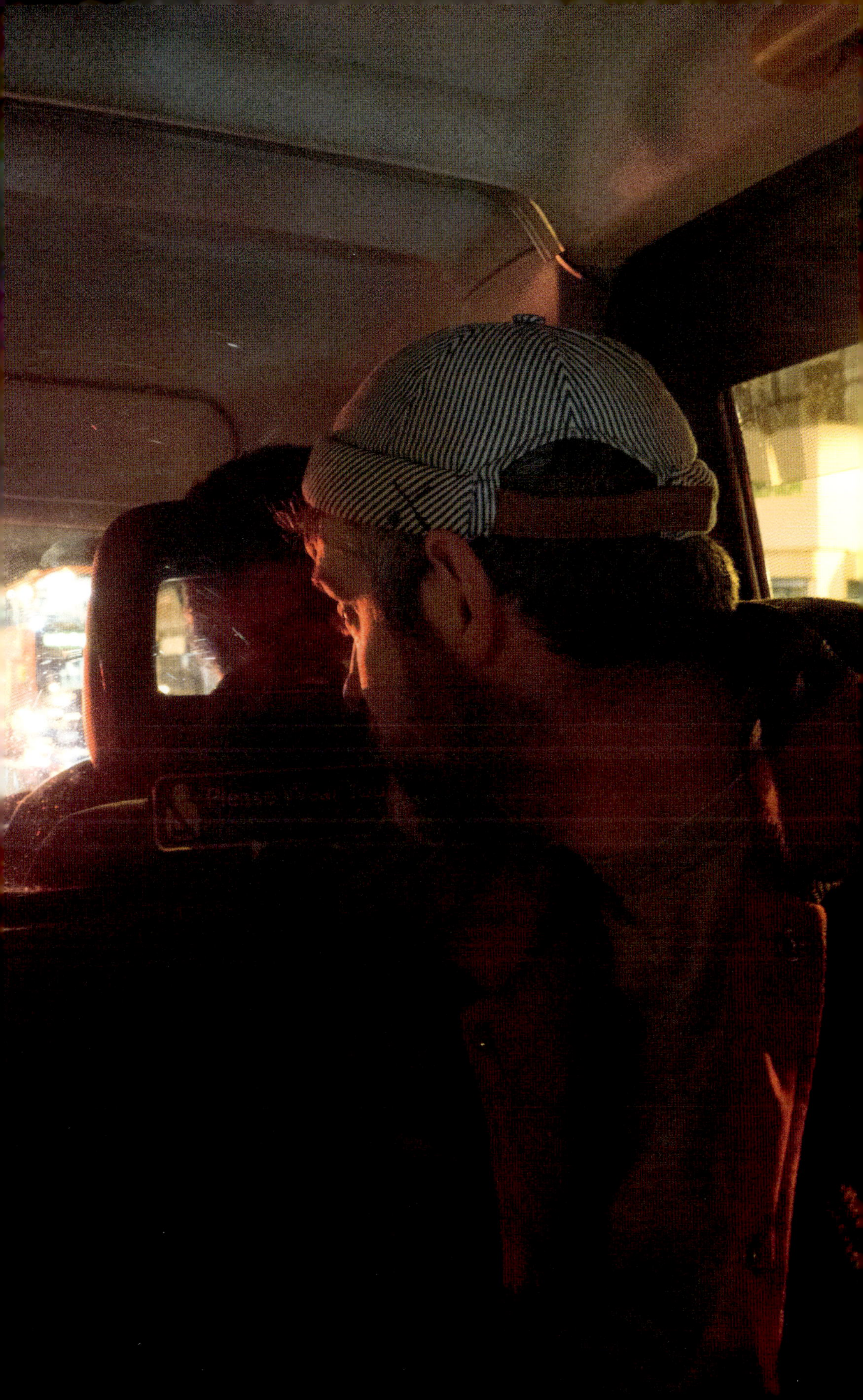
Please

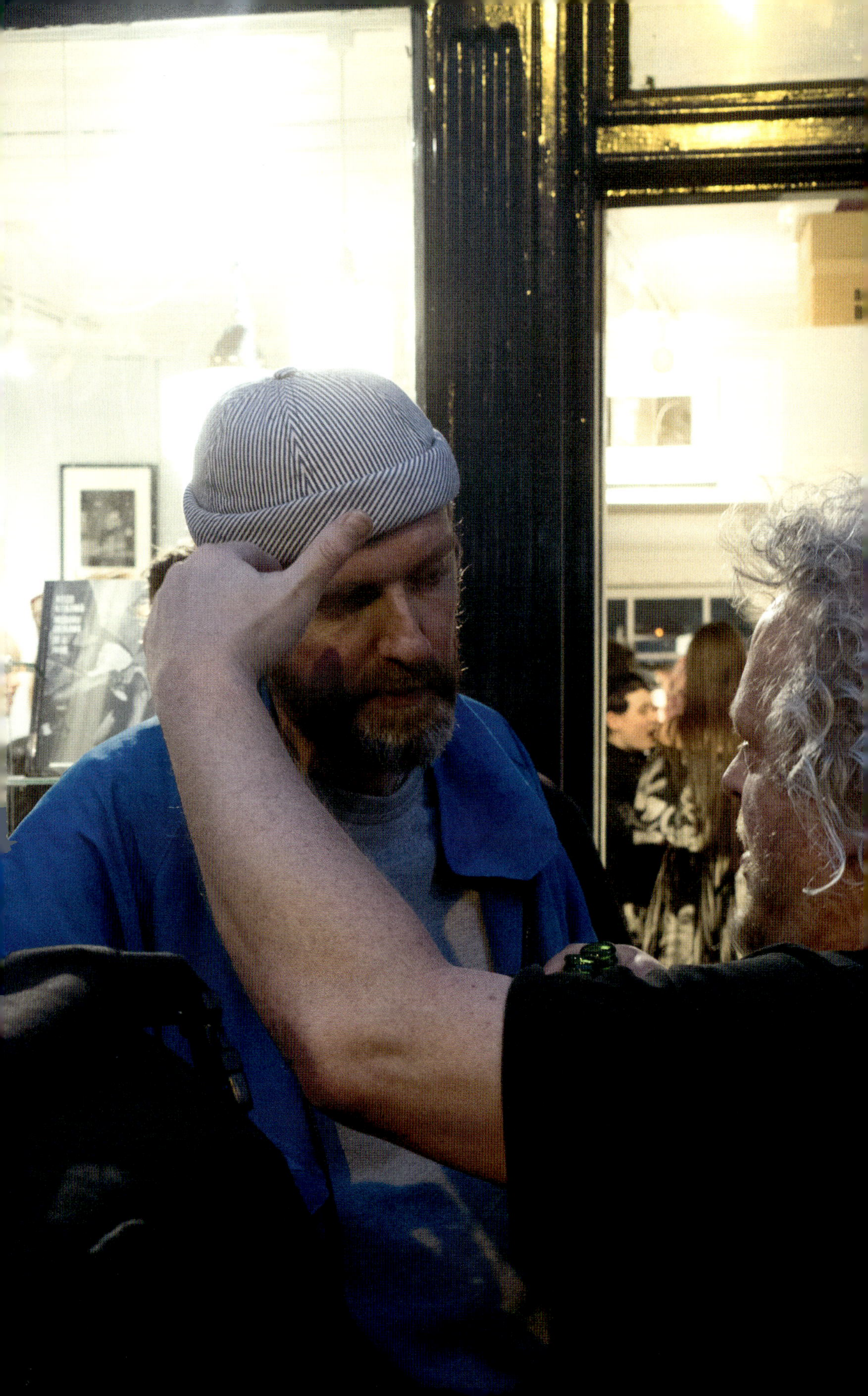

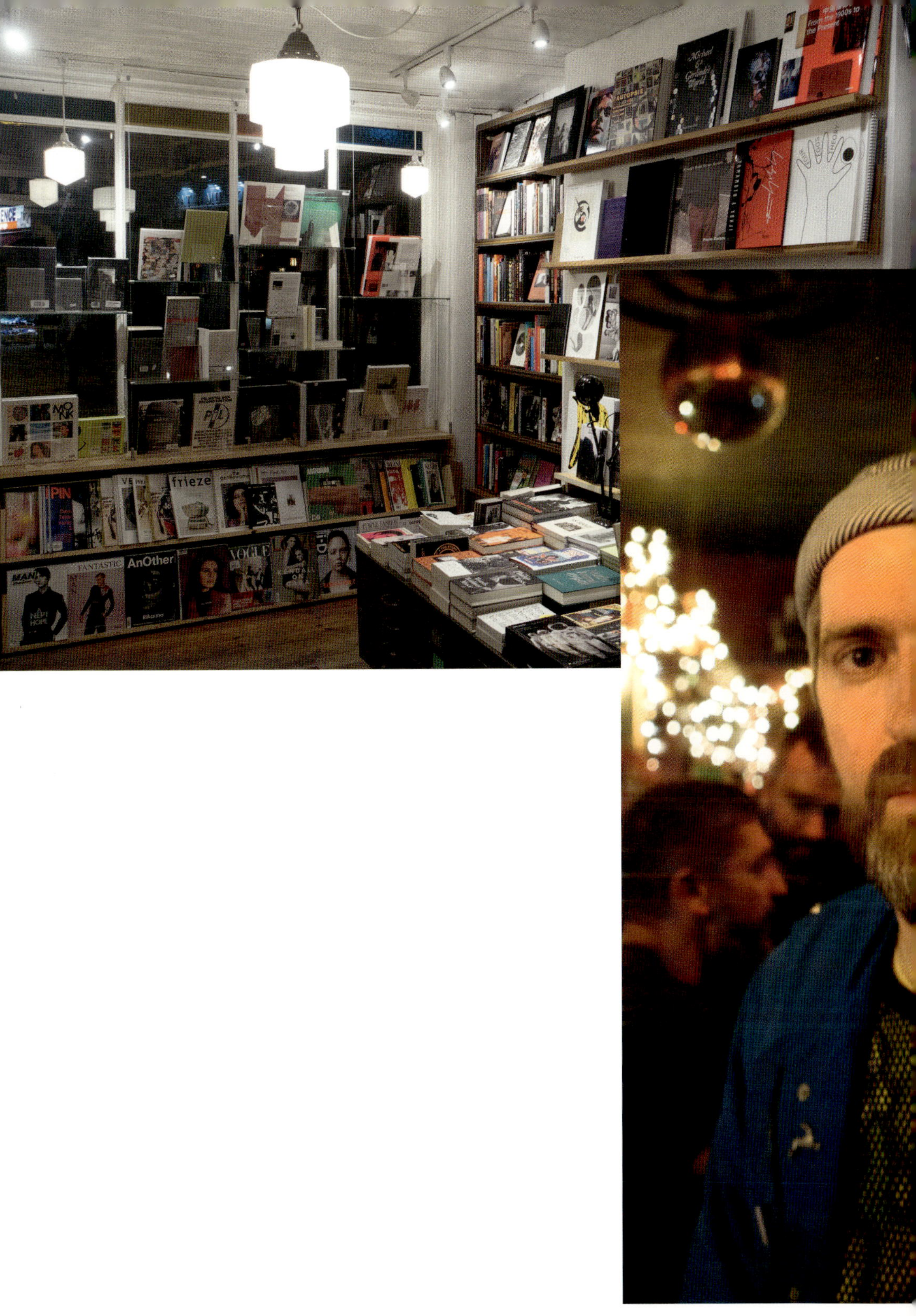

2015

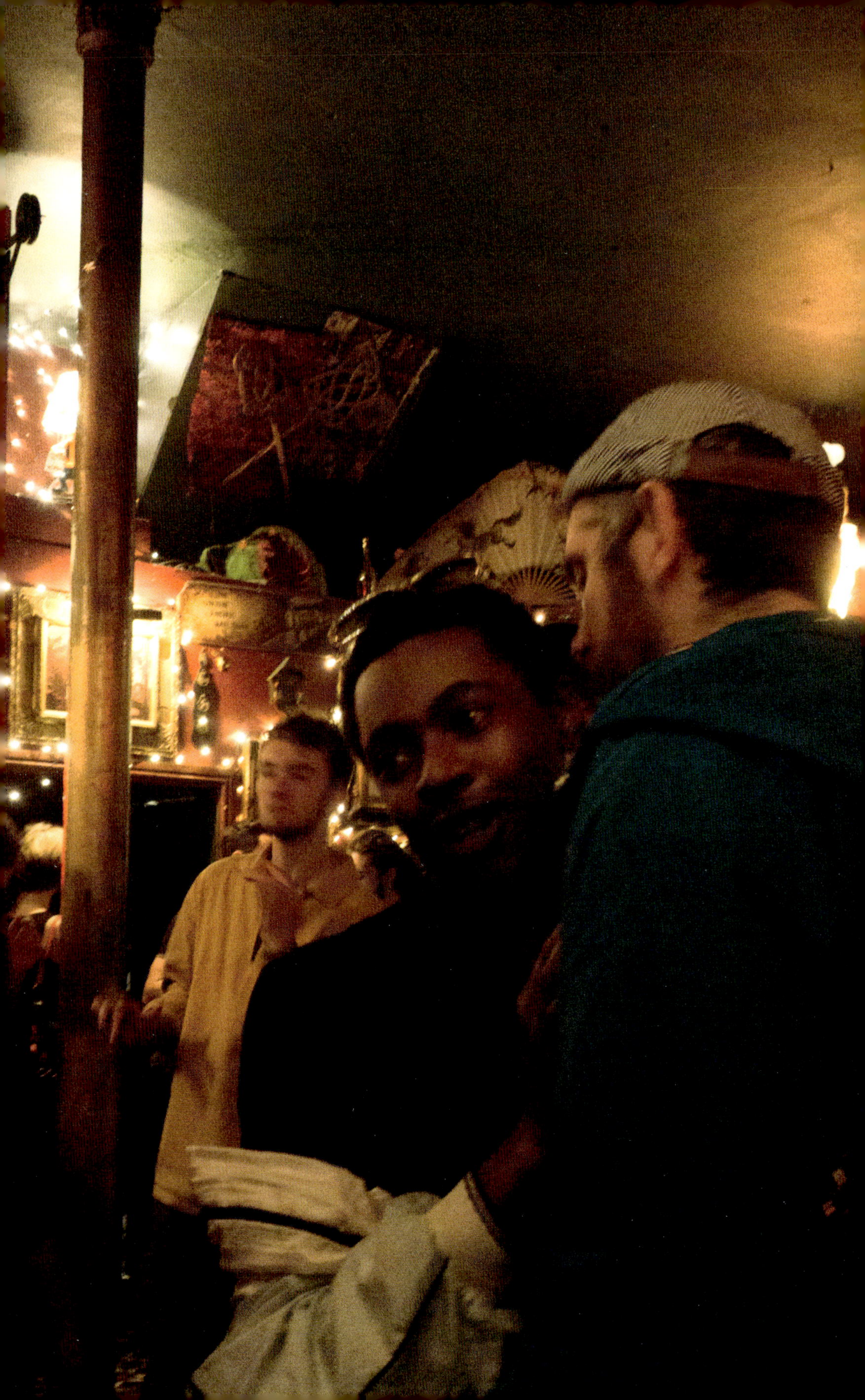

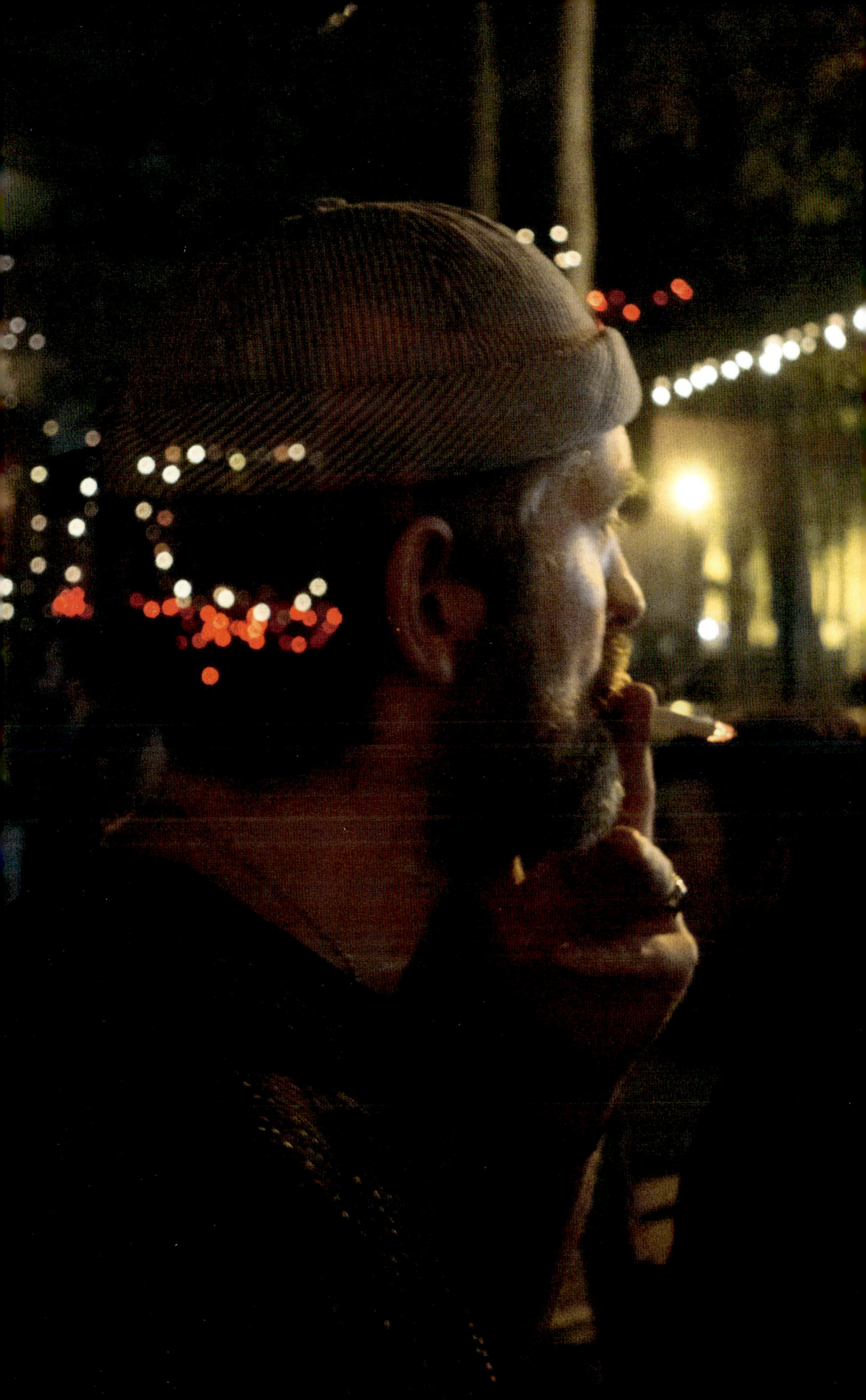

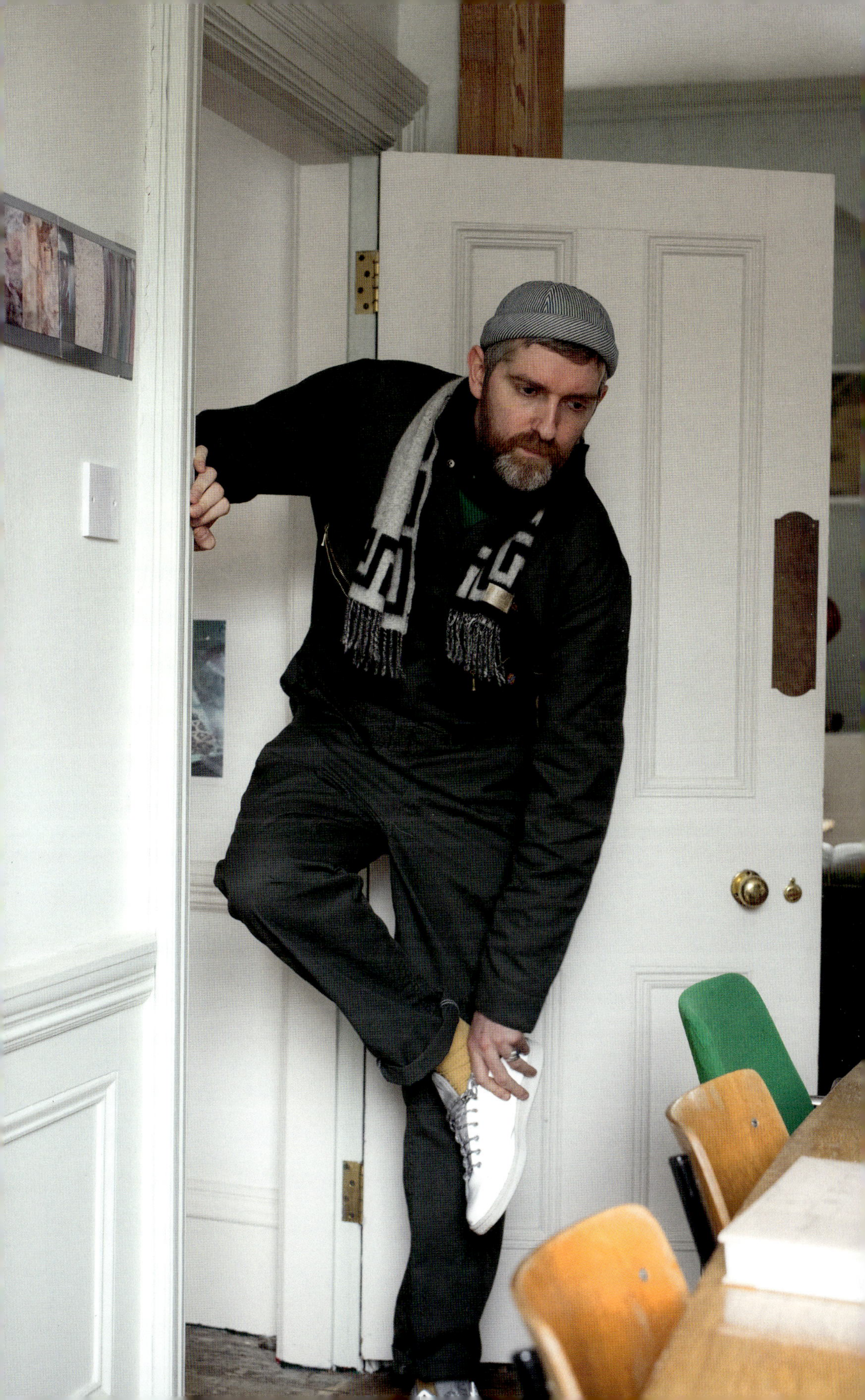

2016

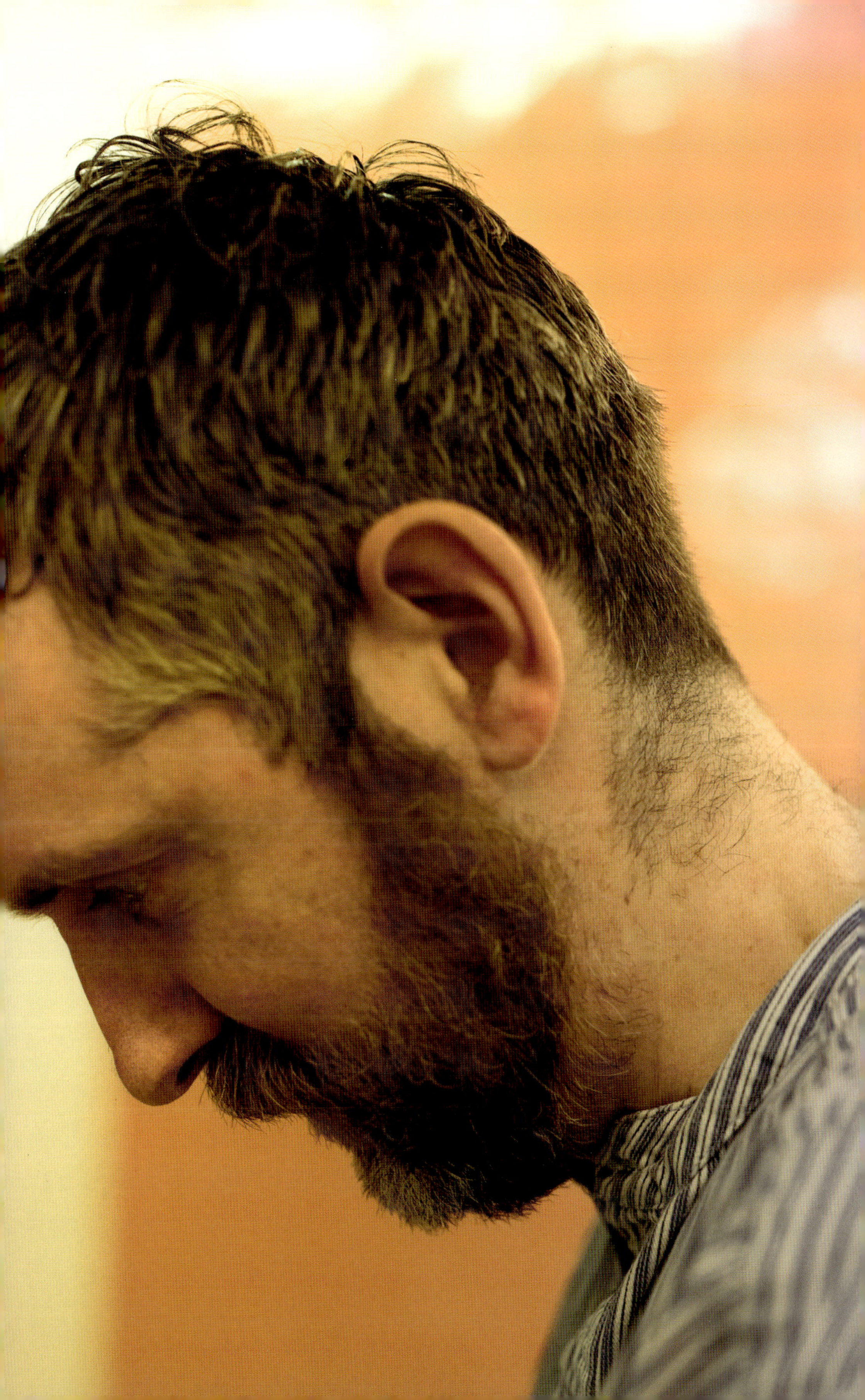

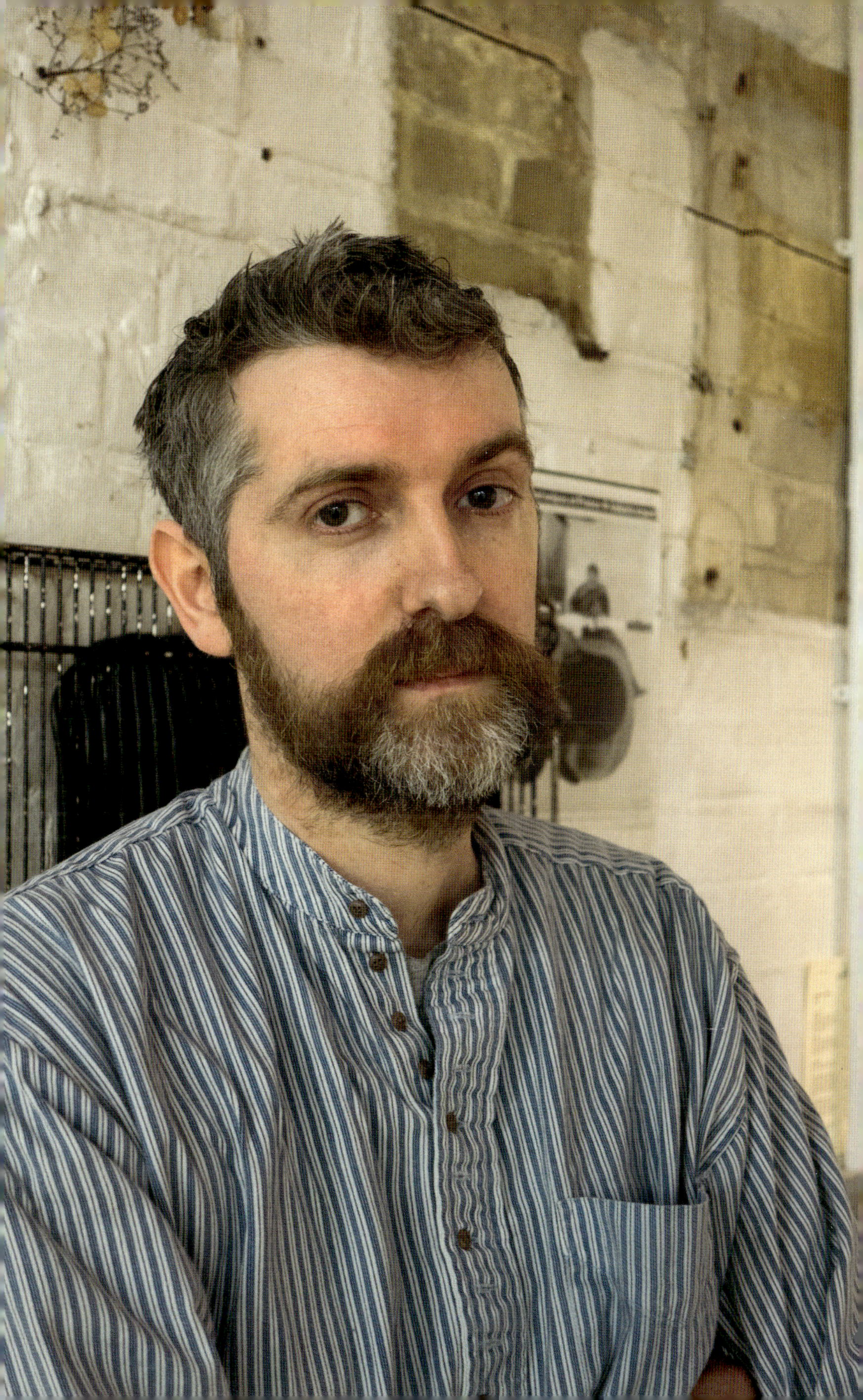

Edited and designed by Wolfgang Tillmans

Introduction: Alex Needham
Typography and Cover Design: Paul Hutchinson

Lithogaphy: Hausstaetter Herstellung, Berlin
Printing: Druckerei Bloch, Berlin

Published by
Verlag der Buchhandlung Walther König, Köln
Ehrenstr. 4, 50672 Köln

Bibliographic information published by the Deutsche Nationalbibliothek
The Deutsche Nationalbibliothek lists this publication in the Deutsche Nationalbibliografie;
detailed bibliographic data are available in the Internet at http://dnb.d-nb.de.

Printed in Germany

Distribution:

Germany & Europe
Buchhandlung Walther König, Köln
Tel. +49 (0) 221 / 20 59 6-53
Fax +49 (0) 221 / 20 59 6-60
verlag@buchhandlung-walther-koenig.de

UK & Ireland
Cornerhouse Publications
HOME
2 Tony Wilson Place
UK - Manchester
M15 4FNFon +44 (0) 161 2123466
Fax +44 (0)161 236 9079
publications@cornerhouse.org

USA & Canada
D.A.P., Distributed Art Publishers
55 Sixth Avenue/ 2nd Floor
USA-New York, NY 10013
Fon +1 (0) 212 627 1999
Fax +1 (0) 212 627 9484
eleshowitz@dapinc.com

ISBN 978-3-86335-941-6